ORGANIZATIONAL COLLABORATION

Many organizations today operate across boundaries – both internal and external to the organization. Exploring concepts and theories about different organizational, inter-organizational and international contexts, this student reader aids understanding of the individual's experience of working within and across such boundaries. The book adopts a critical approach to individual experience and highlights the complexities inherent in these different layers and levels of organizing.

Comprising a collection of key articles and extracts presented in a readable accessible way, this book also features an introductory chapter which provides an overall critique of the book. Each part features a brief introduction before analyzing the following key themes:

- managing aims
- power and politics
- cultural diversity
- international management perspectives
- the darker side of collaborative arrangements.

Some of the readings will specifically address collaboration 'head on' while others will provide an important context or highlight significant theoretical and practical issues that are considered relevant and interesting within the framework of the themes presented. As such, this book differs from existing titles as it sits bestride collaboration and organizational behaviour/theory in order to inform learning of exchange relationships on inter-personal, intra-organizational, and inter-organizational levels. The articles included are selected as critical in approach, straddling and addressing the central contexts described above, and highlighting the experience-centred nature of learning that can be derived from the content presented.

This comprehensive reference will be useful supplementary reading for organizational behaviour courses as well as core reading for those students undertaking research on collaboration.

MariaLaura Di Domenico is Reader in Organizational Behaviour at the University of Surrey School of Management, UK. Prior to this she was Lecturer in Organizational Behaviour at The Open University Business School, UK

Siv Vangen is Senior Lecturer of Management at The Open University Business School, UK. She is co-author, with Chris Huxham, of *Managing to Collaborate* (also published by Routledge)

Nik Winchester is Lecturer in Management at The Open University Business School, UK

Dev Kumar Boojihawon is Lecturer in Strategic Management at The Open University Business School, UK

Jill Mordaunt is Senior Lecturer in Social Enterprise at The Open University Business School, UK. She is co-editor of *Thoughtful Fundraising* (also published by Routledge)

This Reader forms part of the Open University module *Managing across organizational and cultural boundaries* (B325), a 30 credit level three undergraduate module. The course is an optional element for the BA (Hons) Leadership and Management and the BA (Hons) Business Studies.

Opinions expressed in the Reader are not necessarily those of the module team or of The Open University.

Details of this and other Open University modules can be obtained from the Student Registration and Enquiry Service, The Open University, PO Box 197, Milton Keynes MK7 6BJ, United Kingdom: Telephone +44 (0) 845 300 6090, e-mail general-enquiries@open.ac.uk.

Alternatively, you may wish to visit the Open University website at http://www.open.ac.uk, where you can learn more about the wide range of modules and qualifications offered at all levels by The Open University.

ORGANIZATIONAL COLLABORATION

Themes and issues

Edited by

MariaLaura Di Domenico,
Siv Vangen, Nik Winchester,
Dev Kumar Boojihawon
and Jill Mordaunt

LONDON AND NEW YORK

First published 2011
by Routledge
2 Park Square, Milton Park, Abingdon, Oxon OX14 4RN

in association with

The Open University, Walton Hall, Milton Keynes, MK7 6AA,
United Kingdom

Simultaneously published in the USA and Canada
by Routledge
711 Third Avenue, New York, NY 10017

Routledge is an imprint of the Taylor & Francis Group, an informa business

British Library Cataloguing in Publication Data
A catalogue record for this book is available from the British Library.

Library of Congress Cataloging in Publication Data
Organizational collaboration: themes and issues/edited by
MariaLaura Di Domenico . . . [et al.]. -- 1st ed.
p. cm.
Includes bibliographical references and index.
1. Organizational behavior. 2. Interpersonal relations. I. Di
Domenico, Maria Laura. II. Title: Organizational collaboration.
HD58.7.O668744 2011
658--dc22
2011003463

ISBN: 978-0-415-67139-2 (hbk)
ISBN: 978-0-415-67140-8 (pbk)

Typeset in Bembo
by GCS, Leighton Buzzard, Beds.

Printed and bound in Great Britain by
CPI Antony Rowe, Chippenham, Wiltshire

CONTENTS

LIST OF TABLES AND FIGURES

Tables

Figures

ACKNOWLEDGEMENTS

As editors, we feel that the focus of this volume is very apt, not least because of the collaborative enterprise that has led to its creation. In this spirit, many people have helped us to make this project a reality. As such, we would like to extend our sincerest thanks to the whole course team of B325 – Managing Across Organizational and Cultural Boundaries – at the Open University Business School. Special thanks go to the course manager, Colin Stanton. Thanks also to Jenny Powell for her attention to detail in helping to prepare the manuscript.

Our gratitude and thanks for their invaluable help and guidance also go to Gill Gowans, Giles Clark and their colleagues at the co-publishing executive and media department of the Open University. This book would not have been possible without them. We would also like to thank Terry Clague, Commissioning Editor from Routledge who helped to realize the publication of this book.

As the journey leading to the crafting and eventual publication of this book spanned many months, we apologize if we have forgotten to mention anyone who helped us along the way, but we are no less grateful.

The Editors

EDITORIAL ACKNOWLEDGEMENTS

Grateful acknowledgement is made to the following sources:

Chapter 2
Latham, G.P. (2003) 'Learning from practice: Goal setting: A five-step approach to behavior change'. Reprinted from *Organizational Dynamics*, 32 (3), pp. 309–18, with permission from Elsevier.

Chapter 3
Ordónêz, L.D., Schweitzer, M.E., Galinsky, A.D. and Bazerman, M.H. (2009) 'Goals gone wild: The systematic side effects of overprescribing goal setting', *Academy of Management Perspectives*, 23 (1), pp. 6–16. Reproduced with permission of Academy of Management. Permission conveyed through Copyright Clearance Center.

Chapter 4
Hofstede, G., Van Deusen, C.A., Mueller, C.B., and Charles, T.A. (2002) 'What goals do business leaders pursue? A study in fifteen countries', *Journal of International Business Studies*, 33 (4), pp. 785–803. Copyright © Geert Hofstede.

Chapter 5
Gagalyuk, T. and Hanf, J., 'The role of goals in the management of supply chain networks', Conference paper. With permission from the authors.

Chapter 6
Machiavelli, N. (1515) *The Prince*, translated by W.K. Marriott, Chapters 14, 15, 16, 17 and 18. Every effort has been made to contact copyright holders. If any have been inadvertently overlooked the publishers will be pleased to make the necessary arrangements at the first opportunity.

Chapter 7
Anthony, J. (1967) *Management and Machiavelli*. Copyright © 1967 Hodder and Stoughton. Reproduced with permission of John Wiley & Sons, Inc.

Chapter 8
Pfeffer, J. (1992) 'Understanding power in organizations', *Managing with Power*. Copyright © 1992 by the President and Fellows of Harvard College. All Rights Reserved. Further copying without permission of Harvard Business School is prohibited.

Chapter 9
Di Domenico, M., Tracey, P. and Haugh, H. (2009) 'The dialectic of social exchange: theorising corporate-social enterprise collaboration', *Organization Studies*, 30 (8), pp. 887–907. Reprinted by permission of SAGE Publications Ltd.

Chapter 10
McSweeney, B. (2002) 'Hofstede's model of national cultural differences and their consequences', *Human Relations*, 55 (1), pp. 89–118. Copyright © 2002 The Tavistock Institute. Reprinted by permission of SAGE Publications Ltd.

Chapter 11
Schein, E.H. (2004) 'The levels of culture', *Organizational Culture and Leadership*. Copyright © 2004 Jossey-Bass. Reproduced with permission of John Wiley & Sons, Inc.

Chapter 12
Kuenz, J. (1995) 'Working at the rat', *Inside the Mouse: Work and play at Disney World, The Project on Disney*, pp. 110-66. Copyright © 1995 Duke University Press. All rights reserved. Reprinted by permission of the publisher.

Chapter 13
Brett *et al.*, (2006) 'Managing cultural teams', *Harvard Business Review*, 14 (1), November, pp. 84–91, Harvard Business School.

Chapter 14
Contractor, F.J. and Lorange, P. (2002) 'The growth of alliances in the knowledge-based economy', *International Business Review*, Vol. 11, pp. 485–502. Copyright © 2002. Reprinted from International Business, with permission from Elsevier.

Chapter 15
Hamel, G. (1991) 'Competition for competence and inter-partner learning within international strategic alliances', *Strategic Management Journal*, Vol. 12, pp. 83–103. Copyright © John Wiley and Sons, Ltd.

Chapter 16
Hitt, M.A., Lee, H.-U. and Yucel, E. (2002) 'The importance of social capital to the management of multinational enterprises: relational networks among Asian and Western firms', *Asia Pacific Journal of Management*, Vol. 19, Springer. With kind permission from Springer Science+Business Media B.V.

Chapter 17
Bjørn, P. and Ngwenyama, O. (2009) 'Virtual team collaboration: building shared, meaning, resolving breakdowns and creating translucence', *Information Systems Journal*, 19 (3), May, Blackwell Publishing Ltd. John Wiley & Sons, Inc.

Chapter 18
Columbia Accident Investigation Board (CAIB) (2003) 'History as cause: Columbia and Challenger', *CAIB Report Volume 1*, August 2003, Chapter 8, Columbia Accident Investigation Board.

Chapter 19
Jackall, R. (2007) 'Whistleblowing and its quandaries', *Georgetown Journal of Legal Ethics*, 20 (4), pp. 1133-6. Copyright © 2007. Reprinted with permission of the publisher, Georgetown Journal of Legal Ethics.

Chapter 20
Mordaunt, J. (2006) 'The emperor's new clothes: Why boards and managers find accountability relationships difficult', *Public Policy and Administration*, 21 (3), Autumn, pp. 120-34. Copyright © 2006 SAGE Publications Ltd. Reprinted by permission of SAGE Publications Ltd.

Every effort has been made to contact copyright holders. If any have been inadvertently overlooked the publishers will be pleased to make the necessary arrangements at the first opportunity.

General Introduction

1

LEARNING FROM AND THROUGH COLLABORATIONS

MariaLaura Di Domenico

This book is a compilation of articles, put together to support and inform three groups of readers. The first group comprises academics and students with an interest in collaboration and issues pertinent to managing across organizational and cultural boundaries. The second involves practitioners and policy-makers who either plan to be or are already at the sharp end of collaborative activities. The third is the interested layperson who we feel will also gain immensely from reading and critiquing the articles contained in its pages. For our purposes, we take collaboration to refer to the acts of organizing, interacting or managing across inter-personal, intra-organizational or inter-organizational levels. So, whichever of these groups you happen to fall into, we welcome you and trust that you will enjoy and learn from this collection.

So why have we explored the issue of collaboration? Well, collaboration is in many ways a term that is in vogue. For me, at a basic level, collaboration is simply about interactions. Certainly, there are some complex collaborative relationships such as international joint ventures. But fundamentally, collaboration is about exchange relationships between people, groups, organizations or even institutions.

There is no getting away from the fact that organizations are intensely collaborative spheres. People will find either a need or an urge to collaborate with others in some form or another. This may be interpersonal (i.e. between two or more individuals), inter-group within the same organizational context, or even across organizational boundaries. Therefore, the overarching narrative that runs through this book as a whole is the challenge facing individuals and organizations involved with activities of boundary spanning or crossing borders. These borders are varied in nature. For instance, one needs to appreciate the issues that are likely to be brought to bear if concerned with collaboration on levels such as those including intra-organizational (i.e. within an organization such as between departments or functions), inter-organizational (i.e. between two or more organizations), cross-national, intra-national, or cross-cultural.

The book has been divided into parts according to carefully selected and defined themes in order to raise and explore pertinent issues about collaboration, particularly from an organization behaviour/theory perspective. The intention is to take a 'broad brush' and to stimulate thinking about collaboration, particularly in organizational settings. The themes we have selected to orient the articles contained in this collection are:

- managing aims – introduced and edited by Siv Vangen;
- power and politics – introduced and edited by MariaLaura Di Domenico;
- cultural diversity – introduced and edited by Nik Winchester;
- international management perspectives – introduced and edited by Dev Kumar Boojihawon; and
- the darker side of collaborative arrangements – introduced and edited by Jill Mordaunt.

Some of the readings in this volume specifically address collaboration 'head on' while others provide an important context or highlight significant theoretical and practical issues that are considered relevant and interesting within the framework of the themes presented. As such, this book straddles collaboration and organization behaviour/theory in order to inform learning about exchange relationships. We move back and forth in a recursive manner between parallel themes and issues as listed above and the central concern with what it means to collaborate. Not all of the articles are explicitly about collaboration *per se*, or indeed restricted to purely an organizational context. But all are about relationships and interactions. The section editors thus use their articles to essentially tell a story that attempts to link a key theme to collaborative interactions and exchanges.

Why these themes in particular, one may ask? The answer to this is very much related to the historical evolution of this text which derives from our thinking as joint members of an Open University course team. As such, we worked collaboratively to critique and hopefully stimulate learning about the issue of collaborative working. As much as we would have liked, we could not cover all the pertinent issues concerning collaboration. Indeed, that is far more than merely a single volume could reflect at least with sufficient depth or coherency! Therefore, this thematic list is not intended to be exhaustive. Rather, it is intended to highlight what we collectively identify to be key issues, and to encourage readers to investigate further for themselves, and to reflect on how this relates to their own experiences or plans for collaborative working. The articles we include here also refer to other works not to be found in these pages but which the reader can choose to explore.

Another important point to note is that the articles in this book have been edited. We have aimed to remain true to each author's original piece while providing a synthesized text that puts across the core tenets of the piece in what we hope is more nuanced and focused on the issue of collaboration. Any modifications are clearly indicated in the text. However, we have intentionally not altered the original formatting and referencing style of each article. We feel that this approach of careful but limited editing allows us to orient the collection in terms of the themed sections and central narrative of the book whilst also remaining true to the original source.

Hence, the collection of articles in Part I of this book are all concerned with the background work that must be undertaken before any collaboration is entered into, and subsequently once the relationship is formed. All of the chosen articles tackle the issue of managing aims and goal setting. The articles in Part II illustrate the political dimension of our interactions with others and the centrality of power to actions and decision-making. Part III centres on culture. The articles here vividly bring to the fore the importance of the cultural dimension. Part IV considers alliances and collaboration from a distinctly international perspective. Those articles included in Part V invite us to adopt a critical evaluation of collaboration, such as when things go wrong. It also explores the 'darker' side to certain collaborative activities such as those involving more nefarious deeds like corruption.

The articles included are selected as a vehicle to stimulate thinking and discussion, straddling and addressing the central contexts described above, and highlighting the experience-centred nature of learning that can be derived from the content presented. Of course, each article can also be enjoyed individually and from various perspectives that do not always appear (at least perhaps on first reading) to take collaboration specifically into account, as some of the articles were not originally written with this focus in mind. This shows that in some cases we have *extrapolated* relevant ideas and arguments and applied them to collaboration *post hoc*. As such, we invite you, the reader, to do the same.

For us, organization and business studies is crucially an interdisciplinary and interpretive endeavour. Addressing complex and often ambiguous and slippery concepts such as 'collaboration' is certainly challenging but can be rewarding and enjoyable. It also forces us to look beyond a narrow or defined literature base in search of knowledge and inspiration that can cross-fertilize and enhance understanding across subject spheres and boundaries. This edited collection is therefore diverse in content, theoretically and practically rich in scope, and highly versatile.

Thus, each part of this volume contains a collection of articles that are essentially the individual choices and preferences of the respective editors of this volume. As such, we do not hide the fact that this book can only ever provide a partial view of the issues and themes raised. Therein lies both its strength and its weakness. We hope that you, the reader of this book, will approach this edited collection with this in mind. It is not intended to be read in a linear fashion, although you can, of course, read it in this way if you so wish. Each part of the book tackles a different theme and, as such, can be read as a distinct stand-alone section. Alternatively, each article can also be enjoyed and taken on its own merits. Therefore, we present what we regard as interesting pieces or even one or two that are 'little gems' (Machiavelli's *The Prince* certainly falls into the latter category and, in my view, should be essential basic reading for scholars looking at power and politics not just in the realm of organization studies but also in wider society).

Do read or browse the section introductions as well. These have been individually written by the section editors in a bid to provide a short narrative of their views and rationale for their article choices. Thus, you should find that after doing so, the collaborative thread running through each section is evidenced, and the *raison d'être* for its composition made plain. These introductions help to map out the respective thematic and other linkages between articles and how they can be appreciated as a collection.

Reading is like travelling on a metaphorical 'journey' or voyage of discovery. Once embarked upon, the direction of that journey, and the manner in which it is experienced, are expressly for you, the reader, to decide. All journeys are personal in their purpose and impact. The experience of reading this edited collection is likely to be no less so in terms of your own interests and experiences. This was also the case for the five editors of this volume in putting it together. Editing this volume was a collaborative enterprise. Nevertheless, each of us brings our own personal likes and, undeniably, pedagogical biases to bear upon its contents. It involved considerable discussion before eventually settling on our final selections. What we trust that you will find in these pages is a varied and interesting palette of theoretical critique, practical examples and discussion from which you can select.

PART I

Managing aims

Introduction

Siv Vangen

The management of aims, which is the topic of this section, is one of the most important and controversial topics in the study of organizations. Earlier research – which tended to use the term goals rather than aims – focused on whether organizations have goals and whether they can be perceived as goal attaining devices. Without reifying the organization as a single purposeful actor, our starting point here is that goals are conceived of by individuals but are also conceptualized as belonging to organizations, and that organizations are mechanisms through which goals that are beyond the reach of individuals acting on their own can be pursued. In a similar vein, we posit that inter-organizational collaboration provides a mechanism by which organizations seek *Collaborative Advantage,* that is, they jointly seek the achievement of aims that none of them could achieve on their own.

One principle for success that runs through both the literature on organizational behaviour and inter-organizational relations is that aims must be clear, congruent and agreed. However, longstanding debates in the studies of organizations show that it is likely to be problematic in practice. Earlier research focusing on the organizational context addressed a range of different issues and revealed some very important challenges associated with the development and agreement of aims. Yet the field of study became 'intellectually exhausted' and the insights have hardly been considered holistically. Certainly, the process of developing and agreeing aims in collaborations has never been fully problematized.

The principle of congruent aims in collaborative contexts is, in any event, somewhat paradoxical. The heterogeneity of organizations' different resources, experiences and expertise that provides the very basis for *Collaborative Advantage* actually militates against operationalizing the principle because that very heterogeneity leads organizations to seek divergent, and sometimes contradictory benefits from a relationship. The four articles chosen for this section will provide a flavour of the challenges and controversies pertaining to the management of divergent aims in and across organizations.

The first article provides an argument in favour of goal setting; it highlights the importance of setting appropriate goals, the role of goals in motivating employees' behaviour and the relationship between goals and performance. It is one of many articles written by Gary Latham and colleagues who have devoted more than four decades to the generation of a "theory on goal setting". The authors of the theory are industrial-organizational psychologists and the gist of their argument is that goal setting, when done properly, will ensure employee motivation, commitment and performance in organizations. Provided that leaders are clear that their words, actions, performance measurements and rewards are consistent with the organization's goals, then goal setting is presented as something that is relatively unproblematic. However, the goal setting theory has also been subjected to criticism primarily because it does not fully address the complexity of goals in the practice of managing and organizing. Thus, when considered from the perspective of management and organization science, rather than psychology, the goal setting theory is found wanting. The gist of the criticism is the subject of the second article.

In this, Lisa Ordóñez and co-authors argue that the beneficial effects of goal setting have been overstated and that contrary to the goal setting theory, there are a number of systematic, harmful, side effects of goal setting that have been largely ignored. They highlight the difficulties associated with setting goals and argue that arriving at appropriate, specific, timely goals can be so problematic that negative – rather than positive – behaviours follow. Specifically, they suggest that challenging goals can result in unnecessary risk taking and unethical behaviour and have negative psychological consequences for the very people that they intend to motivate. While some of the problems they highlight have been addressed by the authors of the goal setting theory, the wider literature on goals in organizations would support their argument that goal setting is highly problematic and therefore worth making. In particular, in terms of the theme of collaboration that runs through this book, it is important to note their observation that goals can hinder cooperation and collaborative behaviour.

The next two articles look at goals in the context of international collaborations. In the first of these, Geert Hofstede and co-authors offer an account of the differences between goals pursued by leaders in different countries. They argue that if people and operations from different countries are to be successfully integrated, the goals pursued must be clear to everyone involved. Lack of such clarity, they argue, is a fundamental reason why international collaborations fail. Differences in business goals may result from different traditions of corporate governance, differences in business ethics and differences in individual entrepreneurs' values and behaviours. The article investigates whether such effects of national culture still apply or whether as a result of globalization, business people in different countries are starting to embrace similar goals. They conclude that goals are influenced by national cultures and that therefore there are no globally universal business goals. For this reason, they argue, organizations should be careful about entering into cross-national collaborations and be mindful of the risks and costs associated with it.

The fourth and final article by Taras Gagalyuk and Jon Hanf offers a largely positive narrative on the management of goals, highlighting the importance of goal consensus while at the same time alluding to a range of serious managerial tensions. The text derives from research on supply chains and is essentially about the role of "firm" and "network" level goals in managing cooperation and coordination between the supply chain actors. It is argued that a focal actor needs to take a strategic approach to the development of network goals which accounts for the objectives of all the chain actors and is agreed by them. However, a range of tensions inherent in such an approach is also evident: A lead organization both helps and hinders consensus on network level goals, the pursuit of collaborative advantage runs the risk of inter-firm rivalry, compatibility of goals depends on cultural, organizational and strategic fit between partners and finally, while goal incompatibility may necessitate the use of power processes, hierarchical authority can deepen such incompatibilities.

The four articles were selected from a range of possible alternatives because they offer different types of insight pertaining to the principle that organizations and collaborations must have clear, congruent and agreed aims. Taken together they show some important controversies and debates pertaining to the management of aims. They illustrate a key tension in that aims are necessary for individuals and organizations to coordinate their joint actions yet at the same time, focus on aims can cause conflict and hinder cooperative and collaborative behaviour.

2

GOAL SETTING
A five-step approach to behavior change

Gary Latham

Source: *Organizational Dynamics*, 2003, 32 (3), pp. 309–18.

Superordinate goal

A superordinate goal captures the "heart" because it focuses primarily on affect; it appeals to emotion. In doing so, a superordinate goal gives people a cause they can rally around. The purpose of a superordinate or overarching goal is to capture the imagination, and hence to galvanize people to take action. A superordinate goal reflects the power of language expressed in ways that convey to people something they can believe in. Hence a superordinate goal facilitates self-management. It is a "call to arms."

Winston Churchill was a leader in the political arena who would earn an A from psychologists for developing a superordinate goal that appeals to the "heart." When bombs were raining down with devastating effects on London, when flying for the Royal Air force (RAF) was tantamount to suicide because British aeroplanes were inferior to those made in Germany, when England was nearing defeat, Churchill ignited the "will" of the English with such statements as: "... if the British Empire and its Commonwealth last for a thousand years, men will still say: 'This was their finest hour.'" With regard to the RAF, Churchill said that "Never in the field of human conflict was so much owed by so many to so few." And in the blackest hour of World War II, he intoned, "... we shall never surrender."

Another exemplary figure in the political arena was Martin Luther King. Whether he or she resides in Europe or Asia, North or South America, Africa or Australia, everyone recognizes: "I have a dream." Similarly, John F. Kennedy captured the hearts of many Americans in establishing a superordinate goal during his inaugural address: "Ask not what your country can do for you – ask what you can do for your country." Pierre Trudeau, when Prime Minister of Canada, set the overarching goal for Canadians to create "the just society."

In the private sector, Walt Disney was irritated by the fact that children under five years old frequently complain because they cannot go to school. Shortly after they reach the age of five and attend school, however, they whine about having to go to school. Commands from the teacher to sit up straight, sit still, wipe that smile off your face, and stop talking, convince most children that school is less than an ideal place to be. Hence the superordinate goal at the Walt Disney Co. is "learning through entertainment." At Microsoft Corp. in the 1980s the superordinate goal was "information at your fingertips." Among the superordinate goals at General Electric Co. (GE) is the "boundaryless organization." This goal was articulated by former chief executive officer (CEO) Jack Welch as a result of the knowledge that was hoarded within, rather than shared among, divisions of GE.

Bottom-up goals are frequently more powerful than those that are primarily top-down because they are expressed in the language of the employees. Three questions that tap into emotion or affect in developing a "bottom-up" superordinate goal are listed below.

1 Why do we exist as a unit?
2 Who would miss us if we were gone?
3 What is our primary source of discontent?

A newspaper in Washington state, owned by the *Washington Post*, was in danger of being closed because it was consistently in the red, as most readers subscribed to the *Seattle Times*. The answer to the second question posed above was "no one." The sole exception to that answer, of course, was the newspaper's employees. After several hours of brainstorming answers to the first question, a superordinate goal was set around one three letter word: THE, that is, "THE Source of News for the County." There were over 900,000 people in the county where the paper was located. Consequently, the paper shifted its focus on global news to issues of concern to the county's residents. Within one quarter, the paper was profitable, and it remains profitable to the present day.

Maintenance and production employees were at war in a newspaper plant after production employees coined the term "maintenance shuffle." Maintenance employees were described by their production colleagues as being notoriously slow in getting to the work site, and even slower in getting the requested work orders done. As electricians, machinists and journeymen, the maintenance employees took offense to the sobriquet given to them by their relatively uneducated union brothers and sisters in production.

The supervisor called the maintenance people together. With minimum outside help, he was able to get them to focus on answers to the third question posed above, namely, "What is our primary source of discontent?" They were irritated by constantly being put into a reactive mode by production: "Go here;" "Don't go there;" "We now need you over here." In the minds of maintenance employees, the production people had no idea which work orders were a priority to be completed. Maintenance stated that, "Production is making us crazy." Hence the superordinate goal of maintenance became: "We resource those who plan." That is, production units who meet with maintenance on a quarterly basis to set mutually agreed-upon maintenance goals get first priority; production units who inform maintenance of their goals on a quarterly basis get second priority; the remaining production units, those with no goals, are given third priority. As a result of setting this superordinate goal, one cohesive team emerged from these two conflicting parties. Within 18 months, all production and maintenance units were setting mutually agreed-upon goals on a quarterly basis.

The downside of articulating a superordinate goal is that in many organizations it is frequently nothing more than an empty slogan (e.g., "To be the employer of choice"). Hence superordinate goals can become a source of cynicism. They can raise expectations of employees only to have them dashed. The antidote for this cynicism is goal setting.

Goal setting

Whereas a superordinate goal appeals primarily to affect, goal setting is first and foremost a cognitive variable. The purpose of goal setting is to make the superordinate goal concrete, to move it from emotional rhetoric to concrete action steps. To do this, the goal must be specific, measurable, attainable, relevant, and have a time-frame (SMART).

For Walt Disney, the superordinate goal of "learning through entertainment" led to the setting of SMART goals, which in turn led to the construction of the Epcot Center. The goal is for people to be wiser and more knowledgeable at 5 p.m., after an entertaining day in the Center, than they were at 8:55 a.m., while waiting in line. Bill Gates recalled exhausted parents in the 1950s responding to the incessant questions of their children with "look it up in the encyclopedia." His SMART goal was to find a way to enable anyone to learn about anything from computer software run on a desktop in the kitchen.

More than 500 laboratory and field experiments in psychology have shown that urging people to do their best, to "get on this task right away," pales in comparison to the person's performance from setting a SMART goal. This is because a specific high goal allows people to evaluate their performance in relation to the goal, to make adjustments where necessary, to increase their effort, and to persist until the concrete goal is attained. This is difficult if not impossible when employees are told "to do one's best." To achieve concrete goals one must "do what is required." A goal "to do one's best" allows some people to delude themselves into believing they are performing well, while others are unnecessarily critical of their performance. For example, a goal to be "the high quality, low cost space exploration industry in the world" is too vague to affect meaningful behavior. Contrast that vague goal with the SMART goal set by President Kennedy in 1962: "We will put a man on the moon within this decade and return him safely to earth."

Goals are also effective because they provide people with a challenge as well as feelings of accomplishment when progress is made toward goal attainment. Goals even provide meaning to otherwise meaningless tasks. During World War II, the Germans required POWs to shovel dirt into wheelbarrows, empty the wheelbarrows nearby, refill the wheelbarrow, and return the dirt to where it had been dug. Why? Because they wanted to see what people do when the work they perform is void of meaning. What was the result? After several months, people went mad. As a North American psychologist, allow me to repeat the experiment involving dirt, shovel, and "wheelbarrow." Working in dyads, I will only ask that you and your partner set a goal in terms of time to complete the task. In brief, I am simply setting up a relay race for you that has been taking place at picnics for centuries. Goals introduce a sense of fun through competition with self and others.

In the forest products industry, harvesting trees hour after hour can be tiring, monotonous work. When loggers set a specific high goal as to the number of trees each person would cut in a day and in a week, both attendance and performance increased significantly. People bragged about their accomplishments in a manner similar to what one hears on a golf course.

Goals can reduce stress if they are few in number. This is because goals not only provide people with a sense of purpose, they enable people to see the progress they are making in relation to the goals. Goals remove the ambiguity as to the criteria for which you and others will hold yourself accountable. If the goals are too many, such as 37 rather than three to seven, the focus that a goal provides is lost. Setting too many goals invites "cherry picking" the easy ones, and procrastinating on the important ones.

The downside of goal setting is the necessity of finding ways to obtain goal commitment. Without commitment there is no goal. A tool that can be used to understand ways of gaining goal commitment is the empathy box. This box, shown in Figure 2.1, is based on two principles, namely: understand the outcomes

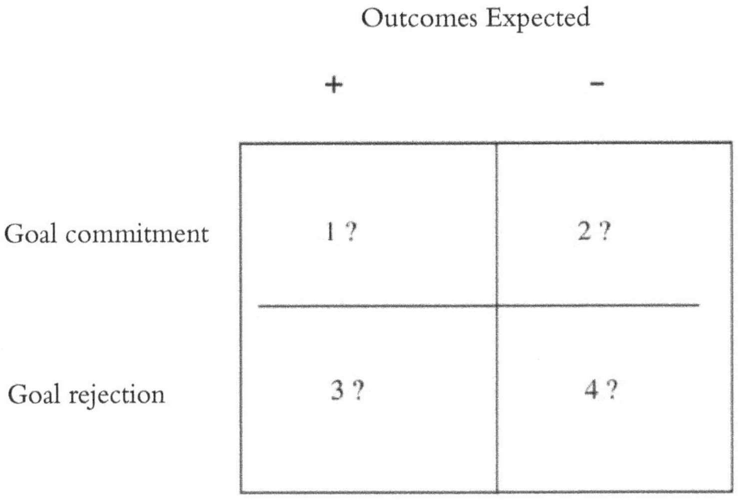

Outcomes Expected

+   –

	Outcomes Expected +	Outcomes Expected –
Goal commitment	1 ?	2 ?
Goal rejection	3 ?	4 ?

FIGURE 2.1 The empathy box

people expect and you will understand their behavior; change the outcomes people expect and you will change their behavior.

I was contacted by a client in the forest products industry whose goal was to reduce theft to $1,000 a year or less. Theft was so bad, that in addition to stealing from the company, employees were even stealing from one another. Consequently, management and the union selected individuals at random for me to interview. As a psychologist, I guaranteed anonymity. Through random selection, I met the thieves. Among their responses to the questions in the empathy box were the following:

Cell 1

What positive outcomes do you expect for being honest? What are the upsides? How will you come out ahead? The most common answer was "nothing."

Cell 2

What negative outcomes do you expect for being honest? What are the downsides? How will you lose? The answers included harassment by and isolation from peers. One supervisor was reprimanded by the HR manager for having grievances filed, due to his catching people who were attempting to remove company material from the site without permission. When other supervisors learned of the reprimand, the mindset adopted among the supervisors was "hear no evil, see no evil."

Cell 3

What positive outcomes do you expect from stealing? What are the upsides? How will you come out ahead? No one was selling the stolen goods, nor were they using them. No one reported theft as a way of expressing anger toward the company. The answers given to us included the "challenge," the "thrill," and the "excitement." The answers included "pride in performance," and, "We are so good, we could steal a headrig from a sawmill." A headrig weighs more than a ton. They even wanted to involve me in their feelings of accomplishment. "Tell us what you want and we will get it out within 45 days."

Cell 4

What negative outcomes do you expect from stealing? What are the downsides? How will you lose? No one feared dismissal. The company has a guaranteed log export policy to Japan. The employees who were stealing belong to a strong militant union. The company does not wish to spark a wildcat strike. At worst, employees who are caught stealing might get suspended. If this occurs, a collection is taken on their behalf in the union hall. Other than a suspension, the thieves feared losing arguments among themselves as to whose turn it was to store the stolen material. "The stuff is clogging up our garages, basements, and attics."

As noted earlier, the value of the empathy box is it provides a systematic way of "walking in the shoes of others." The first principle of the box, as noted above, is if you understand outcomes people expect you will understand their behavior. Why was the goal for honest behavior rejected? Because of the challenge, excitement, and thrill from theft.

The second key principle of the empathy box is that changes in outcome expectancies bring about a change in behavior; in this instance, goal commitment rather than rejection. Thus the fifth question posed to senior management was: "What has to shift, what has to change to get goal commitment, to get people into cell 1?" Clues as to potentially correct answers can usually be found in the answers in cells 2 and 3.

Putting emphasis on cell 4, punishment, should always be viewed as a last resort. Cell 4 is where the IRS and Revenue Canada agents put their emphasis. Failure to pay taxes will lead to the payment of principal plus interest, and if the failure to pay taxes can be proven to be intentional, it can also lead to a jail sentence. A focus on cell 4 can quickly lead to a punishment culture throughout the organization that fosters a mindset among employees to "don't get mad, get even." It's called subversion.

When I presented the results of the empathy box to management, they quickly decided to install hidden cameras and hire Pinkerton detectives to masquerade as employees. "We are going to catch those thieves and we are going to prosecute them." Imagine the surprise of the senior management team when I informed them I had been asked to make those very recommendations to them. "Who asked you to make those recommendations to us?" queried one of the vice-presidents. Who indeed?

Imagine the further surprise of the senior management team when I replied "the thieves." "Why would the thieves ask you to tell us to put in hidden cameras?" "Well, guess what they intend to do with the cameras?" I replied, "Steal them." Installing cameras increases the challenge, the sense of accomplishment. Putting in cameras increases the thrill and excitement of the theft. And more than one thief joked about kidnapping the Pinkerton detectives.

Because the thieves expected to experience fun and excitement from accomplishing theft, the company adopted the policy of a library. On an announced Friday in May, people were informed they could borrow rather than steal what they wanted from the company. Allowing people to borrow equipment from the company caused a fury of activity within the company's legal department. This in turn was a bit of a thrill for all but the lawyers. They produced reams of paper that required the borrower's signature indicating that, should the borrower get hurt while using the equipment, the company was not responsible, etc. The excitement the thieves expected from stealing was now effectively removed.

Again, based on the policy of the library, an amnesty day was announced where people could return that which had been stolen—under the assumption they did not take it, but were returning it for a friend. So much material was returned from the clogged garages, basements, and attics that the company extended the amnesty from a Friday to a Saturday.

Two caveats before leaving the subject of goal setting: First, when people have the necessary knowledge and skill to attain the goal, a performance outcome goal should be set (e.g., revenue to be earned; costs to be reduced). Goals affect choice, effort, and persistence. However, when people lack the knowledge or skill for goal attainment, a SMART learning rather than an outcome goal should be set. A learning goal, as the name implies, focuses attention on the discovery of strategies and skills necessary for goal attainment. Hence, the emphasis is on the development of procedures or systems necessary for mastering the task. Thus a good golfer with a low handicap should set a goal in terms of the desired score. A poor golfer should set a goal in terms of acquiring the skills necessary for using a 3 wood or a 1 driver, or in the adept use of the putter. In short, a learning goal focuses attention on skill or knowledge acquisition rather than on a specific performance outcome. Setting learning goals leads eventually to the ability to profit from setting performance goals.

Second, among the biggest impediments to the effectiveness of goal setting is environmental uncertainty. Information that is true at one point in time may become obsolete at a later point in time due to rapid environmental changes. As uncertainty increases, it becomes increasingly difficult to set a SMART goal. The solution is to set proximal or sub goals in addition to the distal goal.

For example, in organizations where, without warning, there are dramatic price fluctuations, setting a specific high outcome goal can result in profits that are significantly worse than a mindset to "do their best." But, when people set proximal or sub goals in addition to the performance goal, profits are significantly higher than in the case where only a SMART performance goal is set, or when people adopt the abstract goal to do one's best. In highly dynamic settings, it is important to actively search for feedback and react quickly. Sub goals increase error management. Errors provide information as to whether one's picture of reality is congruent with goal attainment. There is an increase in information for people to take into account when proximal or sub goals are set. In addition to the increase in information from setting proximal goals, the attainment of them increases overall goal commitment; it increases the belief that the end goal is indeed attainable.

Integrity

Leaders must model commitment to the superordinate and SMART goals. Hence, an organization's leaders need to take a long look in the mirror to see whether their words and actions are consistent with the superordinate and SMART goals that have been set. To the extent they are not, leaders are a primary source of hypocrisy in the workforce. The problem for leaders is they are often unaware of the signals they send. These signals are frequently inadvertent or unconsciously sent. Thus it is incumbent upon leaders to find ways (e.g. set learning goals) to make people comfortable, informing them of when what they are doing is seen as incongruent to the superordinate or SMART goals. Experience has shown this is often accomplished by informal rather than formal means. That is, it's accomplished through a discussion with people over coffee, in the hallway, at lunch, etc. regarding the following questions:

1 Is the superordinate goal still applicable? Does it still galvanize people?
2 Are we pursuing the right SMART goals? Are they too hard/easy?
3 Are there situational constraints to goal attainment?
4 Is there anything I am saying or doing as the leader of this team that is getting in the way of goal attainment or reducing goal commitment? What would you like to see me start doing, stop doing, or continue doing in this regard?

Accessibility

It is difficult to be an effective leader when you are inaccessible to the people who are on your team. Leaders need to be accessible for at least two reasons: (1) to let people know what they are doing is both noticed and appreciated with regard to goal attainment, and (2) to encourage dissent with the goals that are set.

Just as engineers strengthen and reinforce bridges, leaders need to strengthen and reinforce behavior that is consistent with the superordinate and SMART goals. If this is not done, apathy is the likely outcome. Most people can recall the date they were fired from a job; few of us can recall when apathy set in. When did the excitement for, the challenge of goal attainment dissipate? Apathy is cancer-like, because its onset and growth is usually insidious. Recognizing and acknowledging people is an effective antidote to apathy.

Immediately after World War II, studies were done comparing POWs who died rather quickly, with others, physiologically similar, who survived. An explanation is portrayed in the film *The Bridge on the River Kwai*. When a British soldier was placed in solitary confinement, his goal was to survive in order to increase the morale of the soldiers in the camp. The goal of the soldiers was to "be present" for the person in solitary confinement. How was the latter operationalized? How was it SMART? Immediately upon seeing the soldier emerge from solitary confinement there was a whistle throughout the camp, whereupon all the soldiers stopped what they were doing, stood at attention and saluted. To whom was the salute given? In addition to the soldier who had been in solitary confinement, God, King, and Country. The signal cogently sent to the enemy by the British was: no one could break a British soldier; when you put one British soldier in solitary confinement, you put the entire British army in solitary confinement; when you free one British soldier, you free the entire POW camp. Through goal setting there can be a sense of cohesion, a sense of unity, a sense of one team. Goal setting is the manifestation of needs and values.

This fact is not lost on effective union leaders. Employees have a need to have their welfare taken into account in the organizational decisions that will affect them. Hence union leaders stress the value of solidarity within the workforce. In grievance meetings, in contract negotiations, union leaders set specific concrete goals that reflect needs and values of the employees whom they represent. Lack of attention to the needs, values, and goals of employees usually results in the derailment of the leader, as was shown by the departure of the CEO of American Airlines in the spring of this year.

In organizational settings there is often a desire to change the culture. Culture refers to the shared values and behaviors that differentiate one organization from another. Working with a government-owned nuclear power plant, I found that a relatively effective way to change the culture is to (a) identify the behaviors that define the desired culture, (b) set SMART learning or behavioral goals for teams and individuals, and (c) acknowledge that what people are doing in relation to the goals is noticed and appreciated.

A powerful source of behavior change in relation to goal attainment is one's peers. At monthly staff meetings, people in the nuclear plant go around the table singling out an individual with regard to one behavior that the individual was observed doing in relation to goal attainment. For example, an employee is acknowledged by another for seeking divergent viewpoints before making a decision. The outcome of this acknowledgment is three-fold. First, people on the team learn who is doing what. Second, they learn what is appreciated—and by whom. Third, the person who is engaging in the behavior learns that the behavior is appreciated, and the behavior is reinforced. The outcome people expect as a result of this exercise is that they too will earn the appreciation of their peers if they engage in similar behavior.

This exercise is proving beneficial in shifting the current government/bureaucratic culture of the nuclear plant to that of a privatized customer-driven organization. Table 2.1 shows the behaviors that the organization's leaders identified as characterizing the present versus the desired culture. Employees are given opportunities to acknowledge in team meetings who is doing what to bring about the desired culture change.

A downside of goal setting is people committing to that which they know to be wrong, in order to remain considered by others as part of the team. This phenomenon is called group-think. Engineers know that an O ring is unlikely to seal below 50–55°F. Nevertheless, the pressure from, and excitement among, the team members to meet a launch deadline may overwhelm a person's desire to express dissent. The outcome that one can expect is the disaster of the space shuttle, the *Challenger*.

TABLE 2.1 Culture change

Present Culture	Desired Culture
Internal Focus	External Focus
Gossiping	Communicative
Self-absorption	Self-interest
Transmit	Receive
Pension	Bonus
Silo	Team
Hire clones/subordinates	Hire successors/iconoclasts
Half-empty	Half-full
Nervous	Optimistic

An effective strategy to address group-think is to appoint and rotate "nay sayers" before a final decision is made. Their specific goal is to find one or more fatal flaws in the proposed decision. If the same people are always the nay sayers, their comments will likely be discredited: "Those people are never supportive of anything."

Measurement

An axiom in psychology is that which gets measured, gets done. Measurement conveys loudly and clearly what organizational decision makers believe is important, versus what they say is important. Effective leaders ensure that the measurement system is aligned with the superordinate and SMART goals. If people are rewarded and promoted on metrics that do not support the goals, zealots will remain committed to the goals, everyone else will focus on "that which gets measured."

When dysfunctional behavior is observed, the cause more frequently lies in the goals and/or measurement system than it does in the person who is exhibiting the behavior. For example, to improve the responsiveness of the human resources department to line management, an organization named a line manager as the Director of HR. When I queried the line managers a year later as to how the HR director was doing in his new role, they responded by questioning me as to how HR could ruin a good person so quickly. The mystery was solved when the goals against which he and the HR department were measured were explained to them. Change the goals, change the behavior. That which gets measured against goals almost always gets done.

In a professional consulting firm, people were evaluated on their attainment of revenue goals for new and existing clients. The result led to behavior detrimental to staff development as well as the overall good of the Firm. Partners ignored exhortations by their senior management team to find ways to reduce voluntary staff turnover. The Firm was being hurt in multiple ways: loss of "benchstrength" in terms of staff capable of being promoted to partner; loss of money invested in developing staff who subsequently left the Firm; loss of competent human resources to work on business that the partners were bringing to the Firm. Why would the partners knowingly engage in behavior dysfunctional for both the staff and their Firm? Their paychecks, their year-end bonuses, and their status within the Firm were all based primarily on the client revenue that they generated. Consequently, the partners devoted their time to their clients. Thus the Firm's senior management committee implemented a balanced scorecard where SMART goals are now set for client, people, and the Firm. The formula is multiplicative. Hence the partners have three priorities rather than one. The outcome that a partner can expect from earning a perfect 10 on client and a zero on staff or Firm is to be counseled to leave the organization.

Summary and conclusions

Superordinate goals galvanize and excite people. They give people a cause that they can rally around. The downside is that they can play with people's emotions; they can be a source of cynicism in that they are nothing more than rhetoric. The solution is goal setting. Specific high goals make the superordinate goal concrete. They make clear what people have to do to make the superordinate goal a reality. To gain goal commitment, one must understand the outcomes that people expect from attaining the goal. If the outcomes are positive, goal commitment is likely. In addition, leaders must be sensitive to the signals they send that may be misinterpreted by others as lack of support for the goals. In addition, they have to make people aware that what they accomplish in relation to goal attainment is both noticed and appreciated. However, to minimize group-think regarding the goals that are set, leaders must also encourage dissent with the goals. Finally, leaders must ensure that the measurement system is aligned with the goals. If there is a misalignment, dysfunctional behavior is all but guaranteed.

3

GOALS GONE WILD
The systematic side effects of overprescribing goal setting

Lisa Ordóñez, Maurice Schweitzer, Adam Galinsky and Max Bazerman

Source: Edited from *Academy of Management Perspectives*, 2009, 23 (1), pp. 6–16.

Executive overview

Goal setting is one of the most replicated and influential paradigms in the management literature. Hundreds of studies conducted in numerous countries and contexts have consistently demonstrated that setting specific, challenging goals can powerfully drive behavior and boost performance. Advocates of goal setting have had a substantial impact on research, management education, and management practice. In this article, we argue that the beneficial effects of goal setting have been overstated and that systematic harm caused by goal setting has been largely ignored. We identify specific side effects associated with goal setting, including a narrow focus that neglects non-goal areas, distorted risk preferences, a rise in unethical behavior, inhibited learning, corrosion of organizational culture, and reduced intrinsic motivation. Rather than dispensing goal setting as a benign, over-the-counter treatment for motivation, managers and scholars need to conceptualize goal setting as a prescription-strength medication that requires careful dosing, consideration of harmful side effects, and close supervision. We offer a warning label to accompany the practice of setting goals.

For decades, goal setting has been promoted as a panacea for improving employee motivation and performance in organizations. Across hundreds of experiments, dozens of tasks, and thousands of participants on four continents, the results are clear (Locke and Latham, 1990): Compared to vague, easy goals (e.g. "Do your best"), specific, challenging goals boost performance. In a review of four decades of goal-setting research, Locke and Latham (2006, p. 265) claimed, "So long as a person is committed to the goal, has the requisite ability to attain it, and does not have conflicting goals, there is a positive, linear relationship between goal difficulty and task performance."

In this article, however, we contend that goal setting has been overprescribed.

In particular, we argue that goal setting has powerful and predictable side effects. Rather than being offered as an "over-the-counter" salve for boosting performance, goal setting should be prescribed selectively, presented with a warning label, and closely monitored.

Emblematic examples of goals gone wild

Here are just a few examples of the hazards of indiscriminate goal setting. First, consider Sears, Roebuck and Co.'s experience with goal setting in the early 1990s. Sears set sales goals for its auto repair staff of $147/hour. This specific, challenging goal prompted staff to overcharge for work and to complete unnecessary repairs on a companywide basis (Dishneau, 1992). Ultimately, Sears Chairman Edward Brennan acknowledged that goal setting had motivated employees to deceive customers. Sears' "goal setting process for service advisers created an environment where mistakes did occur," Brennan admitted (Disheau, 1992).

In the late 1990s, specific, challenging goals fuelled energy-trading company Enron's rapid financial success. Ackman (2002) compared Enron's incentive system to "paying a salesman a commission based on the volume of sales and letting him set the price of goods sold." Even during Enron's final days, Enron executives were rewarded with large bonuses for meeting specific revenue goals. In sum, "Enron executives were meeting their goals, but they were the wrong goals," according to employee compensation expert Solange Charas (Ackman, 2002). By focusing on revenue rather than profit, Enron executives drove the company into the ground.

In the late 1960s, the Ford Motor Company was losing market share to foreign competitors that were selling small, fuel-efficient cars. CEO Lee Iacocca announced the specific, challenging goal of producing a new car that would be "under 2,000 pounds and under $2,000" and would be available for purchase in 1970. This goal, coupled with a tight deadline, meant that many levels of management signed off on unperformed safety checks to expedite the development of the car — the Ford Pinto. One omitted safety check concerned the fuel tank, which was located behind the rear axle in less than 10 inches of crush space. Lawsuits later revealed what Ford should have corrected in its design process: The Pinto could ignite on impact. Investigations revealed that after Ford finally discovered the hazard, executives remained committed to their goal and instead of repairing the faulty design, calculated that the costs of lawsuits associated with Pinto fires (which involved 53 deaths and many injuries) would be less than the cost of fixing the design. In this case, the specific, challenging goals were met (speed to market, fuel efficiency, and cost) at the expense of other important features that were not specified (safety, ethical behavior, and company reputation).

As these disasters suggest, the harmful effects of goal setting have received far too little attention in the management literature. Although prior work has acknowledged "pitfalls" of goal setting (Latham and Locke, 2006), we argue that the harmful side effects of goal setting are far more serious and systematic than prior reviews of goal setting have acknowledged.

First, we begin by describing the systematic and predictable ways in which goal setting harms organizations. We describe how the use of goal setting can degrade employee performance by narrowing focus to neglect important but nonspecified goals, motivating risky and unethical behaviors, inhibiting learning, corroding organizational culture, and reducing intrinsic motivation. We argue that, in many situations, the damaging effects of goal setting outweigh its benefits.

Second, we offer a warning label to guide the use of goal setting. We identify specific questions managers should ask in order to ascertain whether the harmful effects of goal setting outweigh the potential benefits. Third, we call for further study of the adverse consequences of goal setting. Given the widespread endorsement and use of goal setting, we argue that its harmful effects deserve additional scholarly and managerial attention.

How goals go wild

Advocates of goal setting argue that for goals to be successful, they should be specific and challenging. Countless studies (see Locke and Latham, 2002, 2006) find that specific, challenging goals motivate performance far better than "do your best" exhortations. According to these findings, specific goals provide clear, unambiguous, and objective means for evaluating employee performance. Specific goals focus people's attention; lacking a specific goal, employee attention may be dispersed across too many possible objectives. In turn, because challenging goals, or "stretch" goals, create a discrepancy between one's current and expected output, they motivate greater effort and persistence.

Although specific, challenging goals can produce positive results, we argue that it is often these same characteristics that cause goals to "go wild."

When goals are too specific

As research has shown, goals focus attention. Unfortunately, goals can focus attention so narrowly that people overlook other important features of a task. Consider Simons and Chabris' (1999; Neisser, 1979) well-known study of inattentional blindness. The researchers asked participants to watch a video in which two groups of players pass basketballs. One group wears white shirts; the other group wears dark shirts. Given the task of counting basketball passes among people wearing only white shirts, people unconsciously block out the black-shirted individuals. As a result of this narrow focus, most participants fail to notice when a man wearing a black gorilla suit saunters into the middle of the screen, pounds his chest, and walks off screen. Intense concentration on the counting task causes people to overlook a striking element of their visual world. This focusing problem has broad application (Bazerman and Chugh, 2006) and direct relevance to goal setting.

Narrow goals

With goals, people narrow their focus. This intense focus can blind people to important issues that appear unrelated to the goal (as in the case of Ford employees who overlooked safety testing to rush the Pinto to market). The tendency to focus too narrowly on goals is compounded when managers chart the wrong course by setting the wrong goal (e.g. setting revenue rather than profit goals at Enron).

Setting appropriate goals is a difficult, intricate process. Suppose that a university department bases tenure decisions primarily on the number of articles professors publish. This goal will motivate professors to accomplish the narrow objective of publishing articles. Other important objectives, however, such as research impact, teaching, and service, may suffer. Consistent with the classic notion that you get what you reward (Kerr, 1975, 1995), goal setting may cause people to ignore important dimensions of performance that are not specified by the goal-setting system.

Staw and Boettger (1990) documented the hazards of narrow focus fostered by goals in a clever study. They asked students to proofread a paragraph that contained both grammatical and blatant content errors. The paragraph was purportedly going to be used in a brochure promoting the business college. The authors found that individuals instructed to "do your best" were more likely to correct both grammatical and content errors than were those who were given explicit goals to correct *either* grammar *or* content. Tenbrunsel, Wade-Benzoni, Messick, and Bazerman (2000) made a related point. They argued that standards, such as the Environmental Protection Agency's standards on pollution, too often focus compliance on specific, measurable goals at the expense of the overall mission of protecting the environment.

When managers set targets for specific dimensions of a problem, they often fail to anticipate the broader results of their directives. Goals "inform the individual about what behavior is valued and appropriate" (Staw and Boettger, 1990, p. 555). The very presence of goals may lead employees to focus myopically on short-term gains and lose sight of the potential devastating long-term effects on the organization.

Too many goals

A related problem occurs when employees pursue multiple goals at one time. Shah, Friedman, and Kruglanski (2002) demonstrated that individuals with multiple goals are prone to concentrate on only one goal. Related research suggests that some types of goals are more likely to be ignored than others. In a stock selection task, Gilliland and Landis (1992) gave participants both quality goals and quantity goals. When quantity and quality goals were both difficult, participants sacrificed quality to meet the quantity goals. Goals that are easier to achieve and measure (such as quantity) may be given more attention than other goals (such as quality) in a multigoal situation.

Inappropriate time horizon

Even if goals are set on the right attribute, the time horizon may be inappropriate. For example, goals that emphasize immediate performance (e.g. this quarter's profits) prompt managers to engage in myopic, short-term behavior that harms the organization in the long run. Cheng, Subramanyam, and Zhang (2005) showed that firms that issued quarterly earnings reports frequently tended to meet or beat analyst expectations, but also tended to invest less in research and development. The effort to meet short-term targets occurred at the expense of long-term growth. Some companies are learning from these mistakes; Coca-Cola announced in 2002 that it would cease issuing quarterly earnings guidance and provide more information about progress on long-term objectives.

The time horizon problem is related to the notion that goals can lead people to perceive their goals as ceilings rather than floors for performance. Just as the pigeons in the Skinner experiments demonstrated "post-pellet pause" (a state of inactivity after their pecking produced the desired pellet of food), once a goal is achieved people pause, relax, and rest. For example, a salesperson, after meeting her monthly sales quota, may spend the rest of the month playing golf rather than working on new sales leads. An excellent example of this problem comes from a study of New York City cab drivers. This study answered the age-old question of why it is so hard to get a cab on a rainy day (Camerer, Babcock, Loewenstein, and Thaler, 1997). Most people blame demand: More people hail cabs when it is raining than when the weather is clear. But as it turns out, supply is another important culprit. Cabs start disappearing more quickly from Manhattan streets on rainy days than on sunny days. Why? Because of the specific daily goal most cab drivers set: to earn double the amount it costs them to rent their cabs for a 12-hour shift. On rainy days, cabbies make money more quickly than on sunny days (because demand is indeed higher), hit their daily goal sooner, and go home (the problem of goals as ceilings). This finding flies in the face of the economic tenet of wage elasticity, which predicts that people should work more hours on days when they can earn more money and less on days when they earn less. If Manhattan taxi drivers used a longer time horizon (perhaps weekly or monthly), kept track of indicators of increased demand (e.g. rain or special events), and ignored their typical daily goal, they could increase their overall wages, decrease the overall time they spend working, and improve the welfare of drenched New Yorkers.

When goals are too challenging

Proponents of goal setting claim that a positive linear relationship exists between the difficulty of a goal and employee performance. Specifically, they argue that goals should be set at the most challenging level possible to inspire effort, commitment, and performance but should not be so challenging that employees see no point in trying. This logic makes intuitive sense, but stretch goals also cause serious side effects, by shifting risk attitudes, promoting unethical behavior, and triggering the psychological costs of goal failure.

Risk taking

As prior work conjectured (Knight, Durham, and Locke, 2001; Neale and Bazerman, 1985) and recent work has demonstrated (Larrick, Heath, and Wu, in press), goal setting distorts risk preferences. Larrick et al. (in press) demonstrated that people motivated by specific, challenging goals adopt riskier strategies and choose riskier gambles than do those with less challenging or vague goals.

Related work has found that goals harm negotiation performance by increasing risky behavior. Negotiators with goals are more likely to reach an inefficient impasse (i.e. failure to reach a profitable agreement) than are negotiators who lack goals (Galinsky, Mussweiler, and Medvec, 2002; Neale and Bazerman, 1985). For example, Galinsky et al. (2002) found that stretch goals increased the number of impasses, and Larrick et al. (in press) found that goals prompted participants to make larger demands that in turn destroyed value. It is also quite easy to imagine that a negotiator who has obtained concessions sufficient to reach his goal will accept the agreement on the table, even if the value-maximizing strategy would be to continue the negotiation process. Clearly, in some domains, goal setting can significantly harm performance rather than promoting better outcomes.

An excessive focus on goals may have prompted the risk-taking behavior that lies at the root of many real-world disasters. The collapse of Continental Illinois Bank provides an example with striking parallels to the collapse of Enron and the financial crisis of 2008. In 1976, when Continental was the ninth-largest bank in the United States, Continental's chairman announced that within five years, the magnitude of the bank's lending would match that of any other bank. To reach this stretch goal, the bank shifted its strategy from conservative corporate financing toward aggressive pursuit of borrowers. Continental allowed officers to buy loans made by smaller banks that had invested heavily in very risky loans. Continental would have become the seventh-largest U.S. bank if its borrowers had been able to repay their loans; instead, following massive loan defaults, the government had to bail out the bank.

In other domains, such as the design process for the Ford Pinto, the perceptual blinders of narrow and challenging goals have had fatal consequences. Kayes (2006) cited the 1996 Mount Everest disaster in which eight climbers died due to the decisions of the two team leaders as an example of "destructive goal pursuit." On Mount Everest, world class high-altitude guides Rob Hall and Scott Fischer identified so closely with the goal of reaching the summit that they made risky decisions that led to their own and six of their clients' deaths. Kayes identified warning signs of leaders who have become excessively fixated on goals: expressing narrowly-defined goals, associating goals with destiny, expressing an idealized future, offering goal-driven justifications, facing public expectations, and attempting to engage in face-saving behavior.

Unethical behavior

Another serious way goal setting can damage organizations is by promoting unethical behavior. At Sears' automotive unit, employees charged customers for unnecessary repairs in order to meet specific, challenging goals. In the late 1980s, Miniscribe employees shipped actual bricks to customers instead of disk drives to meet shipping targets. And in 1993, Bausch and Lomb employees falsified financial statements to meet earnings goals. In each of these cases, specific, challenging goals motivated employees to engage in unethical behavior.

Goal setting has been promoted as a powerful motivational tool, but substantial evidence demonstrates that in addition to motivating constructive effort, goal setting can induce unethical behavior. Surprisingly little research in the goal setting literature has examined what people might do when they have the opportunity to misrepresent their performance or cheat to attain a goal. One of the few studies that looked for a direct link between goal setting and cheating found that participants were more likely to misrepresent their performance level when they had a specific, challenging goal than when they did not, especially when their actual performance level fell just short of reaching the goal (Schweitzer, Ordóñez, and Douma, 2004). Similarly, when senior management gives lawyers and consultants specific, challenging goals for billable hours, they may bill clients for hours they never worked.

Goal setting can promote two different types of cheating behavior. First, when motivated by a goal, people may choose to use unethical methods to reach it. For example, at Sears, mechanics told customers that they needed unnecessary repairs and then performed and charged them for this unneeded work. Second, goal setting can motivate people to misrepresent their performance level – in other words, to report that they met a goal when in fact they fell short. For example, employees at Bausch and Lomb who were driven to reach sales targets reported sales that never took place.

Goal setting, of course, is not the only cause of employee unethical behavior, but it is certainly an important, under-studied ingredient. A number of factors serve as catalysts in the relationship between goal setting and cheating: lax oversight, financial incentives for meeting performance targets (Jensen, 2003; Schweitzer *et al.*, 2004), and organizational cultures with a weak commitment to ethics.

The interplay between organizational culture and goal setting is particularly important. An ethical organizational culture can rein in the harmful effects of goal setting, but at the same time, the use of goals can influence organizational culture. Specifically, the use of goal setting, like "management by objectives," creates a focus on ends rather than means. Barsky (2007) argued that goal setting impedes ethical decision-making by making it harder for employees to recognize ethical issues and easier for them to rationalize unethical behavior. Given that small actions within an organization can have broad implications for organizational culture (Fleming and Zyglidopoulos, 2008), we postulate that aggressive goal setting within an organization increases the likelihood of creating an organizational climate ripe for unethical behavior. That is, not only does goal setting directly motivate unethical behavior, but its introduction may also motivate unethical behavior indirectly by subtly altering an organization's culture. In sum, although many factors contribute to unethical behavior, the point cannot be overstated: Goal setting motivates unethical behavior.

Dissatisfaction and the psychological consequences of goal failure

One problem embedded in stretch goals is the possibility that the goal may not be reached. In negotiations, for example, challenging goals can increase negotiation and task performance but decrease satisfaction with high-quality outcomes (Galinsky *et al.*, 2002; Garland, 1983). These decreases in satisfaction influence how people view themselves and have important consequences for future behavior. Mussweiler and Strack (2000) found that giving someone a challenging goal rather than an easy goal on an attention task or an intelligence test improved performance but left people questioning their concentration abilities and overall intelligence. These goal-induced reductions in self-efficacy can be highly detrimental, because perceptions of self-efficacy are a key predictor of task engagement, commitment, and effort (Bandura, 1977).

Goals, learning, and cooperation

To adapt to a competitive landscape, organizations need employees who are able to learn and collaborate with their colleagues. Goals can inhibit both learning and cooperation.

Goals inhibit learning

When individuals face a complex task, specific, challenging goals may inhibit learning from experience and degrade performance compared to exhortations to "do your best" (Cervone, Jiwani, and Wood, 1991; Earley, Connolly, and Ekegren, 1989; Wood, Bandura, and Bailey, 1990). An individual who is narrowly focused on a performance goal will be less likely to try alternative methods that could help her learn how to perform a task. As an example of this phenomenon, Locke and Latham (2002) described an air traffic controller simulation in which the performance goal interfered with learning in this complex domain (Kanfer and Ackerman, 1989). Overall, the narrow focus of specific goals can inspire performance but prevent learning.

Locke and Latham recommended that "learning goals" be used in complex situations rather than "performance goals." In practice, however, managers may have trouble determining when a task is complex enough to warrant a learning rather than a performance goal. In many changing business environments, perhaps learning goals should be the norm. Even when tasks are complex enough to clearly warrant learning goals, managers face the challenge of identifying the specific, challenging goal levels for learning objectives. Setting the right goals is itself a challenging affair.

Goals create a culture of competition

Organizations that rely heavily on goal setting may erode the foundation of cooperation that holds groups together. Arrow (1973) argued that an exclusive focus on profit maximization can harm altruistic and other-regarding behavioral motives. Similarly, being too focused on achieving a specific goal may decrease extra-role behavior, such as helping coworkers (Wright, George, Farnsworth and McMahan, 1993). Goals may promote competition rather than cooperation and ultimately lower overall performance (Mitchell and Silver, 1990).

When goals harm motivation itself

As goal setting increases extrinsic motivation, it can harm intrinsic motivation engaging in a task for its own sake (Mossholder, 1980; Rawsthorne and Elliot, 1999; Shalley and Oldham, 1985). This is true of rewards in general (Deci, Koestner, and Ryan, 1999), but several studies demonstrate that it is particularly true for goals themselves (Elliot and Harackiewicz, 1996; Rawsthorne and Elliot, 1999).

This problem is important, because managers are likely to overvalue and overuse goals. Although people recognize the importance of intrinsic rewards in motivating themselves, people exaggerate the importance of extrinsic rewards in motivating others (Heath, 1999). In short, managers may think that others need to be motivated by specific, challenging goals far more often than they actually do.

By setting goals, managers may create a hedonic treadmill in which employees are motivated by external means (e.g. goals and rewards) and not by the intrinsic value of the job itself (Deci, 1971, 1975).

Can we set the right goal? The problem of calibration

Proponents of goal setting have long championed the simplicity of its implementation and the efficiency of its effects. In practice, however, setting goals is a challenging process, especially in novel settings.

Goal setting can become problematic when the same goal is applied to many different people. Given the variability of performance on any given task, any standard goal set for a group of people will vary in difficulty for individual members; thus, the goal will simultaneously be too easy for some and too difficult for others. Conversely, idiosyncratically tailoring goals to each individual can lead to charges of unfairness. This has important implications, because employee perceptions of whether rewards fairly match effort and performance can be one of the best predictors of commitment and motivation (Cropanzano, Byrne, Bobocel, and

Rupp, 2001; Walster, Walster, and Berscheid, 1978). For example, salary disparities between executives and lower-level managers predict the organizational exodus of underpaid managers (Wade, O'Reilly, and Pollock, 2006). Both broad-based goals and idiosyncratic goals can lead to problems.

Perverse incentives can also make goal setting politically and practically problematic. When reaching preset goals matters more than absolute performance, self-interested individuals can strategically set (or guide their managers to set) easy-to-meet goals. By lowering the bar, they procure valuable rewards and accolades. Company executives often choose to manage expectations rather than maximize earnings (Bartov, Givoly, and Hayn, 2002). In some cases, managers set a combination of goals that, in aggregate, appears rational, but is in fact not constructive. For example, consider a self-interested CEO who receives a bonus for hitting targets. This CEO may set a mix of easy goals (that she is sure to meet) and "what the hell" difficult goals (that she does not plan to meet). On average, the goal levels may seem appropriate, but this mix of goals may generously reward the CEO (when she meets the easy goals) without motivating any additional effort when the goals are difficult. In reality, CEOs (and many Wall Street executives) face asymmetric rewards – a large bonus for meeting the goal in one year, but no fear of having to return a large bonus the next year for underperforming.

Getting it right: harness the power of goals

There are many ways in which goals go wild: They can narrow focus, motivate risk-taking, lure people into unethical behavior, inhibit learning, increase competition, and decrease intrinsic motivation. At the same time, goals can inspire employees and improve performance. How, then, should we prescribe the use of goal setting? Which systematic side effects of goal setting should we most closely monitor, and how can we minimize the side effects?

Just as doctors prescribe drugs selectively, mindful of interactions and adverse reactions, so too should managers carefully prescribe goals. To do so, managers must consider—and scholars must study—the complex interplay between goal setting and organizational contexts, as well as the need for safeguards and monitoring.

According to General Electric's Steve Kerr, an expert in reward and measurement systems, "most organizations don't have a clue how to manage 'stretch goals'" (Sherman, 1995). He advises managers to avoid setting goals that increase employee stress, to refrain from punishing failure, and to provide the tools employees need to meet ambitious goals. Integrating these ideas, we urge managers to think carefully about whether goals are necessary, and, if so, about how to implement a goal-setting system. In particular, we encourage managers to ask themselves the questions listed in Table 3.1 when considering the use of goals.

TABLE 3.1 Ten questions to ask before setting goals

Question to ask before setting goals	Why is this important to ask?	Possible remediation
Are the goals too specific?	Narrow goals can blind people to important aspects of a problem.	Be sure that goals are comprehensive and include all of the critical components for Firm success (e.g., quantity and quality).
Are the goals too challenging?	What will happen if goals are not met? How will individual employees and outcomes be evaluated? Will failure harm motivation and self-efficacy?	Provide skills and training to enable employees to reach goals. Avoid harsh punishment for failure to reach a goal.
Who sets the goals? People will become more committed to goals they help to set.	At the same time, people may be tempted to set easy-to-reach goals.	Allow transparency in the goal-setting process and involve more than one person or unit.
Is the time horizon appropriate?	Short-term goals may harm long-term performance.	Be sure that short-term efforts to reach a goal do not harm investment in long-term outcomes.
How might goals influence risk taking?	Unmet goals may induce risk taking.	Be sure to articulate acceptable levels of risk.
How might goals motivate unethical behavior?	Goals narrow focus. Employees with goals are less likely to recognize ethical issues, and more likely to rationalize their unethical behavior.	*Multiple* safeguards may be necessary to ensure ethical behavior while attaining goals (e.g. leaders as exemplars of ethical behavior, making the costs of cheating far greater than the benefit, strong oversight).
Can goals be idiosyncratically tailored for individual abilities and circumstances while preserving fairness?	Individual differences may make standardized goals inappropriate, yet unequal goals may be unfair.	If possible, strive to set goals that use common standards and account for individual variation.
How will goals influence organizational culture?	Individual goals may harm cooperation and corrode organizational culture.	If cooperation is essential, consider setting team-based rather than individual goals. Think carefully about the values that the specific, challenging goals convey.
Are individuals intrinsically motivated?	Goal setting can harm intrinsic motivation.	Assess intrinsic motivation and avoid setting goals when intrinsic motivation is high.
What type of goal (performance or learning) is most appropriate given the ultimate objectives of the organization?	By focusing on performance goals, employees may fail to search for better strategies and fail to learn.	In complex, changing environments, learning goals may be more effective than performance goals.

This cautious approach to setting goals is consistent with King and Burton's (2003, pp. 63–64) claim that goals should be used only in the narrowest of circumstances:

> The optimally striving individual ought to endeavor to achieve and approach goals that only slightly implicate the self; that are only moderately important, fairly easy, and moderately abstract; that do not conflict with each other; and that concern the accomplishment of something other than financial gain.

After answering the questions in Table 3.1 and considering this advice, many managers may conclude that goals are not the best way to motivate their employees. At a minimum, we recommend that managers who use goals do so with great caution.

[…]

Conclusion

For decades, scholars have prescribed goal setting as an all-purpose remedy for employee motivation. Rather than dispensing goal setting as a benign, over-the-counter treatment for students of management, experts need to conceptualize goal setting as a prescription-strength medication that requires careful dosing, consideration of harmful side effects, and close supervision. Given the sway of goal setting on intellectual pursuits in management, we call for a more self-critical and less self-congratulatory approach to the study of goal setting.

References

Ackman, D. (2002, March 22). Pay madness at Enron.Forbes.com. Retrieved December 16, 2008, from www.forbes.com/2002/03/22/0322enronpay.html

Arrow, K. (1973). Social responsibility and economic efficiency. *Public Policy*, 21, 300–317.

Bandura, A. (1977). *Social learning theory*. New York: General Learning Press.

Barsky, A. (2007). Understanding the ethical cost of organizational goal-setting: A review and theory development. *Journal of Business Ethics*, 81(1), 63–81.

Bartov, E., Givoly, D., and Hayn, C. (2002). The rewards to meeting or beating earnings expectations. *Journal of Accounting and Economics*, 33(2), 173–204.

Bazerman, M. H., and Chugh, D. (2006). Decisions without blinders. *Harvard Business Review*, 84(1), 88–97.

Camerer, C., Babcock, L., Loewenstein, G., and Thaler, R. (1997). Labor supply of New York City cabdrivers: One day at a time. *The Quarterly Journal of Economics*, 112(2), 407–441.

Cervone, D., Jiwani, N., and Wood, R. (1991). Goal setting and the differential influence of self-regulatory processes on complex decision-making performance. *Journal of Personality and Social Psychology*, 61(2), 257–266.

Cheng, M., Subramanyam, K. R., and Zhang, Y. (2005). *Earnings guidance and managerial myopia* (Working Paper). Los Angeles, CA: University of Southern California.

Cropanzano, R., Byrne, Z. S., Bobocel, D. R., and Rupp, D. E. (2001). Moral virtues, fairness heuristics, social entities, and other denizens of organizational justice. *Journal of Vocational Behavior*, 58(2), 164–209.

Deci, E. L. (1971). Effects of externally mediated rewards on intrinsic motivation. *Journal of Personality and Social Psychology*, 18(1), 105–115.

Deci, E. L. (1975). *Intrinsic motivation*. New York: Plenum.

Deci, E. L., Koestner, R., and Ryan, R. M. (1999). A meta-analytic review of experiments examining the effects of extrinsic rewards on intrinsic motivation. *Psychological Bulletin*, 125(6), 627–668.

Dishneau, D. (1992, June 22). Sears admits mistakes, takes workers off commission. The Associated Press.

Earley, P. C., Connolly, T., and Ekegren, G. (1989). Goals, strategy development, and task performance: Some limits on the efficacy of goal setting. *Journal of Applied Psychology*, 74(1), 24–33.

Elliot, A. J., and Harackiewicz, J. M. (1996). Approach and avoidance achievement goals and intrinsic motivation: A mediational analysis. *Journal of Personality and Social Psychology*, 70(3), 461–475.

Fleming, P., and Zyglidopoulos, S. C. (2008). The escalation of deception in organizations. *Journal of Business Ethics*, 81(4), 837–850.

Galinsky, A. D., Mussweiler, T., and Medvec, V. H. (2002). Disconnecting outcomes and evaluations: The role of negotiator focus. *Journal of Personality and Social Psychology*, 83(5), 1131–1140.

Garland, H. (1983). Influence of ability, assigned goals, and normative information on personal goals and performance: A challenge to the goal attainability assumption. *Journal of Applied Psychology*, 68(1), 20–30.

Gilliland, S. W., and Landis, R. S. (1992). Quality and quantity goals in a complex decision task: Strategies and outcomes. *Journal of Applied Psychology*, 77(5), 672–681.

Heath, C. (1999). On the social psychology of agency relationships: Lay theories of motivation overemphasize extrinsic incentives. *Organizational Behavior and Human Decision Processes*, 78(1), 25–62.

Jensen, M. C. (2003). Paying people to lie: The truth about the budgeting process. *European Financial Management*, 9(3), 379–406.

Kanfer, R., and Ackerman, P. L. (1989). Motivation and cognitive abilities: An integrative/aptitude-treatment interaction approach to skill acquisition. *Journal of Applied Psychology*, 74(4), 657–690.

Kayes, D. C. (2006). *Destructive goal pursuit: The Mount Everest disaster*. Basingstoke, England: Palgrave Macmillan.

Kerr, S. (1975). On the folly of rewarding A, while hoping for B. *Academy of Management Journal*, 18(4), 769–783.

Kerr, S. (1995). On the folly of rewarding A, while hoping for B. *Academy of Management Executive* (1993), 9(1), 7–14.

King, L. A., and Burton, C. M. (2003). The hazards of goal pursuit. In E. Chang and L. Sanna (Eds). *Virtue, vice, and personality: The complexity of behavior* (pp. 53–69). Washington, DC: American Psychological Association.

Knight, D., Durham, C. C., and Locke, E. A. (2001). The relationship of team goals, incentives, and efficacy to strategic risk, tactical implementation, and performance. *Academy of Management Journal*, 44(2), 326–338.

Larrick, R. P., Heath, C., and Wu, G. (in press). Goal-induced risk taking in negotiation and decision making. *Social Cognition*.

Latham, G.P., and Locke, E.A. (2006). Enhancing the benefits and overcoming the pitfalls of goal settings. *Organizational Dynamics*, 35(4), 332–340.

Locke, E. A., and Latham, G. P. (1990). *A theory of goal setting and task performance*. Englewood Cliffs, NJ: Prentice-Hall College Division.

Locke, E. A., and Latham, G. P. (2002). Building a practically useful theory of goal setting and task motivation: A 35-year odyssey. *American Psychologist*, 57(9), 705–717.

Locke, E. A., and Latham, G. P. (2006). New directions in goal-setting theory. *Current Directions in Psychological Science*, 15(5), 265–268.

Mitchell, T. R., and Silver, W. S. (1990). Individual and group goals when workers are interdependent: Effects on task strategies and performance. *Journal of Applied Psychology*, 75(2), 185–193.

Mossholder, K. W. (1980). Effects of externally mediated goal setting on intrinsic motivation: A laboratory experiment. *Journal of Applied Psychology*, 65(2), 202–210.

Mussweiler, T., and Strack, F. (2000). The "relative self": Informational and judgmental consequences of comparative self-evaluation. *Journal of Personality and Social Psychology*, 79(1), 23–38.

Neale, M. A., and Bazerman, M. H. (1985). The effect of externally set goals on reaching integrative agreements in competitive markets. *Journal of Occupational Behaviour*, 6(1), 19–32.

Neisser, U. (1979). The concept of intelligence. *Intelligence*, 3(3), 217–227.

Rawsthorne, L. J., and Elliot, A. J. (1999). Achievement goals and intrinsic motivation: A meta-analytic review. *Personality and Social Psychology Review*, 3(4), 326–344.

Schweitzer, M. E., Ordóñez, L., and Douma, B. (2004). Goal setting as a motivator of unethical behavior. *Academy of Management Journal*, 47(3), 422–432.

Shah, J. Y., Friedman, R., and Kruglanski, A. W. (2002). Forgetting all else: On the antecedents and consequences of goal shielding. *Journal of Personality and Social Psychology*, 83(6), 1261–1280.

Shalley, C. E., and Oldham, G. R. (1985). Effects of goal difficulty and expected external evaluation on intrinsic motivation: A laboratory study. *Academy of Management Journal*, 28(3), 628–640.

Sherman, S. (1995, November). Stretch goals: The dark side of asking for miracles. *Fortune*, 132(10), 231.

Simons, D. J., and Chabris, C. F. (1999). Gorillas in our midst: Sustained inattentional blindness for dynamic events. *Perception*, 28(9), 1059–1074.

Staw, B. M., and Boettger, R. D. (1990). Task revision: A neglected form of work performance. *Academy of Management Journal*, 33(3), 534–559.

Tenbrunsel, A. E., Wade-Benzoni, K. A., Messick, D. M., and Bazerman, M. H. (2000). Understanding the influence of environmental standards on judgments and choices. *Academy of Management Journal*, 43(5), 854–866.

Wade, J. B., O'Reilly, C. A., and Pollock, T. G. (2006). Overpaid CEOs and underpaid managers: Fairness and executive compensation. *Organization Science*, 17(5), 527–544.

Walster, E., Walster, G. W., and Berscheid, E. (1978). *Equity theory and research*. Boston, MA: Allyn & Bacon.

Wood, R., Bandura, A., and Bailey, T. (1990). Mechanisms governing organizational performance in complex decision-making environments. *Organizational Behavior and Human Decision Processes*, 46(2), 181–201.

Wright, P. M., George, J. M., Farnsworth, S. R., and McMahan, G. C. (1993). Productivity and extra-role behavior: The effects of goals and incentives on spontaneous helping. *Journal of Applied Psychology*, 78(3), 374 –381.

4

WHAT GOALS DO BUSINESS LEADERS PURSUE?
A study in fifteen countries

Geert Hofstede, Cheryl Van Deusen, Carolyn Mueller, Thomas Charles, The Business Goals Network

Source: Edited from *Journal of International Business Studies*, 2002, 33 (4), pp. 785–803. Copyright © Geert Hofstede.

Introduction

Throughout history, people from different countries and different walks of life have traded and made productive deals while pursuing their own very different goals. Trading partners don't need to share goals and values. In international trade, differences in goals are useful to know but not an impediment.

This situation changes when businesses from different countries enter into shared operations like strategic alliances, joint ventures, acquisitions and mergers. The management of such operations needs parties to be of one mind about the goals the operation pursues. Not only do "too many cooks spoil the broth" but the success of most ventures depends on interactions with their environment; and different environments hold different expectations. Thus global companies acquiring local businesses or merging with other global companies may find themselves acting as company owner in a setting for which they are ill prepared. Their new host countries present them with different expectations about the goals they will pursue, which does have profound implications for their relationships with local stakeholders like co-owners, shareholders, employees, unions, customers, suppliers and authorities.

In spite of their increasing frequency, international ventures do not have a high success rate. Strategic alliances, if they do not already break down in the negotiation stage, often fall short of their promises. Joint ventures remain costly drains on resources and eventually disappear. International acquisitions are resold. Mergers announced with great enthusiasm crash after some years, leaving a trail of broken careers and even ruined personal health of major proponents.

At the time such deals are concluded, those responsible think too often in terms of size and price only, showing naive optimism about the execution of their decision. While integrating people and operations from different countries is a difficult task, it can be and has been done successfully where the goals pursued were clear to everyone. When this is not the case, where leading persons involved hold different implicit goals, attempts at integration at lower levels will fail and the new venture is almost certain to get into trouble. Such fundamental goal disparities often go unrecognized or remain taboo. We believe this is a main reason for the failures and disappointing results in international ventures.

The national component in business goals: a review of the literature

The risks and disasters of international ventures have been known for decades. The road to internationalization is lined with wrecks. The management literature prefers describing successes rather than failures, but business sections in daily newspapers continue to announce broken dreams. […].

One hurdle to be overcome is different traditions of corporate governance. Equally developed and sometimes neighboring countries maintain very different ownership and governance systems, with little sign of convergence. Pedersen and Thomsen (1997), studying the ownership of the 100 largest business corporations in each of 12 European countries, reported that in Britain 61% of the 100 largest companies had many small shareholders, in Austria and Italy no large companies at all had this ownership type. Such differences are evidently historically rooted but they are maintained by different conceptions about the goals of business. These conceptions are part of national value systems, which belong to national cultures (Hofstede, 2001). […]

Li and Guisinger (1991) found that foreign entries in the U.S.A. from culturally distant countries were more likely to fail than were those from culturally close countries. Barkema, Bell and Pennings (1996) analyzed survival rates of foreign entries by Dutch companies and found these to decrease with cultural distance, but more for joint ventures and acquisitions than for Greenfield starts, and more for partly owned than for wholly-owned subsidiaries. They explained this by the need for "doublelayered acculturation" in the riskier cases. Barkema and Vermeulen (1997) in an extended set of Dutch foreign entries found the failure rate of joint ventures to be related to differences in Uncertainty Avoidance and to […] Long Term Orientation [Hofstede, 1980]. Luo (1999) found the performance of foreign joint ventures in China to be negatively associated with the cultural distance between the partners. A dissenting voice was heard from Morosini, Shane and Singh (1998), who in a set of foreign acquisitions into and from Italy found the acquired companies' sales growth in the two years after the acquisition to be positively related to the cultural distance of the partners. They suggested that the variety may have led to synergy. As the different studies used different success criteria, their results are not fully comparable. In the majority of cases, cultural differences seem to spell trouble.

The literature on business ethics shows extensive proof of the influence of nationality on values; that is feelings of right and wrong. For example, Schlegelmilch and Robertson (1995) showed that both country and industry affected the ethical perceptions of senior executives in the U.S.A. and European countries. Nakano (1997) found that Japanese and U.S. managers differed strongly in their ethics orientations. McDonald and Kan (1997) demonstrated differences in ethical perceptions between expatriate and local managers in Hong Kong. A worldwide survey of business ethics by Enderle (1997) reported significant country differences. Whitcomb, Erdener and Li (1998) showed differences between Chinese and U.S. managers in scenario based ethical decision-making exercises. Baker and Veit (1998) compared North American and Pacific Rim (i.e. Hong Kong, Japan, Singapore and Thailand) nations and found differences in the ethical principles of investment professionals. Priem, Worrell and Walters (1998) showed differences in moral judgment between respondents from rich and from poor countries. Stevenson and Bodkin (1998) even found significant differences in a cross-national comparison of U.S. and Australian university students' perceptions of right and wrong in sales practices.

Cross-national differences in business goals can also be traced in comparative studies on entrepreneurship, in spite of common traits of entrepreneurs across borders (McGrath and McMillan, 1992). Baum, Olian and Erez (1993) contrasted the needs of entrepreneurs and managers in Israel versus the U.S.A. Holt (1997) found both similarities and consistent differences between the values and behaviors of entrepreneurs in China and the U.S.A. Wildeman, Hofstede, Noorderhaven, Thurik, Verhoeven and Wennekers (1999) reported large differences in the levels of self-employment across 23 OECD countries, and related these to the goals of persons in these countries starting their own business. Many comparative studies have shown cross-national differences in individuals' values (England, 1975; Hofstede, 1980, 1997, 2001; Schwartz, 1994; Smith, 1996). These affect people in business as much as anybody else. For example, they affect what is considered fair compensation (Pennings, 1993; Hundley and Kim, 1997). They also affect concepts of desirable leadership traits (e.g. Koopman, Den Hartog and Konrad, 1999).

On the other hand forces of globalization of business, modern communication services, ease of transportation and international education could reduce the importance of local and national cultures, as suggested by, for example, Kumar and Thibodeaux (1998) and Salk and Brannen (2000). Being exposed to similar business contexts, business people in different countries might increasingly start embracing similar goals.

The present study, based on data about the goals of business leaders collected in the later 1990s, will show to what extent this "shrinking world" has wiped out effects of national cultures, or whether persistent national cultural differences have so far survived globalization.

Method and data

[…] Our strategy was to use the shared perceptions of well-informed third persons: Junior managers and professionals working during the day and attending evening

MBA classes at local universities. Of course the perceptions we measured were in the eyes of the beholders; but these beholders were cultural insiders, sharing the national cultures of the business leaders they reported on. [...]

Goals will vary between individuals, based on their personality, education, age, prosperity and experience. [...] What we were after was to see what national components these goals, as perceived by insiders, contained. Our data were collected with a standard "Questionnaire about Business Goals".[...] Fifteen different relevant goals [...] were put in questionnaire format, and respondents were asked to score their importance [...]. The present paper compares 21 groups from 16 universities, with students from 15 countries. They are listed in Table 4.1.

TABLE 4.1 Numbers of respondents from 21 country/university groups

Respondents	Country	University
93	Australia (AUL)	R.M.I.T. Melbourne
38	Bahamas (BAH)	Nova Southeastern U.
96	Brazil (BRA)	Fundaçao Dom Cabral, Belo Horizonte
23	China except Hong Kong (CHI)	R.M.I.T. Melbourne U. of Hawaii Ball State U. (Indiana) U. of Colorado-Boulder U. of N. Florida
190	France (FRA)	I.A.E.'s Paris, Grenoble, Lyon, Montpellier, Strasbourg
84	Germany (GER)	European Business School
42	Great Britain (GBR)	Henley Management College
101	Hong Kong (HOK)	U. of HK Business School
105	Hungary (HUN)	International Mgmt. Center
99	India (IND)	Goa Institute of Mgmt.
45	Jamaica (JAM)	Nova Southeastern U.
110	Netherlands (NET)	Tilburg University
72	New Zealand (NZL)	University of Auckland (AUK)
34	New Zealand (NZL)	Henley Management College (HEN)
65	Panama (PAN)	Nova Southeastern U.
148	USA	Ball State U., IN (BAL)
191	USA	U. of Colorado (COL)
115	USA	U. of North Florida (FLO)
102	USA	St. Louis U., MO (SLU)
30	Hawaii-Caucasians (USH-CAU)	University of Hawaii
31	Hawaii-Asians (USH-ASI)	University of Hawaii
1,814	ALL COUNTRIES	ALL UNIVERSITIES

Results

Comparing "Tycoon" with "Self"

Table 4.2 shows the 15 goals in their overall order of importance across all 21 country/university groups, giving equal weights to both genders and both age categories [under and over the age of 30]. The "tycoon" column refers to the "typical successful businessperson in your country" and the "self" column to the goals claimed for oneself. Low ranks and positive scores stand for "more important." The comparison between "tycoon" and "self" shows that:

1   Growth and continuity of the business are the leading goals both for tycoon and for self, but more strongly for the tycoon.
2   This year's profits, personal wealth and power were rated as very important for the tycoon, but less so for the self. "Power" is the goal for which the scores show the largest difference between tycoon and self.
3   Creating something new, profits 10 years from now, staying within the law, responsibility towards employees, respecting ethical norms and responsibility towards society were rated important for the self, but less for the tycoon.
4   Gambling spirit, patriotism and family interests were ranked lowest for both tycoon and self.

TABLE 4.2 Mean rated importance of 15 business goals across 21 country/university groups

	For Tycoon		For Self	
(standardized data; rank 1 = most important)	*Rank*	*Score*	*Rank*	*Score*
growth of the business	1	1.26	1	1.00
continuity of the business	2	1.05	2	.86
this year's profits	3	1.01	9	.26
personal wealth	4	.83	10	.08
power	5	.68	12	−.62
honor, face, reputation	6	.47	7	.48
creating something new	7	.21	6	.49
profits 10 years from now	8	.15	5	.56
staying within the law	9	−.12	4	.59
responsibility towards employees	10	−.30	3	.64
respecting ethical norms	11	−.52	8	.30
responsibility towards society	12	−.82	11	−.06
game and gambling spirit	13	−1.09	14	−1.57
patriotism, national pride	14	−1.26	13	−1.28
family interests	15	−1.56	15	−1.73

So the average respondent felt that: My priorities will be with being responsible towards employees, staying within the law and focusing on the long term, but my country's "tycoons" are mainly after the short term, wealth and power. We interpret this as a self-serving bias which is a common trait of human perception: Seeing one's own motives as noble, but other people's motives less so. [...] Further comparisons in this paper between countries and universities will obviously be based on the scores for "tycoon," not on the biased "self" scores. [...]

Country/University clusters

The present article focuses on the comparison across country/university groups. [...]

In the dendrogram (Table 4.3) we read that the two U.S. universities of Colorado and North Florida have produced the most similar scores (one point distance on the horizontal scale). The other two mainland U.S. universities and the ethnic Caucasians in Hawaii have also produced quite similar scores. The five U.S. universities form one close cluster with no more than three points mutual distance.

The two New Zealand groups also produced very similar scores, as shown by their tight clustering. None of the other groups share the same nationality, and none of them produced clusters as tight as the U.S. and New Zealand groups did. So the dendrogram proves that respondents from the same countries scored more similarly than those from the same universities (like the Henley Management College groups from New Zealand and Great Britain and the Nova Southeastern University groups from Bahamas, Jamaica and Panama). [...]

The similarity of answers deriving from the same country proves the reliability of the goals list as an instrument for detecting country effects. Groups from different countries also clustered, albeit somewhat less tightly than groups from the same country. If we consider groups with a mutual distance of less than ten points in Table 4.3 as belonging to a common cluster, five clusters remain. Two of these can be logically subdivided into political/geographical sub clusters (1ab and 4ab). The clustering structure to be read from Table 4.3 becomes:

1a All U.S. universities except the Asians in Hawaii.
1b New Zealand and Great Britain.
2   India, Jamaica and Bahamas (all three former parts of the British empire).
3   Panama, Australia, France, Brazil and Hungary. Panama, France and Brazil are the Latin countries in our population. Australia remarkably does not cluster with Britain and New Zealand. Hungary is our only East European country.
4a Hong Kong and the Hawaiian Asians, both affluent groups with an Asian ancestry.
4b Germany and the Netherlands, non-Anglo West European countries.
5   The mainland Chinese expatriate students in the U.S.A. and in Australia.

TABLE 4.3 Hierarchical cluster analysis of 21 groups on 15 business goals for "Tycoon"

Dendrogram using average linkage between groups

				Rescaled	Distance	Cluster	Combine
C A S E		0	5	10	15	20	25
Ctry	Univ	+--------	+--------	+--------	+--------	+--------	---+

1a
USA	COL
USA	FLO
USA	SLU
USA	BAL
USA	CAU

1b
NZL	HEN
NZL	AUK
GBR	HEN

2
IND	GIM
JAM	NSU
BAH	NSU

3
PAN	NSU
AUL	RMT
FRA	ULP
BRA	FDC
HUN	IMC

4a
| HOK | HKU |
| USH | ASI |

4b
| GER | EBS |
| NET | TIL |

5
| CHI | VAR |

For abbreviations see Table 4.1

Goal priorities according to country clusters

Table 4.4 lists the six most important goals attributed to business tycoons for each of the clusters, in order of importance. At first sight the lists look rather similar. Growth of the business, continuity of the business and reputation are mentioned in all seven cultures and sub clusters. This year's profits and personal wealth occur six times, power four times, profits 10 years from now and creating something new each two times, and staying within the law once. This apparent similarity is due to the fact that the 15 goals in the list are of unequal weight; [...] goals like growth and continuity have such a strong general appeal that they will figure high on any list. Other items among our 15 are more specific and produced larger differences between clusters, but this is not evident from the top six goals in Table 4.4.

The differences between the country clusters became more clearly visible after we eliminated the overall attractiveness of each goal. This was done by once more standardizing the scores, this time across the seven (sub)clusters. Our data have

TABLE 4.4 Six most important perceived goals of "Tycoons" in each of seven (sub)clusters of countries

---

Cluster 1a (U.S.A.)
growth of the business
this year's profits
personal wealth
power
continuity of the business
honor, face, reputation

Cluster 2 (India, Jamaica, Bahamas)
continuity of the business
growth of the business
this year's profits
personal wealth
power
honor, face, reputation

Cluster 3 (Latin countries, Australia, Hungary)
growth of the business
this year's profits
continuity of the business
personal wealth
power
honor, face, reputation

Cluster 4a (HKong, Hawaii-Asian)
growth of the business
personal wealth
continuity of the business
creating something new
honor, face, reputation
profits 10 years from now

Cluster 5 (China)
growth of the business
continuity of the business
power
honor, face, reputation
this year's profits
profits 10 years from now

Cluster 1b (Britain, New Zealand)
this year's profits
growth of the business
continuity of the business
staying within the law
personal wealth
honor, face, reputation

Cluster 4b (Germany, Netherlands)
continuity of the business
growth of the business
creating something new
honor, face, reputation
this year's profits
personal wealth

---

thus been standardized twice, first across the 15 goals (eliminating response sets of country/university groups), and second across 7 (sub)clusters (eliminating the overall attractiveness per goal). The results are listed in Table 4.5. which reflects the full variety in the choices from different clusters. Even if certain goals, like family interests, were overall given lower priority than growth, continuity and profits, their attributed importance did vary considerably between country clusters, and this is what Table 4.5 shows.

TABLE 4.5 Six relatively most important perceived goals of "Tycoons" in each of seven (sub)clusters of countries

---

Cluster 1a (U.S.A.) "the Executive"

growth of the business
this year's profits
personal wealth
power
staying within the law
respecting ethical norms

Cluster 1b (Britain, New Zealand)
"the Manager"

this year's profits
staying within the law
responsibility twds employees
continuity of the business
patriotism, national pride
respecting ethical norms

Cluster 2 (India, Jamaica, Bahamas) "the Family Manager"

continuity of the business
family interests
patriotism, national pride
personal wealth
profits 10 years from now
this year's profits

Cluster 3 (Latin countries, Australia, Hungary) "the Family Entrepreneur"

family interests
personal wealth
power
this year's profits
game and gambling spirit
growth of the business

Cluster 4a (HKong, Hawaii-Asian)
"the Entrepreneur"

profits 10 years from now
creating something new
game and gambling spirit
growth of the business
honor, face, reputation
personal wealth

Cluster 4b (Germany, Netherlands)
"the Founder"

responsibility twds employees
responsibility twds society
creating something new
game and gambling spirit
continuity of the business
honor, face, reputation

Cluster 5 (China) "the Mandarin"

respecting ethical norms
patriotism, national pride
honor, face, reputation
power
responsibility towards society
profits 10 years from now

Discussion

Archetypes of business leaders

Each of the (sub)clusters has its own profile of top-ranked business goals, according to Table 4.5. Each of these profiles reflects an "archetypal" business leader whom our MBA respondents thought of when scoring the questionnaire. In this section we name and describe these seven archetypes.

Cluster la in Table 4.5 is a tight group composed of all five U.S. universities, producing very similar rankings in spite of their geographical distance (they were located in Colorado, Florida, Hawaii, Indiana and Missouri). The only U.S. citizens not in this cluster are the ethnic Asian Americans in Hawaii. In the mainstream U.S. cluster, MBA students perceived their business leaders as focusing on growth and this year's profits, on personal wealth and power, on staying within the law, and on respecting ethical norms.

These goals provide a shorthand description of the U.S. business ethos. There is a focus on the "bottom line" or short term, and getting bigger is almost synonymous with getting better; there is a general respect for wealthy persons and wealth is considered the prime measure of success and human worth; there is a belief in power; there is a constant concern with the law in a country with the highest per capita density of lawyers and the largest number of lawsuits in the world; and at the same time a concern with moral and ethical rectitude supported by a multitude of religious communities. All of these form part and parcel of the U.S. national culture. [...]

As a unique term for describing the archetypal U.S. business leader reflected by these goals we chose the Executive. Executives in this case are defined as high-status and well-paid professionals in charge of a business they run on behalf of anonymous shareholders, without forgetting themselves.

Cluster lb in Table 4.5 unites the U.S.A.'s Anglo-cousins from Britain and New Zealand. They share the U.S. concern for short-term profits, laws, and respecting ethical norms, but their political and industrial environment has been marked by strong labor parties and trade unions. This accounts for the prominent place of the goal responsibility towards employees on their ranking, which was missing on the U.S. list. They stress continuity rather than growth, and successful business is part of their national pride.

As a unique term for describing the archetypal British/New Zealand business leader reflected by this slightly different set of goals we chose the Manager. The term manager rather than executive stresses the relationship with the employees who are managed.

Cluster 2 in Table 4.5 contains three non-Western members of the British Commonwealth: Bahamas, India and Jamaica. Their goals extend the British stress on this year's profits, continuity and patriotism to profits 10 years from now. They add personal wealth (like the Americans) but especially family interests, suggesting that business leadership in these countries is associated with family companies – which, in fact, are the dominant type of local businesses. As a unique term for describing the archetypal business leader in these former British colonies we chose the Family Manager.

Cluster 3 in Table 4.5 contains the Latin countries Brazil, France and Panama, as well as Australia and Hungary. Compared to Cluster 2 they lack the longer-term goals of continuity and profits 10 years from now. To the family business goals of personal wealth and family interests they explicitly add the goal of power. Here, for the first time, game and gambling spirit is also recognized as a prime goal of business tycoons. Australia is the only Anglo-country that did not cluster with its cultural sisters. The Australian MBAs associated their country's business tycoons no longer with traditional Anglo-values but rather with the more cosmopolitan values mix of the new Australians immigrated from various other parts of the world. Hungary as the only East-European country in our set also appears to fit into this values set. As a unique term for describing the archetypal business leader in this group of countries we chose the Family Entrepreneur.

Cluster 4a in Table 4.5 combined the Hong Kong Chinese MBAs with the Asian-American MBAs from the University of Hawaii. The latter, as we saw, are the only U.S. citizen group outside the tight five-U.S.-universities Cluster la. The combining of these two groups into one cluster is remarkable: Both reside on the margin between "East" and "West" in a part of the globe where "East" lies to the West of "West", and vice versa. They combine Eastern and Western values, usually very successfully. They take a long-term view, with profits 10 years from now before this year's profits. Creating something new and game and gambling spirit suggest a creative entrepreneurship. They are seen as focusing on growth rather than continuity, and on face and wealth for themselves. As a unique term for describing the archetypal business leader in these groups on the fringe between East and West we chose the Entrepreneur.

Cluster 4b in Table 4.5 combines two non-Anglo European countries, Germany and the Netherlands. The goals attributed to their tycoons differ from those elsewhere by a heavy stress on the social role of the business towards employees and towards society at large. At the same time they share the creative entrepreneurship goals creating something new and game and gambling spirit and the concern for honor and face with their colleagues from Cluster 4a at the opposite side of the globe. They are seen as aiming for continuity rather than growth. As a unique term for describing the archetypal business leader in these industrial European countries we chose the Founder whose goals are more directed towards the business empire to be created than towards personal wealth or power.

Cluster 5 in Table 4.5 contains one single group, the combined mainland Chinese expatriate students studying in Australia and the U.S.A. The goals they attribute to their business leaders are noble: Respecting ethical norms, patriotism, responsibility towards society. At the personal level their rewards are seen as face and power. Profit goals are 10 years from now. As an archetype for such a business leader we chose the classic Chinese Mandarin.

Conclusion

By describing the profiles of business leader goals in the previous section as "archetypes" we have already expressed our belief in their deep historical roots. These differences are not short-term and accidental. The historical origins of national differences in management were dramatically illustrated by the French sociologist Philippe d'Iribarne (1989, 1994) who compared work-floor relations in technologically identical aluminum smelters in France, the U.S.A. and the Netherlands. He related these to the social and political traditions of these countries dating from at least the 17th century and found three different basic principles: honor for France, the fair contract for the U.S.A., and consensus for the Netherlands. The unique traditions of each country have been maintained in their institutions like families, schools and forms of government and they are also conserved in differences in national cultures in the sense of "software of the mind" (Hofstede, 1997), that is patterns of thinking, feeling and acting that differentiate one country from another and continue to be transferred from generation to generation.

Nobel Prize laureate Douglass North (1990), the father of institutional economics, has classified cultural factors as "informal constraints" on societies, and has put them on an equal level with formal constraints via institutions. We believe that claiming either a priority or a causality link between "institutions" and "cultures" is useless hair-splitting. Institutions are the crystallizations of culture, and culture is the substratum of institutional arrangements. For example, the differences found in Table 4.5 in the relative importance attributed to family interests between and even within parts of the world are reflected in the role of families in business ownership.

The results of our comparative study of perceived goals of successful businesspersons show that the national component in goals is real and robust. There are no globally universal business goals. Globalization is often more a slogan and wishful thinking than a reality. The national origin of an enterprise continues to matter; it matters precisely in one of the most profound issues in the management of the enterprise, the goals held by its leaders. An appeal to a shared rationality will not be enough. Nationality constrains rationality. In decisions about international ventures, this fact should be taken into account more seriously than is usually the case. Parties should think twice before entering any cross-national venture, and estimate the risks and cost attached to cooperating across their national borders. If they decide to go ahead they should devote sustained top-management attention and high-quality resources to monitoring and managing the consequences of goal discrepancies.

References

Baker, H. Kent and E. Theodore Veit. 1998. A Comparison of Ethics of Investment Professionals: North America versus Pacific Rim Nations. *Journal of Business Ethics*, 17(8): 917–37.

Barkema, Harry G. and Freek Vermeulen. 1997. What Differences in the Cultural Backgrounds of Partners are Detrimental for International Joint Ventures? *Journal of International Business Studies*, 28(4): 845–64.

Barkema, Harry G., John H.J. Bell and Johannes M. Pennings. 1996. Foreign Entry, Cultural Barriers, and Learning. *Strategic Management Journal*, 17, 151–66.

Baum, J. Robert, Judy D. Olian and Miriam Erez. 1993. Nationality and Work Role Interactions: A Cultural Contrast of Israeli and U.S. Entrepreneurs' versus Managers' Needs. *Journal of Business Venturing*, 8(6): 499–512.

d'Iribarne, Philippe. 1989. *La Logique de l'Honneur: Gestion des Entreprises et Traditions Nationales*. Paris: Editions du Seuil.

———.1994. The Honor Principle in the Bureaucratic Phenomenon. *Organization Studies*, 15(1): 81–97.

Enderle, Georges. 1997. A Worldwide Survey of Business Ethics in the 1990s. *Journal of Business Ethics*, 16(14): 1475–83.

England, George W. 1975. *The Manager and his Values: An International Perspective from the U.S., Japan, Korea, India and Australia*. Cambridge, MA: Ballinger.

Hall, Pamela L. and Terrell G. Williams. 1998. Marketing/Finance Executives' Personal and Business Value Perspectives: Implications for Marketing-Focused Management. *International Journal of Value-Based Management*, 11(2): 125–57.

Hofstede, Geert. 1980. *Culture's Consequences: International Differences in Work-Related Values*. Beverly Hills, CA: Sage.

———.1997. *Cultures and Organizations: Software of the Mind*. New York: McGraw-Hill.

———. 2001. *Culture's Consequences: Comparing Values, Behaviors, Institutions and Organizations across Nations*. Second Edition. Thousand Oaks, CA: Sage.

Holt, David H. 1997. A Comparative Study of Values among Chinese and U.S. Entrepreneurs: Pragmatic Convergence between Contrasting Cultures. *Journal of Business Venturing*, 12(6): 483–505.

Hundley, Greg and Jooyup Kim. 1997. National Culture and the Factors Affecting Perceptions of Pay Fairness in Korea and the United States. *The International Journal of Organizational Analysis*, 5(4): 325–41.

Koopman, Paul L., Deanne N. den Hartog and Edvard Konrad. 1999. National Cultures and Leadership Profiles in Europe. *European Journal of Work and Organization Psychology*, 8(4): 503–20.

Kumar, Kamalesh and Mary S. Thibodeaux. 1998. Differences In Value Systems of Anglo-American and Far Eastern Students: Effects of American Business Education. *Journal of Business Ethics*, 17(3): 253–62.

Li, Jiatao and Stephen Guisinger. 1991. Comparative Business Failures of Foreign-Controlled Firms in the United States. *Journal of International Business Studies*, 22, 209–24.

Luo, Yadong. 1999. Time-Based Experience and International Expansion: The Case of an Emerging Economy. *Journal of Management Studies*, 36, 505–34.

March, James G. and Johan P. Olsen. 1976. *Ambiguity and Choice in Organizations*. Bergen, Norway: Universitetsforlaget.

McDonald, Gael M. and Kan, Pak Cho. 1997. Ethical Perceptions of Expatriate and Local Managers in Hong Kong. *Journal of Business Ethics*, 16(15): 1605–23.

McGrath, Rita Gunther and Ian C. McMillan. 1992. More Like Each Other than Anyone Else? A Cross-Cultural Study of Entrepreneurial Perceptions. *Journal of Business Venturing*, 7(5): 419–29.

Morosini, Piero, Scott A. Shane and Harbir Singh. 1998. National Cultural Distance and Cross-Border Acquisition. *Journal of International Business Studies*, 29, 137–58.

Nakano, Chiaki. 1997. A Survey Study on Japanese Managers' Views on Business Ethics. *Journal of Business Ethics*, 16(16): 727–35.

North, Douglass. 1990. *Institutions, Institutional Change and Economic Performance*. Cambridge: Cambridge University Press.

Pedersen, Torben and Steen Thomsen. 1997. European Patterns of Corporate Ownership: A Twelve-Country Study. *Journal of International Business Studies*, 28(4): 759–78.

Pennings, Johannes M. 1993. Executive Reward Systems: A Cross-National Comparison. *Journal of Management Studies*, 30(2): 261–80.

Priem, Richard, Dan Worrell and Bruce Walters. 1998. Moral Judgment and Values in a Developed and Developing Nation: A Comparative Analysis. *Journal of Business Ethics*, 17(5): 491–501.

Salk, Jane and Mary Yoko Brannen. 2000. National Culture, Network and Individual Differences in a Multinational Management Team. *Academy of Management Journal*, 43(2): 191–202.

Schlegelmilch, Bodo B. and Diana C. Robertson. 1995. The Influence of Country and Industry on Ethical Perceptions of Senior Executives in the U.S. and Europe. *Journal of International Business Studies*, 26(4): 859–81.

Schwartz, Shalom H. 1994. Beyond Individualism/Collectivism: New Cultural Dimensions of Values. In U. Kim, H.C. Triandis, C. Kagitcibasi, S.C. Choi and G. Yoon, editors, *Individualism and Collectivism: Theory, Method and Applications* (85–119). Thousand Oaks, CA: Sage.

Smith, Peter B. 1996. National Cultures and the Values of Organizational Employees: Time for Another Look. In P. Joynt and M. Warner, editors, *Managing across Cultures: Issues and Perspectives* (92–102). London: Thomson.

Stevenson, Thomas H. and Charles D. Bodkin. 1998. A Cross-National Comparison of University Students' Perceptions Regarding the Ethics and Acceptability of Sales Practices. *Journal of Business Ethics*, 17(1): 45–55.

Whitcomb, Laura L., Carolyn B. Erdener and Chen Li. 1998. Business Ethical Values in China and the U.S. *Journal of Business Ethics*, 17(8): 839–52.

Wildeman, Ralph E., Geert Hofstede, Niels G. Noorderhaven, A. Roy Thurik, Wim H.J. Verhoeven and Alexander R.M. Wennekers. 1999. *Culture's Role in Entrepreneurship: Self-Employment out of Dissatisfaction*. Rotterdam, Netherlands: Rotterdam Institute for Business Economic Studies (RIBES).

5

THE ROLE OF GOALS IN THE MANAGEMENT OF SUPPLY CHAIN NETWORKS

Taras Gagalyuk and Jon Hanf

Introduction

Several studies on the effects of foreign direct investments (FDI) in the agribusiness of Central and East-European countries (CEEC) show that foreign investors exert significant efforts to arrange well-functioning supply chain networks (Swinnen 2006, Reardon *et al.* 2007). To raise the level of quality of their suppliers, foreign retailers and food manufacturers introduce chain-wide management concepts to optimize inter-firm relationships with local suppliers.

Supply chain networks embody collaboration of more than two firms (Omta *et al.* 2001). Their members maintain highly-intensive and recurrent interactions with each other based on formal and informal contracts (Burr 1999). To support its structure and strategic nature, a focal actor tends to set the network strategy and coordinate its implementation in a hierarchical manner (Jarillo 1988; Sanders 2005). This focal actor is typically recognized by the consumers as "responsible" for the specific product (Hanf and Kühl 2005). The managerial task of the focal actor is to deal with problems of cooperation and coordination (Gulati *et al.* 2005). While the problems of cooperation arise from the conflicts of interests, the problems of coordination originate from unawareness of the existing interdependencies or the lack of one's knowledge about the behavior of others. More specifically, problems of cooperation and coordination can be viewed as a consequence of distinctive goals that are established at the firm and network levels of collaboration (Duysters *et al.* 2004).

Whereas the establishment of clear goals is recognized as a prerequisite of a firm strategic success (Simon 1964, Porter 1980), the importance of network goals for the network's strategy and (chain) management is still poorly understood. In this chapter therefore, our aim is to provide a theoretical elaboration on the role that network goals play in strategic chain management. Specifically, the following questions are explored: What are the network goals? How can these goals affect chain management? How does chain management deal with network goals in the agri-food supply chains of the CEEC?

Supply chain network goals

A major challenge facing the focal company of a supply chain network is the structuring of the exchange relationships so that its suppliers and customers remain in the relationships and act in the best interests of all the parties (Jap and Ganesan 2000). Consequently, from the focal company's perspective, it is necessary to develop a strategic approach which accounts for the objectives of all the chain actors and is agreed upon by them.

In the inter-organizational literature, such an approach is defined as a collective strategy (Bresser and Harl 1986). Starting from the work by Astley and Fombrun (1983), a number of studies (e.g. Bresser and Harl 1986, Sjurts 2000) have addressed collective strategies as a type of strategy implemented for and by collaborating organizations. Because collaboration *per se* implies joint work of numerous actors to achieve common goals (e.g. Chen *et al*. 1998, Huxham and Vangen, 2005), collective strategies can be subsumed as those aiming to create a framework for the achievement of common goals.

In supply chain networks, adoption of the collective strategy is most often initiated by the focal actor who goes beyond addressing its own goals and proposes ways to achieve network goals. In this context, several authors (e.g. Duysters *et al*. 2004, Contractor *et al*. 2006) argue that the network's management should specifically involve mechanisms to maintain exchange relationships and achieve goals set at least at two levels; the network and firm levels. The focal firm, as a strategy-setting element of the supply chain network, has to take particular interest in the achievement of both. In this context, we understand the network-level goals as the predefined set of outcomes which can be achieved only if all the network actors work together to achieve them.

Such goals can be regarded as common to or shared by all the network members, and their achievement is the essence of collaboration (Huxham and Vangen 2005). Provan and Kenis (2008) provide examples of network-level goals in the public sector, e.g. strengthened community capacity to solve public problems; regional economic development; responsiveness to natural or made-made disasters, etc. In food supply chain networks, the achievement of total chain quality can be considered as an example of the network-level goal. The goal of total chain quality requires that all the food chain actors efficiently and effectively work together to address increasing consumers' demands and minimize the risk of food scandals. Providing solutions for such complex issues requires multilateral coordination and more than just achieving the goals of individual organizations (O'Toole 1997). Furthermore, unclear definition of common goals or lack of agreement upon them is the main reason why 50 per cent of all inter-organizational projects fail (Brinkhoff and Thonemann, 2007).

However, in contrast to participant-governed networks with all the actors knowledgeable about network-level goals (Provan and Kenis 2008), supply chain networks are in most cases deliberately engineered by the focal actor. This implies that the focal firm is responsible not only for implementation of collective strategies but also for setting network level goals (Schermerhorn 1975, Lorenzoni and Baden-Fuller 1995). Therefore, the commonness of goals in a supply chain network largely depends on the efforts by the focal firm and, thus, the focal firm has to ensure that all the members pursue network-level goals (Kochan *et al.* 1976, Doz *et al.* 2000). For example, performance of a just-in-time (JIT) system introduced by a retailer can not be analyzed only by benefits to this retailer. Reduction of inventory in terms of JIT requires that a retailer's suppliers substantially improve their quality and that there is a low level of holdups at each upstream stage of a supply chain (Davy *et al.* 1992).

However, the sole focus on network-level goals does not encompass measures of the network's effectiveness entirely. One has to consider also firm-level goals because networks involve relationships among individual firms. Although effective functioning of the network requires goal consensus among the members (Doz *et al.* 2000, Provan and Kenis 2008), each actor enters the network with its own objectives. An endeavor to achieve them can affect the achievement of network-level goals (Wathne and Heide 2004, Winkler 2006). Firm-level goals might include, for example, access to resources or markets, increased sales, risk reduction, etc. Furthermore, non-achievement of goals of the particular members can lead to the network's collapse if these members cannot be equally substituted (e.g., Park and Ungson 1997 and 2001). Therefore, analyses of whole networks have to consider not only the network level but also the firm level (Table 5.1).

TABLE 5.1 Examples of the supply chain network's goals

Network goals	
Firm-level goals	*Network-level goals*
Access to input and sales markets	Partner reliability
Reduction of environmental uncertainty	Chain transparency
Access to knowledge, etc.	Chain quality
	End consumer satisfaction, etc.

For a network to perform effectively, it is of particular importance that the goals set at the different levels are achieved to a satisfactory extent. Additionally, the network's management, i.e., the focal company, has to consider specific interrelationships that can occur between goals of the different levels and can create conditions either favoring or constraining the achievement of the whole network's goals. In other words, effectiveness of the supply chain network is subject to influence by network goals.

How can network goals affect strategic chain management?

Goals in supply chain networks can be grouped into three categories: compatible, conflicting, and indifferent goals (Table 5.2).

TABLE 5.2 Interrelationships between firm-level and network-level goals

Goal interrelationship	Preconditions	Outcomes
Compatible	High level of ideological agreement on the nature of tasks and the appropriate approaches to these tasks (Frazier 1983); insensitivity of the organizational domain issue (Schermerhorn 1975).	No serious transaction and coordination costs; trust among partners; commitment to collective interests; improvement of transactional efficiency (Park and Ungson 2001).
Conflicting	Structural differentiation (Kochan et al. 1976); differences in policies and procedures used to achieve individual members' goals (Brown and Day 1981) and common goals (Frazier and Summers 1984); distinctive interests with regard to actions to be undertaken (Frazier 1983); each party has its own business philosophy and interests (Eliashberg and Michie 1984).	Relationship break off (Kumar and van Dissel 1996); negative effect on network satisfaction and network continuity (Bradford et al. 2004); communication difficulties (Leonidou et al. 2008).
Indifferent	No interest overlap; no overlap of actions derived from autonomous, independent decisions.	Indirectly positive or negative.

Compatible goals are the goals that can nurture the achievement of each other; without having compatible goals at the firm level, the achievement of network-level goals is most probably impossible. For instance, at the network level, the goal set by the focal company may be to achieve a certain level of chain quality based on the introduction of a tracking and tracing system. One individual network actor complementary goal in this case could be to gain necessary knowledge from a supply chain network about requirements of a corresponding certification scheme. If network actors lack such knowledge, then the achievement of chain quality is problematic.

Compatible goals may exist as a result of a high level of agreement on the nature of, and approaches to, tasks to be undertaken by individual actors (Frazier 1983). As each member of a network specializes in performing particular functions, such an agreement indicates the members' awareness and readiness to contribute to the achievement of network-level goals.

Conflicting goals are the goals that can hinder the achievement of each other. As individual actors have different characteristics, tasks, responsibilities and reward expectations, their goals can conflict with network-level goals (Kochan *et al.* 1976, Huxham and Vangen 2005). Very often, conflicting goals arise not because of goal incompatibility itself but because of disagreement on how to achieve common goals (e.g. Brown and Day 1981). Conflicting goals can become apparent, for example, due to actors' distinctive views on transaction-specific investments, e.g. needed to install electronic data interchange (Jap and Ganesan 2000). Coping with such goals requires additional efforts by the network's management. This is not surprising because compliance of individual exchange partners with the network is crucial to the achievement of network goals and, therefore, for network functioning (Doz *et al.* 2000).

Indifferent goals are the goals of the different network levels that have no impact on each other. Indifferent goals exist because there is no overlap of individual interests and actions with those of the network level. For instance, a network-level goal of total chain quality can have no relation to the firm-level goal of gaining a higher reputation from participating in a network. These goals, however, can indirectly influence the network's effectiveness. For example, unsatisfactory perceptions of reputation effects from cooperation can reduce the individual firm's desire to contribute to chain quality improvement.

By including the interrelationships between goals set at the different network levels in collective strategies, the focal company creates preconditions for the achievement of network goals and thereby makes the network perform effectively.

Supply chain network management

Integration of the exchange partners requires that the supply chain network's management properly deals with the problems of cooperation and coordination (Gulati *et al.* 2005, Hanf and Dautzenberg 2006, Xu and Beamon 2006). Because problems of cooperation arise due to conflicts of interests, the cooperation task is to align the interests of the participating actors or, in other words, motivate them to work together (Gulati *et al.* 2005). The accomplishment of this task is typically addressed by the implementation of partnering strategies that generally aim to design the relationships within the supply chain (Mentzer *et al.* 2000). Formal partnering strategies mechanisms include contracting, common ownership of assets, monitoring, sanctions, rewards and the prospect of future interactions (Williamson 1985, Gulati *et al.* 2005). Identification and embeddedness serve as informal mechanisms (Granovetter 1985, Kogut and Zander 1996, Gulati and Sytch 2007).

The problems of coordination appear as a consequence of uncertainty about the actions of interdependent actors. Therefore, coordination is related to joint actions and can be generally referred to as the alignment of actions (Gulati *et al.* 2005, Payan 2007). The fulfillment of this task consists in gaining or transferring knowledge about the behavior of interdependent actors and the character of existing interdependences. The alignment of actions in supply chain networks is addressed by implementation of the supply chain management strategies (Simatupang *et al.* 2002). Generally, supply chain management strategies should involve the mechanisms named in the coordination literature. Formal coordination mechanisms include programming, hierarchy and feedback (Thompson 1967) whereas informal mechanisms incorporate shared experience, leadership, culture, norms and values (Kogut and Zander 1996).

In the process of structuring long-term exchange relationships, the focal company has to develop simultaneously the partnering and supply chain management strategies as components of the overall collective strategy derived from the whole network's goals (Hanf and Dautzenberg 2006). Particularly, the alignment of interests and actions is crucial to a) facilitate and maintain the goals' commonality, and b) mediate interrelationships between goals of different levels. In other words, it is necessary to reach consensus on network-level goals via attaining goal compatibility[1] between the network and firm levels, and simultaneously arrange the network's harmonious work to achieve both network-level and firm-level goals.

Goal consensus

As shown by Provan and Kenis (2008) in their study on goal-directed networks in the public sector, the extent of goal consensus among the actors can differ across the different types of networks. In this context, in networks possessing lead organizations, there will be a moderately low level of agreement on network-level goals. This statement can be regarded as partially true for such an interfirm cooperation form as the supply chain network. Obviously, each firm enters a supply chain network with its own reasons to cooperate. Nevertheless, single firms have to take into account that the network has its own rules (including goals) which should be followed (Dyer and Nobeoka 2000). Furthermore, since the focal company deliberately organizes the supply chain network and makes decisions about the network-level goals (Lorenzoni and Lipparini 1999), it is especially in the interest, and within the grasp, of the focal company that the other network actors agree upon the network-level goals.

Although joint action does not automatically imply the need for common goals, cooperation with common goals creates long-term collaborative advantages and is even necessary (Pitsis *et al.* 2004). By reaching an agreement among the network members on such goals as total chain quality or chain transparency, the focal company creates initial conditions for collaboration and stabilizes the network relationships because goal commonality also serves as an integrating mechanism (Winkler 2006). To the extent that the parties' goals become aligned *ex ante*, the

---

[1]Goal consensus and goal compatibility are typically viewed as synonyms in interorganizational research because they have to be achieved simultaneously and most often require similar mechanisms (e.g. Kochan *et al.* 1976, Frazier 1983, Provan and Kenis 2008). We, nevertheless, view them separately because, in terms of supply chain networks, we see goal consensus as agreement on *what* should be achieved, and goal compatibility as agreement on *how* it should be achieved.

likelihood of subsequent motivation-related problems is greatly reduced (Wathne and Heide 2004: 75). However, collaborative advantages are often future-oriented and more uncertain than individual goals; therefore, the network faces the risk of interfirm rivalry (Park and Ungson 2001). In order to reduce the risk and facilitate the achievement of the network's goals, the issue of goal commonality has to be explicitly addressed by the supply chain network's management.

While a number of authors suggest that goal consensus arises from domain similarity (e.g. van de Ven 1976, Doz *et al.* 2000), partnering and supply chain management strategies play an important role in maintaining agreement on network-level goals. In particular, such informal mechanisms of cooperation and coordination as identification, embeddedness, shared experience, norms and values enable actors to agree on goals (Wathne and Heide 2004, Gulati *et al.* 2005). Besides, the focal company should pay attention to sharing appropriate information about network-level goals. Otherwise, for the other network actors, these goals will remain the firm-level goals of the focal company (Gagalyuk and Hanf 2008). Additionally, communication is the way the other network actors participate in the decision-making process (Mohr and Nevin 1990). Appropriate communication, thus, creates preconditions for actors to consent on goals as it helps clarify the extent the network-level goals are compatible with the firm-level ones.

Goal compatibility

Consensus on network-level goals depends on firms' perceptions of compatibility with their own goals on an ongoing basis (Doz 1996). Perceived incompatibility of goals leads to conflict among network actors and makes them perform worse (Provan and Kenis 2008). Therefore, the task of the focal company is to maintain goal compatibility between the different levels of the supply chain network.

The degree of goal compatibility is generally measured by how compatible social and organizational characteristics of the network actors are (Smith *et al.* 1995, Doz *et al.* 2000, Provan and Kenis 2008). The social context in which partners operate is partly defined by the cultural and institutional backgrounds of the partners. Furthermore, the similarity of cultural values may reduce misunderstanding between the partners while lack of fit with a partner's culture leads to poor communication and mutual distrust (Park and Ungson 2001: 44). Not only similarities in cultural values but also the perceived status and legitimacy of partners as well as perceptions of procedural justice influence goal compatibility among network actors (Doz *et al.* 2000).

Additionally, the extent to which the firm-level objectives match the network-level goals depends on organizational compatibility (White and Siu-Yun Lui 2005). Dissimilarities in organizational structures and processes can create problems in coordination by causing disagreements over operating strategies, policies, and methods. Organizational dissimilarities are typically manifested in differences of capabilities and strategies of firms. Therefore, opinions of the network actors about managerial routines, marketing policies, quality control, etc. may differ from those of the focal company (Park and Ungson 2001: 45).

Thus, it is necessary to ensure a certain level of cultural, organizational and strategic fit of the network actors. In general, where goal compatibility is absent, there is a need for a power process (Kochan *et al.* 1976, Frazier 1983). The notion of power typically arouses associations with explicit domination of one actor over the others. Indeed, the focal actor can employ hierarchical mechanisms (e.g. control, sanctions) to make the participants comply with the network-level goals. However, not always acting in such a way will have positive effects on partner compliance. Moreover, the exercise of power based on coercive sources, e.g. financial penalties or withholding of important support (Goodman and Dion 2001), can aggravate communication difficulties caused by cultural dissimilarities and elevate any underlying causes of conflict to a manifest state (Leonidou *et al.* 2008: 93). Thus, the use of hierarchical authority can deepen incompatibility between the network-level and firm-level goals, especially in the case of great cultural and geographic distance (Leonidou 2004).

On account of this, partnering and supply chain management strategies include also mechanisms which represent non-coercive bases of power. The use of such mechanisms as rewards, identification, and information exchange enhances the partners' willingness to exert effort for the network-level goals (Gulati *et al.* 2005, Leonidou *et al.* 2008). Furthermore, such a mechanism as recommendations helps to achieve the desired perceptual change of objectives and subsequent performance of the intended behaviors (Frazier and Summers 1984: 45).

However, not only the fit of culture, resources and strategies of the single firms should be attained. The effective use of the cooperation and coordination mechanisms requires (and enables) deployment of network-specific structural factors which can be also referred to as alliance capabilities (Kale *et al.* 2002) or network-level competencies (Provan and Kenis 2008). In this context, a dedicated alliance function allows developing of network management routines needed to maintain cooperation and information exchange among actors (Ireland *et al.* 2002). In a supply chain network, it is especially important that the focal company performs such a function and has corresponding competencies matching the needs of the whole network. Possession of network-level competencies enhances communication and knowledge transfer within the network and thereby provides an understanding of partners' goals, interests and expectations.

Overall, in ensuring goal compatibility, an emphasis has to be primarily put on the development of partnering strategies, since their task is to align the interests of the network actors or, in other words, to motivate them to work together. As known, motives serve as the causes that lead individuals to select some goals rather than others (Simon 1964). Therefore, interest alignment can be defined as the degree to which the members of the organization are motivated to behave in line with organizational goals (Gottschalg and Zollo 2007). The function of supply chain management strategies is to enable communication of goals among actors via organization of the programming and feedback processes. Altogether, appropriate implementation of the partnering and supply chain management strategies contributes to the achievement of the network-level and firm-level goals (Ireland *et al.* 2002).

Successful food chain management in CEEC

The achievement of goals generally means success. This section draws on expert interviews to provide practices and evidence of successful supply chain networks' management in the agribusiness of CEE countries along with examples of how food chain management deals with network goals.

A high level of awareness of network goals is demonstrated by companies in the agribusiness of CEEC. Multinationals see the issue of chain quality and therewith connected partner reliability as the main goals to be achieved at the network level. Therefore, they introduce chain management concepts as part of their strategic framework used internationally. This use of chain management is apparent in the rolling out of global IT-standards as well as supply chain management techniques. For example, moving abroad, German multinationals such as Metro Group and Rewe primarily install their purchasing, IT and total quality departments. There is recognition behind these activities that network-level goals have to be established with local suppliers on an ongoing basis. Additionally, to ensure goal commonality multinationals introduce such programming tools as private quality standards. Examples of quality standardization include GLOBALGAP, BRC, ISO 9000 and HACCP (Gawron and Theuvsen 2008).

Multinational retailers and food manufacturers also consider firm-level goals of their local partners and try to ensure compatibility with network-level goals where this compatibility may be absent. Due to the prevalence of small- and medium-size enterprises as well as households in agricultural production, the use of necessary and recommended inputs is often a problem as farmers face a financial burden. Furthermore, due to numerous non-payments and delays experienced in the 1990s, farmers perceive prompt cash payments from downstream partners as a benefit (Swinnen 2006). However, given the high volatility of business environment in some of CEEC, multinational companies are interested in more than just providing their partners with inputs and cash payments. Satisfaction of their requirements includes compliance with the basic level of quality. Therefore, they use different coordination schemes to assure quality. For example, in Bulgaria, Romania, Moldova, Ukraine and Russia, dairy processors assure quality supplies by leasing cooling tanks to farmers as part of their contracts (Top Agrar 2004, Gorton *et al.* 2006, Swinnen 2006). Except for input and loan support, there is evidence of support on quality expertise and training for specialists as is the case with dairy processor Wimm Bill Dann and brewery holding Interbrew in Russia (Swinnen 2006).

Goal compatibility at the firm level is also achieved through enrollment of some informal mechanisms like identification. Foreign companies establish cooperation with local suppliers by using their general cooperativeness and reputation aspects. Local companies are very proud to work with well-known multinationals. Moreover, non-compliance with their cooperation principles may have negative reputation consequences (Swinnen 2006). Additionally, multinational companies use coercive mechanisms like control and sanctions. Well-branded multinationals have their own quality control departments where they conduct random product quality testing. Furthermore, purchasing departments evaluate delivery quality. Suppliers' non-compliance leads to fees and, as a last resort, sanctions. Joint problem solving and knowledge sharing are used to help partners succeed. Thus, acting as focal companies, well-branded retailers and food manufacturers smooth over social and organizational inconsistencies of their suppliers, promote trust among the partners, and thereby make them work to achieve the network-level goal of chain quality. However, intensive implementation of chain management concepts is still impeded by high riskiness and unfavorable institutional environment: bank loans are unsafe, corruption is present, property rights are weakly protected, etc. On account of this, foreign companies that invest on a long-term basis are obliged to properly consider possible short-term risks. There is a conflict between long-term orientation of chain management and the need to produce high returns on investments in short terms. To solve this dilemma, foreign companies try to establish long-term relationships with their local suppliers.

Conclusion

As a type of strategic networks (Gulati *et al.* 2000), supply chain networks manifest goal-orientation themselves and involve traditionally self-oriented participants. Consequently, one of the main points that should be addressed by the network's management is the tension between intra- and inter-organizational goals. To deal with this task properly, it is necessary to gain an understanding of goals set in the supply chain network.

The supply chain network's focal actor is a brand-owner, a food manufacturer or a food retail company, whose concern about chain quality requires maintaining of tight and long-term exchange relationships with the chain partners. To structure such relationships so that the partners simultaneously comply with the overall network's requirements and are satisfied by collaboration, the focal company has to align the interests and the actions of the involved parties. By ensuring goal commonality among actors and goal compatibility between the network and firm levels, the network's management paves the way for attaining beneficial outcomes at both levels. In particular, attention must be paid to management of conflicting goals since they negatively influence network effectiveness. Conflicting goals arise due to a number of factors that stem from cultural, resource and strategic differences. Only real understanding of these aspects can help organize the harmonious work of the network actors to achieve both network-level and firm-level goals.

References

Astley, W.G., Fombrun, C.J. 1983. Collective strategy: Social ecology of organizational environments. *Academy of Management Review* 8: 576–587.

Bradford, K.D., Stringfellow, A., Weitz, B.A. 2004. Managing conflict to improve the effectiveness of retail networks. *Journal of Retailing* 80: 181–195.

Bresser, R.K.F., Harl, J.E. 1986. Collective strategy: Vice or virtue? *Academy of Management Review* 11: 408–427.

Brinkhoff, A., Thonemann, U.W. 2007. Perfekte Projekte in der Lieferkette. *Harvard Business Manager* 7: 6–9.

Brown, J.R., Day, R.L. 1981. Measures of manifest conflict in distribution channels. *Journal of Marketing Research* 18 (3): 263–274.

Burr, B. 1999. Koordination durch Regeln in selbstorganisierenden Unternehmensnetzwerken. *Zeitschrift für Betriebswirtschaft* 69 (10): 1159–1179.

Chen, C.C., Chen, X.P., Meindl, J.R. 1998. How can cooperation be fostered? The cultural effects of individualism and collectivism. *Academy of Management Review* 23 (2): 285–304.

Contractor, N.S., Wasserman, S., Faust, K. 2006. Testing multitheoretical, multilevel hypotheses about organizational networks: An analytic framework and empirical example. *Academy of Management Review* 31 (3): 681–703.

Davy, J.A., White, R.E., Merritt, N.J., Gritzmacher, K. 1992. A derivation of the underlying constructs of just-in-time management systems. *Academy of Management Journal* 35(3): 653–670.

Doz, Y.L. 1996. The evolution of cooperation in strategic alliances: Initial conditions or learning processes? *Strategic Management Journal* 17, Special Issue: Evolutionary Perspectives on Strategy: 55–83.

Doz, Y.L., Olk, P.M., Smith Ring, P. 2000. Formation processes of R&D consortia: Which path to take? Where does it lead? *Strategic Management Journal* 21: 239–266.

Duysters, G., Heimeriks, K.H., Jurriens, J.A. 2004. An integrated perspective on alliance management. *Journal on Chain and Network Science* 4: 83–94.

Dyer, J.H., Nobeoka, K. 2000. Creating and managing a high-performance knowledge sharing network: the Toyota case. *Strategic Management Journal* 21 (3): 345–367.

Eliashberg, J., Michie, D.A. 1984. Multiple business goals sets as determinants of marketing channel conflict: An empirical study. *Journal of Marketing Research* 21 (1): 75–88.

Ellram, L.M., Zsidisin, G.A., Siferd, S.P., Stanly, M.J. 2002. The impact of purchasing and supply management activities on corporate success. *The Journal of Supply Chain Management* 38 (1): 4–17.

Frazier, G.L. 1983. Interorganizational exchange behavior in marketing channels: A broadened perspective. *Journal of Marketing* 47 (4): 68–78.

Frazier, G.L., Summers, J.O. 1984. Interfirm influence strategies and their applications within distribution channels. *Journal of Marketing* 48 (3): 43–55.

Gagalyuk, T., Hanf, J.H. 2008. Successful management of supply chain networks: What is missing, what are the goals? Paper presented at the 8th International Conference on Management in AgriFood Supply Chains and Networks, Ede, The Netherlands, May 28–30, 2008.

Gawron, J.-C., Theuvsen, L. 2008. Certification schemes in the European agrifood sector: Overview and opportunities for Central and Eastern Europe. Paper presented at IAMO Forum 2008 "Agri-Food Business: Global Challenges – Innovative Solutions", Halle (Saale), Germany, June 25–27, 2008.

Goodman, L.E., Dion, P.A. 2001. The determinants of commitment in the distributor–manufacturer relationship. *Industrial Marketing Management* 30 (3): 287–300.

Gorton, M., Dumitrashko, M., White, J. 2006. Overcoming supply chain failure in the agrifood sector: A case study from Moldova. *Food Policy* 31: 90–103.

Gottschalg, O., Zollo, M. 2007. Interest alignment and competitive advantage. *Academy of Management Review* 32 (2): 418–433.

Granovetter, M. 1985. Economic action and social structure: The problem of embeddedness. *American Journal of Sociology* 91: 481–510.

Gulati, R., Nohria, N., Zaheer, A. 2000. Strategic Networks. *Strategic Management Journal* 21: 203–216.

Gulati, R., Lawrence, P.R., Puranam, P. 2005. Adaptation in vertical relationships: Beyond incentive conflicts. *Strategic Management Journal* 26: 415–440.

Gulati, R., Sytch, M. 2007. Dependence asymmetry and joint dependence in interorganizational relationships: Effects of embeddedness on a manufacturer's performance in procurement relationships. *Administrative Science Quarterly* 52: 32–69.

Hanf, J., Kühl, R. 2005. Branding and its consequences for the German agribusiness. *Agribusiness: An International Journal* 21: 177–189.

Hanf, J.H., Dautzenberg, K. 2006. A theoretical framework of chain management. *Journal on Chain and Network Science* 6: 79–94.

Huxham, C, Vangen, S. 2005. Managing to collaborate: The theory and practice of collaborative advantage. Abingdon: Routledge.

Ireland, R.D., Hitt, M.A., Vaidyanath, D. 2002. Alliance management as a source of competitive advantage. *Journal of Management* 28 (3): 413–446.

Jap, S.D., Ganesan, S. 2000. Control mechanisms and the relationship life cycle: Implications for safeguarding specific investments and developing commitment. *Journal of Marketing Research* 37 (2): 227–245.

Jarillo, J.C. 1988. On strategic networks. *Strategic Management Journal* 9: 31–41.

Kale P., Dyer J.H., Singh H. 2002. Alliance capability, stock market response, and long-term alliance success: the role of the alliance function. *Strategic Management Journal* 23: 747–767.

Kochan, T.A., Cummings L.L., Huber, G.P. 1976. Operationalizing the concepts of Goals and goal incompatibilities in organizational behavior research. *Human Relations* 29 (6): 527–544.

Kogut, B., Zander, U. 1996. What firms do. Coordination, identity and learning. *Organization Science* 7: 502–518.

Kumar, K., van Dissel, H.G. Sustainable collaboration: Managing conflict and cooperation in interorganizational systems. *MIS Quarterly* 20 (3): 279–300.

Leonidou, L. C. 2004. An analysis of the barriers hindering small business export development. *Journal of Small Business Management* 24(3): 279–302.

Leonidou, L.C., Talias, M.A., Leonidou C.N. 2008. Exercised power as a driver of trust and commitment in cross-border industrial buyer–seller relationships. *Industrial Marketing Management* 37: 92–103.

Lorenzoni, G., Baden-Fuller, C. 1995. Creating a strategic center to manage a web of partners. *California Management Review* 37 (3): 146–163.

Lorenzoni, G., Lipparini, A. 1999. The leveraging of interfirm relationships as a distinctive organizational capability: A longitudinal study. *Strategic Management Journal* 20 (4): 317–338.

Mentzer, J.T., Min, S., Zacharia, Z.G. 2000. The nature of inter-firm partnering in supply chain management. *Journal of Retailing* 76: 549–568.

Mohr, J., Nevin, J.R. 1990. Communication strategies in marketing channels: A theoretical perspective. *Journal of Marketing* 54 (3): 36–51.

Omta, A.W.F., Trienekens, J.H., Beers, G. 2001. Chain and network science: A research framework. *Journal on Chain and Network Science* 1 (1): 1–6.

O'Toole, Jr., L.J. 1997. Treating networks seriously: Practical and research-based agendas in public administration. *Public Administration Review* 57 (1): 45–52.

Park, S.H., Ungson, G.R. 1997. The effect of national culture, organizational complementarity, and economic motivation on joint venture dissolution. *The Academy of Management Journal* 40 (2), Special Research Forum on Alliances and Networks: 279–307.

Park, S.H., Ungson, G.R. 2001. Interfirm rivalry and managerial complexity: A conceptual framework of alliance failure. *Organization Science* 12 (1): 37–53.

Payan, J.M. 2007. A review and delineation of cooperation and coordination in marketing channels. *European Business Review* 19 (3): 216–233.

Pitsis, T.S., Kornberger, M., Clegg, S. 2004. The art of managing relationships in interorganizational collaboration. *M@n@gement* 7 (3): 47–67.

Porter, M.E. 1980. Competitive advantage: Techniques for analyzing industries and competitors. New York: The Free Press.

Provan, K.G., Kenis, P. 2008. Modes of network governance: Structure, management, and effectiveness. *Journal of Public Administration Research and Theory* 18 (2): 229–252.

Reardon, T., Henson, S., Berdegué, J. 2007. "Proactive fast tracking" diffusion of supermarkets in developing countries: Implications for market institutions and trade. *Journal of Economic Geography* 7 (4): 399–431.

Sanders, N.R. 2005. IT alignment in supply chain relationships: A study of supplier benefits. *The Journal of Supply Chain Management* 41 (2): 4–13.

Schermerhorn, Jr., J.R. 1975. Determinants of interorganizational cooperation. *Academy of Management Journal* 18 (4): 846–856.

Simatupang, T.M., Wright, A.C., Sridharan, R. 2002. The knowledge of coordination for supply chain integration. *Business Process Management Journal* 8: 289–308.

Simon, H., 1964. On the concept of organizational goal. *Administrative Science Quarterly* 9 (1): 1–22.

Sjurts, I., 2000. Kollektive Unternehmensstrategie. Grundfragen einer Theorie kollektiven strategischen Handelns. Wiesbaden: Habilitation.

Smith, K.G., Carroll, S.J., Ashford, S.J. 1995. Intra- and interorganizational cooperation: Toward a research agenda. *Academy of Management Journal* 38 (1): 7–23.

Swinnen, J.F.M. 2006. The dynamics of vertical coordination in agrifood chains in Eastern Europe and Central Asia. Implications for policy and World Bank operations. The World Bank.

Thompson, J.D. 1967. *Organizations in Action.* New York: McGraw-Hill.

Top Agrar. 2004. Russische Milchviehhalter bekommen neue Melktechnik. *Top Agrar,* May 6.

Van de Ven, A.H. 1976. On the nature, formation and maintenance of relations among organizations. *Academy of Management Review* 1 (4): 24–36.

Wathne, K.H., Heide, J.B. 2004. Relationship governance in a supply chain network. *Journal of Marketing* 68: 73–89.

White, S., Siu-Yun Lui, S. 2005. Distinguishing costs of cooperation and control in alliances. *Strategic Management Journal* 26: 913–932.

Williamson, O.E. 1985. *The economic institutions of capitalism.* New York: The Free Press.

Winkler, I. 2006. Network governance between individual and collective goals: Qualitative evidence from six networks. *Journal of Leadership and Organizational Studies* 12 (3): 119–134.

Xu, L., Beamon, B.M. 2006. Supply chain coordination and cooperation mechanisms: An attribute-based approach. *The Journal of Supply Chain Management* 42 (1): 4–12.

PART II

Power and politics

Introduction

MariaLaura Di Domenico

The following collection of four articles is grouped around the loose central theme of power and politics. As organizations are manifestly social entities, power and politics are ubiquitous elements in their make-up. Often used synonymously, they are also inherently interwoven and as such are treated in many ways as inseparable issues. They are arguably key to any critical appreciation of the interactions within organizations and also across the boundaries which separate organizations. The overarching narratives or thematic drivers that run throughout this book as a whole are the challenges or controversies facing individuals and organizations involved with activities of crossing 'borders' or boundaries of one type or another. Thus, various issues inherent in power and politics, and how these are played out, often become more pertinent and potentially magnified when considering these added layers of complexity inherent in cross-boundary working.

There is a wealth of research on power and politics in the context of organizational and work settings in organization studies and adjacent fields such as sociology and psychology. It would be a challenge to do full justice to these topics in terms of coverage and scope of relevant issues. Therefore, and in line with the other parts of this book, these articles have been chosen with the aim of providing a flavour of these issues – a personal repertoire if you will. They are those that *I* have found useful and pertinent and are my choices within the restrictions of being able to select only four pieces as vehicles for highlighting and exploring the importance and omnipresence of issues of power and politics in organizations of various genres, and our social interactions within and across their boundaries.

I start the journey then with excerpts from a classic work that has stood the test of time in terms of its relevance and impact on philosophical reasoning, despite the original version being written as far back as 1532. This work is Niccolò Machiavelli's *The Prince*. Is it still relevant to contemporary challenges and controversies for organizations, you may be thinking? My answer to this question is a resounding and unequivocal 'yes'. Indeed, in a lot of higher education institutions, this piece features as required reading for students reading for degrees in moral philosophy. It is no less relevant to students of organization and management studies. It has much to teach us. Actually, that sounds rather passive. To rephrase, not only do we have much to learn from this text, but it also encourages us to question received wisdom. We are pushed outside our moral comfort zone to debate the efficacy and ethics of its doctrine. *The Prince* caused a great deal of outrage when it was first published. Much of it appears to advocate taking advantage of one's power base in order to manipulate and take advantage of the weaknesses of others through politicking and other means. We can see these practices taking place all around us. One could argue that, to a greater or lesser extent, the desire to be 'on top', 'win out' or even to 'get one over' on competitors is a natural manifestation of the human condition. If you go along with Machiavelli's world view, although there is no reason that you should, you may think that these may even be the traits of the more successful individual – akin to the Prince maintaining a hold on power and his reign for as long as possible.

The second excerpt builds on the first. This is taken from the book by Anthony Jay, *Management and Machiavelli*. The title gives a useful signposting for its core thesis – that of relating Machiavelli's work to management and organizations. This helps us on our travels but for me doesn't quite get us there. Although the focus on management and managers *per se* (as opposed to the multitude of roles to be found within organizations) is for me its main limiting feature, it does argue a convincing case for considering Machiavelli's work more closely. Hence my rationale for the inclusion of this second piece.

Next I offer to you a piece by Jeffrey Pfeffer, considered by many as somewhat of a 'guru', at least when it comes to the study of power, of contemporary management and organization studies taught in Business Schools. There are many pieces that he has written which could have been selected, but I chose this one as it is very accessible and helpfully unpacks the notion of power in organizations – making it a very worthy choice!

My final, more humble, offering has much more of a personal note to it. This is an edited part of an article that I co-wrote with two colleagues on the issue of organizational collaboration. This is very contemporary in focus, as it deals with social enterprises – organizations that combine social goals with an ethos of wealth creation – and their partnerships with private sector firms. Drawing upon actual practical examples, this examination of corporate-social enterprise collaboration takes us beyond the micro level of interpersonal relations to consider exchanges and linkages at the level of the firm. The argument relayed here is that corporate-social enterprise collaborations are shaped by three key issues, namely (1) the value that each member of the collaboration attributes to the inputs of their partner, (2) the competing practices and priorities intrinsic to the corporation and the social enterprise, and (3) the expected benefits of the collaboration to each partner. Tensions, and potential power imbalances, stem from the differences in corporations' and social enterprises' goals, ownership structures, governance mechanisms and lines of accountability. These may give rise to disharmony and even the abandonment of the collaboration by one or both partners. There is also a danger that the development of partnership maturity may not be an equitable process with one organization seeking to imitate the other. Power inequity and domination is therefore likely (although not inevitable) in such collaborative ventures.

Overall, when taken together, these four articles provide a 'way in' to accessing some of the complex, contested and challenging issues relevant to power and politics. Although linked, in many ways they are a heterogeneous collection, as each is distinct in what it offers and contributes to the book. The fourth piece on corporate-social enterprise collaborations tackles the issue of cross boundary working 'head on'. The first three articles do not do this as explicitly as they are more concerned with the influence of power and politics in inter-personal interactions. Therefore, we need to read what they have to say about power and politics in a broader sense in order to extrapolate these 'lessons' to inform our judgements and interpretations of organizational collaborative activities of different hues. Therefore, from the start, Machiavelli's work requires you to take a 'step back' to consider how it can help us to make sense of political and other modes of power in an alternative context (i.e. organizational) and temporal age (i.e. contemporary society). This sets the scene for the latter three articles which look squarely in the face of organizational life and invite us to follow suit to digest their ideas about the varieties of power and politics in organizational interactions, and our experiences of them in everyday life.

6

THE PRINCE

Niccolò Machiavelli (translated and edited by W.K. Marriott)

Chapters XIV, XV, XVI, XVII and XVIII

Chapter XIV – That which concerns a prince on the subject of the art of war

A prince ought to have no other aim or thought, nor select anything else for his study, than war and its rules and discipline; for this is the sole art that belongs to him who rules, and it is of such force that it not only upholds those who are born princes, but it often enables men to rise from a private station to that rank. And, on the contrary, it is seen that when princes have thought more of ease than of arms they have lost their states. And the first cause of your losing it is to neglect this art; and what enables you to acquire a state is to be master of the art. Francesco Sforza, through being martial, from a private person became Duke of Milan; and the sons, through avoiding the hardships and troubles of arms, from dukes became private persons. For among other evils which being unarmed brings you, it causes you to be despised, and this is one of those ignominies against which a prince ought to guard himself, as is shown later on. Because there is nothing proportionate between the armed and the unarmed; and it is not reasonable that he who is armed should yield obedience willingly to him who is unarmed, or that the unarmed man should be secure among armed servants. Because, there being in the one disdain and in the other suspicion, it is not possible for them to work well together. And therefore a prince who does not understand the art of war, over and above the other misfortunes already mentioned, cannot be respected by his soldiers, nor can he rely on them. He ought never, therefore, to have out of his thoughts this subject of war, and in peace he should addict himself more to its exercise than in war; this he can do in two ways, the one by action, the other by study.

As regards action, he ought above all things to keep his men well organized and drilled, to follow incessantly the chase, by which he accustoms his body to hardships, and learns something of the nature of localities, and gets to find out how the mountains rise, how the valleys open out, how the plains lie, and to understand the nature of rivers and marshes, and in all this to take the greatest care. Which knowledge is useful in two ways. Firstly, he learns to know his country, and is better able to undertake its defence; afterwards, by means of the knowledge and observation of that locality, he understands with ease any other which it may be necessary for him to study hereafter; because the hills, valleys, and plains, and rivers and marshes that are, for instance, in Tuscany, have a certain resemblance to those of other countries, so that with a knowledge of the aspect of one country one can easily arrive at a knowledge of others. And the prince that lacks this skill lacks the essential which it is desirable that a captain should possess, for it teaches him to surprise his enemy, to select quarters, to lead armies, to array the battle, to besiege towns to advantage.

Philopoemen,[1] Prince of the Achaeans, among other praises which writers have bestowed on him, is commended because in time of peace he never had anything in his mind but the rules of war; and when he was in the country with friends, he often stopped and reasoned with them: "If the enemy should be upon that hill, and we should find ourselves here with our army, with whom would be the advantage? How should one best advance to meet him, keeping the ranks? If we should wish to retreat, how ought we to pursue?" And he would set forth to them, as he went, all the chances that could befall an army; he would listen to their opinion and state his, confirming it with reasons, so that by these continual discussions there could never arise, in time of war, any unexpected circumstances that he could not deal with.

But to exercise the intellect the prince should read histories, and study there the actions of illustrious men, to see how they have borne themselves in war, to examine the causes of their victories and defeat, so as to avoid the latter and imitate the former; and above all do as an illustrious man did, who took as an exemplar one who had been praised and famous before him, and whose achievements and deeds he always kept in his mind, as it is said Alexander the Great imitated Achilles, Caesar Alexander, Scipio Cyrus. And whoever reads the life of Cyrus, written by Xenophon, will recognize afterwards in the life of Scipio how that imitation was his glory, and how in chastity, affability, humanity, and liberality Scipio conformed to those things which have been written of Cyrus by Xenophon. A wise prince ought to observe some such rules, and never in peaceful times stand idle, but increase his resources with industry in such a way that they may be available to him in adversity, so that if fortune chances it may find him prepared to resist her blows.

---

[1]Philopoemen, "the last of the Greeks," born 252 B.C., died 183 B.C.

Chapter XV – Concerning things for which men, and especially princes, are praised or blamed

It remains now to see what ought to be the rules of conduct for a prince towards subject and friends. And as I know that many have written on this point, I expect I shall be considered presumptuous in mentioning it again, especially as in discussing it I shall depart from the methods of other people. But, it being my intention to write a thing which shall be useful to him who apprehends it, it appears to me more appropriate to follow up the real truth of the matter than the imagination of it; for many have pictured republics and principalities which in fact have never been known or seen, because how one lives is so far distant from how one ought to live, that he who neglects what is done for what ought to be done, sooner effects his ruin than his preservation; for a man who wishes to act entirely up to his professions of virtue soon meets with what destroys him among so much that is evil.

Hence it is necessary for a prince wishing to hold his own to know how to do wrong, and to make use of it or not according to necessity. Therefore, putting on one side imaginary things concerning a prince, and discussing those which are real, I say that all men when they are spoken of, and chiefly princes for being more highly placed, are remarkable for some of those qualities which bring them either blame or praise; and thus it is that one is reputed liberal, another miserly, using a Tuscan term (because an avaricious person in our language is still he who desires to possess by robbery, whilst we call one miserly who deprives himself too much of the use of his own); one is reputed generous, one rapacious; one cruel, one compassionate; one faithless, another faithful; one effeminate and cowardly, another bold and brave; one affable, another haughty; one lascivious, another chaste; one sincere, another cunning; one hard, another easy; one grave, another frivolous; one religious, another unbelieving, and the like. And I know that every one will confess that it would be most praiseworthy in a prince to exhibit all the above qualities that are considered good; but because they can neither be entirely possessed nor observed, for human conditions do not permit it, it is necessary for him to be sufficiently prudent that he may know how to avoid the reproach of those vices which would lose him his state; and also to keep himself, if it be possible, from those which would not lose him it; but this not being possible, he may with less hesitation abandon himself to them. And again, he need not make himself uneasy at incurring a reproach for those vices without which the state can only be saved with difficulty, for if everything is considered carefully, it will be found that something which looks like virtue, if followed, would be his ruin; whilst something else, which looks like vice, yet followed brings him security and prosperity.

Chapter XVI – Concerning liberality and meanness

Commencing then with the first of the above-named characteristics, I say that it would be well to be reputed liberal. Nevertheless, liberality exercised in a way that does not bring you the reputation for it, injures you; for if one exercises it honestly and as it should be exercised, it may not become known, and you will not avoid the reproach of its opposite. Therefore, any one wishing to maintain among men the name of liberal is obliged to avoid no attribute of magnificence; so that a prince thus inclined will consume in such acts all his property, and will be compelled in the end, if he wish to maintain the name of liberal, to unduly weigh down his people, and tax them, and do everything he can to get money. This will soon make him odious to his subjects, and becoming poor he will be little valued by any one; thus, with his liberality, having offended many and rewarded few, he is affected by the very first trouble and imperilled by whatever may be the first danger; recognizing this himself, and wishing to draw back from it, he runs at once into the reproach of being miserly.

Therefore, a prince, not being able to exercise this virtue of liberality in such a way that it is recognized, except to his cost, if he is wise he ought not to fear the reputation of being mean, for in time he will come to be more considered than if liberal, seeing that with his economy his revenues are enough, that he can defend himself against all attacks, and is able to engage in enterprises without burdening his people; thus it comes to pass that he exercises liberality towards all from whom he does not take, who are numberless, and meanness towards those to whom he does not give, who are few.

We have not seen great things done in our time except by those who have been considered mean; the rest have failed. Pope Julius the Second was assisted in reaching the papacy by a reputation for liberality, yet he did not strive afterwards to keep it up, when he made war on the King of France; and he made many wars without imposing any extraordinary tax on his subjects, for he supplied his additional expenses out of his long thriftiness. The present King of Spain would not have undertaken or conquered in so many enterprises if he had been reputed liberal. A prince, therefore, provided that he has not to rob his subjects, that he can defend himself, that he does not become poor and abject, that he is not forced to become rapacious, ought to hold of little account a reputation for being mean, for it is one of those vices which will enable him to govern.

And if any one should say: Caesar obtained empire by liberality, and many others have reached the highest positions by having been liberal, and by being considered so, I answer: Either you are a prince in fact, or in a way to become one. In the first case this liberality is dangerous, in the second it is very necessary to be considered liberal; and Caesar was one of those who wished to become pre-eminent in Rome; but if he had survived after becoming so, and had not moderated his expenses, he would have destroyed his government. And if any one should reply: Many have been princes, and have done great things with armies, who have been considered very liberal, I reply: Either a prince spends that which is his own or his subjects' or else that of others. In the first case he ought to be sparing, in the second he ought not to neglect any opportunity for liberality. And to the prince who goes forth with his army, supporting it by pillage, sack, and extortion, handling that which belongs to others, this liberality is necessary, otherwise he would not be followed by soldiers. And of that which is neither yours nor your subjects' you can be a ready giver, as were Cyrus, Caesar, and Alexander; because it does not take away your reputation if you squander that of others, but adds to it; it is only squandering your own that injures you.

And there is nothing wastes so rapidly as liberality, for even whilst you exercise it you lose the power to do so, and so become either poor or despised, or else, in avoiding poverty, rapacious and hated. And a prince should guard himself, above all things, against being despised and hated; and liberality leads you to both. Therefore it is wiser to have a reputation for meanness which brings reproach without hatred, than to be compelled through seeking a reputation for liberality to incur a name for rapacity which begets reproach with hatred.

Chapter XVII – Concerning cruelty and clemency, and whether it is better to be loved than feared

Coming now to the other qualities mentioned above, I say that every prince ought to desire to be considered clement and not cruel. Nevertheless he ought to take care not to misuse this clemency. Cesare Borgia was considered cruel; notwithstanding, his cruelty reconciled the Romagna, unified it, and restored it to peace and loyalty. And if this be rightly considered, he will be seen to have been much more merciful than the Florentine people, who, to avoid a reputation for cruelty, permitted Pistoia to be destroyed.[2] Therefore a prince, so long as he keeps his subjects united and loyal, ought not to mind the reproach of cruelty; because with a few examples he will be more merciful than those who, through too much mercy, allow disorders to arise, from which follow murders or robberies; for these are wont to injure the whole people, whilst those executions which originate with a prince offend the individual only.

And of all princes, it is impossible for the new prince to avoid the imputation of cruelty, owing to new states being full of dangers. Hence Virgil, through the mouth of Dido, excuses the inhumanity of her reign owing to its being new, saying:

> "Res dura, et regni novitas me talia cogunt Moliri, et late fines custode tueri."[3]

Nevertheless he ought to be slow to believe and to act, nor should he himself show fear, but proceed in a temperate manner with prudence and humanity, so that too much confidence may not make him incautious and too much distrust render him intolerable.

---

[2] During the rioting between the Cancellieri and Panciatichi factions in 1502 and 1503.
[3] ... against my will, my fate

> A throne unsettled, and an infant state,
> Bid me defend my realms with all my pow'rs,
> And guard with these severities my shores.
>
> Christopher Pitt.

Upon this a question arises: whether it be better to be loved than feared or feared than loved? It may be answered that one should wish to be both, but, because it is difficult to unite them in one person, it is much safer to be feared than loved, when, of the two, either must be dispensed with. Because this is to be asserted in general of men, that they are ungrateful, fickle, false, cowardly, covetous, and as long as you succeed they are yours entirely; they will offer you their blood, property, life, and children, as is said above, when the need is far distant; but when it approaches they turn against you. And that prince who, relying entirely on their promises, has neglected other precautions, is ruined; because friendships that are obtained by payments, and not by greatness or nobility of mind, may indeed be earned, but they are not secured, and in time of need cannot be relied upon; and men have less scruple in offending one who is beloved than one who is feared, for love is preserved by the link of obligation which, owing to the baseness of men, is broken at every opportunity for their advantage; but fear preserves you by a dread of punishment which never fails.

Nevertheless a prince ought to inspire fear in such a way that, if he does not win love, he avoids hatred; because he can endure very well being feared whilst he is not hated, which will always be as long as he abstains from the property of his citizens and subjects and from their women. But when it is necessary for him to proceed against the life of someone, he must do it on proper justification and for manifest cause, but above all things he must keep his hands off the property of others, because men more quickly forget the death of their father than the loss of their patrimony. Besides, pretexts for taking away the property are never wanting; for he who has once begun to live by robbery will always find pretexts for seizing what belongs to others; but reasons for taking life, on the contrary, are more difficult to find and sooner lapse. But when a prince is with his army, and has under control a multitude of soldiers, then it is quite necessary for him to disregard the reputation of cruelty, for without it he would never hold his army united or disposed to its duties.

Among the wonderful deeds of Hannibal this one is enumerated: that having led an enormous army, composed of many various races of men, to fight in foreign lands, no dissensions arose either among them or against the prince, whether in his bad or in his good fortune. This arose from nothing else than his inhuman cruelty, which, with his boundless valour, made him revered and terrible in the sight of his soldiers, but without that cruelty, his other virtues were not sufficient to produce this effect. And short-sighted writers admire his deeds from one point of view and from another condemn the principal cause of them. That it is true his other virtues would not have been sufficient for him may be proved by the case of Scipio, that most excellent man, not only of his own times but within the memory of man, against whom, nevertheless, his army rebelled in Spain; this arose from nothing but his too great forbearance, which gave his soldiers more license than is consistent with military discipline. For this he was upbraided in the Senate by Fabius Maximus, and called the corrupter of the Roman soldiery. The Locrians were laid waste by a legate of Scipio, yet they were not avenged by him, nor was the insolence of the legate punished, owing entirely to his easy nature. Insomuch that someone in the Senate, wishing to excuse him, said there were many men who knew much better how not to err than to correct the errors of others. This disposition, if he had been continued in the command, would have destroyed in time the fame and glory of Scipio; but, he being under the control of the Senate, this injurious characteristic not only concealed itself, but contributed to his glory.

Returning to the question of being feared or loved, I come to the conclusion that, men loving according to their own will and fearing according to that of the prince, a wise prince should establish himself on that which is in his own control and not in that of others; he must endeavour only to avoid hatred, as is noted.

Chapter XVIII – Concerning the way in which princes should keep faith

[...]

Everyone admits how praiseworthy it is in a prince to keep faith, and to live with integrity and not with craft. Nevertheless our experience has been that those princes who have done great things have held good faith of little account, and have known how to circumvent the intellect of men by craft, and in the end have overcome those who have relied on their word. You must know there are two ways of contesting,[4] the one by the law, the other by force; the first method is proper to men, the second to beasts; but because the first is frequently not sufficient, it is necessary to have recourse to the second. Therefore it is necessary for a prince to understand how to avail himself of the beast and the man. This has been figuratively taught to princes by ancient writers, who describe how Achilles and many other princes of old were given to the Centaur Chiron to nurse, who brought them up in his discipline; which means solely that, as they had for a teacher one who was half beast and half man, so it is necessary for a prince to know how to make use of both natures, and that one without the other is not durable. A prince, therefore, being compelled knowingly to adopt the beast, ought to choose the fox and the lion; because the lion cannot defend himself against snares and the fox cannot defend himself against wolves. Therefore, it is necessary to be a fox to discover the snares and a lion to terrify the wolves. Those who

---

[4]"Contesting," i.e. "striving for mastery." Mr Burd points out that this passage is imitated directly from Cicero's "De Officiis": "Nam cum sint duo genera decertandi, unum per disceptationem, alterum per vim; cumque illud proprium sit hominis, hoc beluarum; confugiendum est ad posterius, si uti non licet superiore."

rely simply on the lion do not understand what they are about. Therefore a wise lord cannot, nor ought he to, keep faith when such observance may be turned against him, and when the reasons that caused him to pledge it exist no longer. If men were entirely good this precept would not hold, but because they are bad, and will not keep faith with you, you too are not bound to observe it with them. Nor will there ever be wanting to a prince legitimate reasons to excuse this non-observance. Of this endless modern examples could be given, showing how many treaties and engagements have been made void and of no effect through the faithlessness of princes; and he who has known best how to employ the fox has succeeded best.

But it is necessary to know well how to disguise this characteristic, and to be a great pretender and dissembler; and men are so simple, and so subject to present necessities, that he who seeks to deceive will always find someone who will allow himself to be deceived. One recent example I cannot pass over in silence. Alexander the Sixth did nothing else but deceive men, nor ever thought of doing otherwise, and he always found victims; for there never was a man who had greater power in asserting, or who with greater oaths would affirm a thing, yet would observe it less; nevertheless his deceits always succeeded according to his wishes,[5] because he well understood this side of mankind.

> Alexander never did what he said, Cesare never said what he did.
>
> Italian Proverb.

Therefore it is unnecessary for a prince to have all the good qualities I have enumerated, but it is very necessary to appear to have them. And I shall dare to say this also, that to have them and always to observe them is injurious, and that to appear to have them is useful; to appear merciful, faithful, humane, religious, upright, and to be so, but with a mind so framed that should you require not to be so, you may be able and know how to change to the opposite.

And you have to understand this, that a prince, especially a new one, cannot observe all those things for which men are esteemed, being often forced, in order to maintain the state, to act contrary to fidelity,[6] friendship, humanity, and religion.

---

[5] "Nondimanco sempre gli succederono gli inganni (ad votum)." The words "ad votum" are omitted in the Testina edition, 1550.

[6] "Contrary to fidelity" or "faith," "contro alla fede," and "tutto fede," "altogether faithful," in the next paragraph. It is noteworthy that these two phrases, "contro alla fede" and "tutto fede," were omitted in the Testina edition, which was published with the sanction of the papal authorities. It may be that the meaning attached to the word "fede" was "the faith," i.e. the Catholic creed, and not as rendered here "fidelity" and "faithful." Observe that the word "religione" was suffered to stand in the text of the Testina, being used to signify indifferently every shade of belief, as witness "the religion," a phrase inevitably employed to designate the Huguenot heresy. South in his Sermon IX, p. 69, ed. 1843, comments on this passage as follows: "That great patron and Coryphaeus of this tribe, Nicolo Machiavel, laid down this for a master rule in his political scheme: 'That the show of religion was helpful to the politician, but the reality of it hurtful and pernicious.'"

Therefore it is necessary for him to have a mind ready to turn itself accordingly as the winds and variations of fortune force it, yet, as I have said above, not to diverge from the good if he can avoid doing so, but, if compelled, then to know how to set about it.

For this reason a prince ought to take care that he never lets anything slip from his lips that is not replete with the above-named five qualities, that he may appear to him who sees and hears him altogether merciful, faithful, humane, upright, and religious. There is nothing more necessary to appear to have than this last quality, inasmuch as men judge generally more by the eye than by the hand, because it belongs to everybody to see you, to few to come in touch with you. Every one sees what you appear to be, few really know what you are, and those few dare not oppose themselves to the opinion of the many, who have the majesty of the state to defend them; and in the actions of all men, and especially of princes, which it is not prudent to challenge, one judges by the result.

For that reason, let a prince have the credit of conquering and holding his state, the means will always be considered honest, and he will be praised by everybody; because the vulgar are always taken by what a thing seems to be and by what comes of it; and in the world there are only the vulgar, for the few find a place there only when the many have no ground to rest on.

One prince[7] of the present time, whom it is not well to name, never preaches anything else but peace and good faith, and to both he is most hostile, and either, if he had kept it, would have deprived him of reputation and kingdom many a time.

---

[7]Ferdinand of Aragon.

7

MANAGEMENT AND MACHIAVELLI

Anthony Jay

Source: Edited from *Management and Machiavelli*. 1967. Hodder and Stoughton.

Chapters I, III and XXVII

I Management and Machiavelli

It must all have been so easy in the nineteenth century. You built your factory, you installed your machines, you hired your labour and you bought your raw materials, and there you were – a full-blown manufacturer. Of course you had problems; your product had to reach a standard of performance and a competitive price, you had to get it to where people could buy it, you needed capital to expand or break into new markets. But these have always been the problems of men who make and sell; they are the framework in which the industrialist has always expected to operate and the soil in which he flourishes. He sees, or feels in his bones, something that people would pay money for if it were obtainable, he knows how he can make it at a cost which will leave him a profit margin, and he has the drive to raise the capital, build the factory, and start producing and selling. This is the primal, rudimentary urge of the entrepreneur industrialist; the essentials have not changed throughout history, and presumably they will never change.

But today there is something else the industrialist has to master, and it is called the science of management. The simple days of just the boss and the labour force are over: between the two has come the 'hierarchy', the 'management structure', the 'chain of command'. There is little point in examining the reasons for this; they are too complex in detail, and too simple in essence. [...] [T]oday, most business organisations are far too large and complicated to be run by a single policy-former and decision-taker. They have to be managed. Sometimes it seems that the old problems of making well and selling well become insignificant compared with the ghastly new problem of managing well. Management is the great new preoccupation of the Western world. [...] The wealth of nations depends increasingly on the quality of managers, and an ever-growing number of the best people are managers, or intend to be managers, while all the rest find their lives directly and sharply affected by the decisions and actions of managers.

Almost more surprising than the rapid growth and spread of management is the apparent novelty of it. The study of the sciences has also developed with staggering speed [...] but science has a long and distinguished ancestry, whereas management appears to have dropped out of nowhere. [...]

How can this have happened? How can the human race have suddenly adapted itself in millions to such a new basic institution? Only, I suggest, because management is not a new basic institution at all. It is a very ancient art.

[...]

Whether a tenable economic theory of business enterprise will ever be found, I do not know. And perhaps it does not matter; because I believe there is a tenable political theory of business enterprise. The new science of management is in fact only a continuation of the old art of government, and when you study management case-histories side by side with political history, you realise that you are only studying two very similar branches of the same subject. Each illuminates the other, but since history has been studied to excess, and management hardly at all, it is not surprising that it is management situations which are illuminated more often.

It was Machiavelli who brought this truth home to me. Machiavelli is not at the moment required reading in business colleges or on management training courses. Professor Butterfield, in his introduction to the Everyman edition,[1] claims no modern relevance for his writings: "The chief significance of his work today," he says, "lies in the fact that it marks a stage in the development of the scientific method, whether in statecraft, or in general political analysis, or in the broader fields of history." And yet Machiavelli, however marginal his relevance to academic historians, is in fact bursting with urgent advice and acute observations for top management of the great private and public corporations all over the world. You only have to know how to look for it.

Although the connection became clear to me in a sudden flash [...] I can see that I had been working towards it for some time. I was one of the middle management of a large and growing corporation of some 20,000 people with a gross revenue around £40 million a year. I was fascinated, perhaps (in view of my lowly position) precociously fascinated, with the problems of management and leadership and organisation, not just of that particular corporation but of any modern corporation that faces the problems of great size and continued growth. It seemed to me then that this scale of operation was still, for most industrial nations, such a new one that we were all probing, pioneering and guessing, with few helpful precedents and little accumulated wisdom to guide us; each firm was working by trial and error, and all too often repeating the errors of others rather than learning from them.

---

[1] *The Prince*, trans. W. K. Marriott, Introduction by H. Butterfield. London: Dent/Everyman, 1958.

I was discussing this at lunch with a friend who is Chairman of an industrial engineering group. I asked if he and his fellow managers had formulated any laws or amassed a body of folk-wisdom about the right way to treat a firm when you have taken it over. He had made some extremely interesting observations from his own experience: one of them was that a staff of four hundred represents the critical number in a firm taken over. It is the number which separates the personal boss from the high-level manager. A man may run a firm of four hundred or fewer staff extremely well, but that is the maximum you can run personally, knowing all their names, without too much delegated authority. If you expand that firm to, say, 1,100, you may destroy him: instead of all being people he knows by name, they become pegs on a board; instead of just doing and deciding he has to do a lot of explaining and educating; instead of checking up on everything himself, he has to institute a system and establish procedures. All this demands skills quite different from those he built his success on, and ones which he may well lack.

This however was only an isolated observation. There did not seem to be any generally accepted body of opinion, any guiding principles, for the taking over of firms, even though it was (and is) one of the chief problems facing thousands of top managements all over the Western world. Many managers had made their own observations, but they were not collated [...]

The next day, while this conversation was very much in my mind, I was reading Machiavelli's *The Prince*. I thought I was browsing agreeably among the remote political problems of Renaissance Italian states; when suddenly I encountered a sentence which was so utterly relevant to the previous day's discussion that in a few seconds it transformed my attitude to the book, to Machiavelli, to management and to political history. It seemed like a direct answer to the question of how you make a taken-over firm into a part of your own organisation, capable of operating to the same standards and worthy to carry a part of your reputation. The passage (Chapter III) read:

> The other and better course is to send colonies to one or two places, which may be as keys to that state, for it is necessary either to do this or else to keep there a great number of cavalry and infantry. A prince does not spend much on colonies, for with little or no expense he can send them out and keep them there, and he offends a minority only of the citizens from whom he takes lands and houses to give them to the new inhabitants; and those whom he offends, remaining poor and scattered, are never able to injure him; whilst the rest being uninjured are easily kept quiet, and at the same time are anxious not to err for fear it should happen to them as it has to those who have been despoiled. In conclusion, I say that these colonies are not costly, they are more faithful, they injure less, and the injured, as has been said, being poor and scattered, cannot hurt. Upon this, one has to remark that men ought either to be well treated or crushed, because they can avenge themselves of lighter injuries, of more serious ones they cannot; therefore the injury that is to be done to a man ought to be of such a kind that one does not stand in fear of revenge.

In other words, "Put small management teams of your own into one or two key factories, because otherwise you'll use up half your staff in giving orders and issuing requests, and then checking that they've been properly fulfilled. By comparison a management team does not cost much, and the only people who will be upset are the former managers whose jobs they have taken over. And since they are no longer in the firm they cannot cause any trouble, while the rest of the staff will not protest as long as they still have their old jobs, particularly while they have the example of the sacked managers to keep them on their toes. The guiding principle is that senior men in taken-over firms should either be warmly welcomed and encouraged, or sacked; because if they are sacked they are powerless, whereas if they are simply downgraded they will remain united and resentful and determined to get their own back." This, though Machiavelli does not mention it in this context, is the principle on which the Romans founded their Empire (which was one of the most spectacular examples of successful large-scale management); generosity (full Roman citizenship) or brutality (executions and enslavement, full military garrisons) but not the sort of half-hearted severity that left the defeated enemy resentful and still in being. Since reading that passage I have tried out Machiavelli's principle on several managers who have had to cope with takeovers; they are with him to a man.

Of course this might simply have been a happy coincidence. Many writers have taken elegant analogies from history – the BBC has been most persuasively compared with the democratic centralism of the Kremlin – to decorate or illuminate their observations on management. But this seemed altogether too close to be an accident; and the next chapter, when looked at in this new light, also became extremely relevant and up-to-date:

> The principalities of which one has record are found to be governed in two different ways: either by a prince, with a body of servants, who assist him to govern the kingdom as ministers by his favour and permission; or by a prince and barons, who hold that dignity by antiquity of blood and not by grace of the prince. Such barons have states and their own subjects, who recognize them as lords and hold them in natural affection. The examples of these two governments in our time are the Turk and the King of France. The entire monarchy of the Turk is governed by one lord, the others are his servants: and, dividing his kingdom into sanjaks, he sends there different administrators and shifts and changes them as he chooses. But the King of France is placed in the midst of an ancient body of lords, acknowledged by their own subjects, and beloved by them; they have their own prerogatives, nor can the king take these away except at his peril.

Anyone who has worked in large organisations must instantly recognise these two basic methods of management. The Civil Service is well known to be Turkish in outlook, rotating managers (especially at the lower levels) at a hectic speed. The Foreign Office is particularly religious in its observance, making sure that none of its embassy staffs stay for more than a few years in one place. This, according to Machiavelli, ensures that the goodwill and hopes of benefit of the foreign governments are directed towards the central government in London, and not to the person of its representative. It is the sort of organisation which often develops under a very tough and strong top man: according to Machiavelli, it is very hard to force or intrigue your way to the top of such an organisation, but comparatively easy to run it once you are there.

At the other pole, the Frankish organisation, it is much easier to take over the top position but much harder to achieve anything when you reach it. When a strong and active leader is succeeded by a weak or lazy one, the organisation will tend to revert from Turkish to Frankish – the barons are strong when the king is weak. Oxford and Cambridge Universities are notorious examples of the Frankish system – it is entirely suitable that the body appointed to inquire into the running of Oxford University should have been known as the Franks Commission. The feudal baronies are the colleges, and the Heads of Colleges rule them from appointment until retirement with as much freedom from interference as they can arrange. And they arrange it very well; the central government of the university comes under the Chancellor, a figurehead, and the Vice-Chancellor, who is the Head of one of the colleges appointed for one year only in strict rotation – an excellent way to ensure that the power of the colleges is never reduced. It is the autonomy of the colleges and the impotence of the University which has always defeated University reform.

[...]

A few pages later there is another parallel, of particular significance to the manufacturing industries. To translate it into modern terms, Machiavelli discusses whether you should, ideally, manufacture and assemble your product entirely in your own works, or whether you should contract it out to associated companies, or to independent contractors. He argues that associated companies are liable to their own industrial disputes and production and delivery crises, which are beyond your control and of a higher priority to them than your order; that independent contractors will delay or scamp your work if a much more lucrative urgent contract crops up; that if you succeed with a product which another firm is making for you, then you place yourself at their mercy; and that you should therefore make everything you possibly can in your own shop. Few production managers would question this conclusion. In fact he expresses it in terms of whether you should defend your state with an army formed by your own citizens, or with auxiliaries, or with mercenaries; he points out that allies may withdraw (or withhold) their troops if they are attacked themselves, or, if they fight and win, that they will then start dictating to you: that mercenaries are always liable to desert to another prince, or even to your enemy, if he pays better: and that an army of your own citizens is the only one you can really trust. The differences are differences of application: the principle, being rooted in human nature, is the same in both cases, and is just as valid now as it was 450 years ago.

The root of the matter is that the great modern corporations are so similar to independent or semi-independent states of the past that they can only be fully understood in terms of political and constitutional history, and management can only be properly studied as a branch of government.

III *The Machiavelli method*

It is of course the increasing size of firms and corporations which makes it possible to study them in political terms. A small family firm can only be compared with a small feudal estate, and since both are entirely and personally run by the head of the family there is little revelation in the comparison. It is only as the commercial and industrial enterprises become as great and as complex as they are today that they begin to take on the apparatus of States and need to be studied as political institutions.

Some firms reach great size through their own organic growth, without any mergers or takeovers. [...] But these are the minority; most big firms today have grown by acquisition, with the extremely complex problem of integrating all the different units they have absorbed, of digesting what they have swallowed. This, of course, is the problem I started with, the discussion about how to treat a taken-over firm, for which there were no established precedents. And yet it is hardly possible to read history without stumbling over precedents on every page. For example, the best-known event in English history, the Norman Conquest in 1066, was one of the most brilliant and ruthless takeovers ever recorded. Not the Battle of Hastings, which was just a battle, but the twenty years which followed it. In that time William I removed all but two of the major English landowners from their manors and replaced them with his own Normans – usually waiting for the excuse provided by an act of disobedience or rebellion: just like the Chief Executive of a taking-over firm replacing every senior executive of the acquired firm with one of his own men the instant [the former] question a decision. Most of the land which he did not keep in the family or the Church went to just ten Normans – a very reasonable span of command. The Domesday Book was the most detailed inventory ever made of capital assets and the annual revenue to be expected from them – and William was ahead of most modern managers in having the whole inventory checked by a team of assessors independent of those who took it. His Normans had to agree an annual production target before being given the land – taxes and mounted knights – and agree to attend central committees – the Royal Courts and Councils. He also imposed a central personnel policy – in 1086 he made all the principal sublandowners in the realm swear to obey him, even against their own feudal overlords. Wherever an existing institution worked satisfactorily, he left it unchanged: where there was resistance, he was utterly ruthless. [...]

In fact the takeover problem, so far from being new, has been the major preoccupation of government for hundreds of years. To quote Professor Butterfield again:

> The work of fusing the smaller units into a monarchy, and turning the monarchy into a 'state', the inhabitants into a 'nation' was the main function of the institution of kingship in Europe between the tenth and the eighteenth centuries.

I suspect that many people in top management today will instantly recognise that sentence as a neat statement of their own problem. Many of our large companies and corporations have become monarchies by a succession of mergers and takeovers, but they know that they are not yet a state, and their employees are not yet a nation. Their problems are the same because the circumstances which brought about the situation were the same: the King wanted the small principality perhaps to secure a frontier, perhaps for its agricultural wealth, as a Managing Director wants a small firm to consolidate a section of the market or augment his plant and labour force. The small principality and the small firm often welcome this absorption as an alternative to annihilation by another more powerful rival. But having acquired the principality the King finds it defends the frontier badly, leaves half its taxes uncollected, is liable to revolution which may spread, and sends its quota of troops to the national army underequipped, badly trained and with low morale. The Managing Director may find the firm he has taken over makes an uncompetitive product, has hopeless labour relations, a chaotic accounting system, uneducated management, and a poor sales force. He has, however, eight centuries of experience to draw on. The wisdom of princes is at the disposal of managers.

So we come back to Machiavelli. It is a pity that his name has become synonymous with sinister and unscrupulous intrigue, 'murderous Machiavel'. It is also unjust; his main purpose was simply to analyse what practices had brought political success in the past, and to deduce from them what principles ought to be followed for political success in the present. It was an honest attempt at scientific inquiry; not surprisingly many of the courses which he discovered had brought political success were not such as to bring moral acclaim as well. [...] As a result he has been held up to obloquy as an advocate of wicked and immoral actions, whereas his message is only: "If political success is what you want, this seems to be the most effective way to achieve it." *The Prince* is a work of extreme realism intended to sort out some guiding principles, based on his own experience of government, his deductions from observing the government of others, and his analysis of history, for the benefit of Giuliano de' Medici when he should take over his new principality. It is a selection of case-histories of government on a number of well defined and important questions: "Concerning the way to govern cities or principalities which lived under their own laws before they were annexed", "Concerning cruelty and clemency, and whether it is better to be loved than feared", "Concerning the secretaries of princes", "Why the princes of Italy have lost their states" and so on. It does not build a coherent system of political philosophy: it is essentially empirical, pragmatic and practical.

I have called [my] book *Management and Machiavelli* not because it is based on Machiavelli's arguments but because it is based on his method, the method of taking a current problem and then examining it in a practical way in the light of the experiences of others who have faced a similar problem in the past. The problems are those of the large corporations in the twentieth century; the experiences are drawn indiscriminately from corporations and states, but because the latter are so much more fully and more truthfully documented, political history has proved a richer source than management case-history. And like Machiavelli I have found problems on which, for lack of any other source, my own experience has had to provide most of my evidence; in particular for the chapters on creativeness. But whatever the source, I have tried to keep [my] book, too, empirical, pragmatic and practical. It is not a search for instances of history repeating itself or a system of management philosophy, but like *The Prince* an attempt to analyse current and relevant management problems in the light of experience, observation and history. Above all it is about leadership; Machiavelli called his book *The Prince*, and not something like *The Art of Government*, because he saw success and failure for states as stemming directly from the qualities of the leader. Success and failure for corporations also stem directly from the qualities of their leaders: management techniques are obviously essential, but what matters is leadership. The word 'leadership' has fallen into disrepute of recent years, chiefly because of the old Victorian concept of leadership as something that any middle-class English boy could be taught in ten years at boarding school before being sent out to govern the lesser breeds. It was a quality that did not need any specialist knowledge or qualification and one that was opposed to originality and imagination and nonconformism. It is now becoming accepted that leadership is not necessarily hindered by a deep knowledge and lifelong experience of the area in which it is leading, even if the battle to establish imagination as a pre-requisite of leadership is not yet won. But we are now in danger of overcompensation, of accepting the rival heresy that success in industry can be achieved not by leadership at all, but by management science, without a man of courage and vision and experience at the head of the enterprise to tell the management scientists what to study and for what purpose.

The trouble is that too much writing on management has been concerned not to examine it but to attack or defend it; and not on the legitimate grounds of whether it has been successful or unsuccessful, but in a fruitless quest to establish that its ultimate purpose and effects are moral, or alternatively immoral. [...]

The only helpful way to examine organizations and their management is as something neither moral nor immoral, but simply a phenomenon; not to look for proof that industry is honourable or dishonourable, but only for patterns of success and failure, growth and decay, strife and harmony, and for the forces which produce them. A great volume of this sort of study has been applied to the *minutiae* of management, and those who are concerned with accounting systems or sales incentive schemes or media selection have a considerable library of dispassionate scientific analysis and recommendation to guide them. But the men concerned with the organisation as a whole have little beyond their own experience, the advice and warnings of their friends, a number of published case-histories and a few disguised tracts.

Perhaps this is not surprising. The simple business of designing and making a product which does what you said it would, and delivering it to the person who ordered it, on the day you promised, for the price you agreed, and then collecting the money and recording the whole transaction somewhere where you can find it when you want – to do this on a large scale and stay in business requires quite a number of separate bits of efficiency. Leaders of expanding organisations have an urgent need for this sort of efficiency, and there are not enough men who possess it. But there is an alternative: a highly efficient system, which can be operated by managers of much less natural ability with some confidence of success and little fear of disaster. And since most of these systems and practices and techniques can be taught and explained and written down in pamphlets or books, there is now a great volume of writing on all these practical aspects of management. But leading the whole organisation needs wisdom and flair and vision, and they are another matter; they cannot be reduced to a system and incorporated into a training manual. And yet, as corporations grow larger and larger, it becomes more and more important to understand how they work, what forces operate within them and upon them, what makes for health or sickness, success or failure. Perhaps we cannot draw up rules for all occasions, but by a judicious use of the Machiavelli method we can learn to recognise which situations and problems are common to large organisations, and see the different results that tend to be brought about by different courses of action. [...] And so this is an attempt to detach managers, if only briefly, from their preoccupation with Inventory Management and Discounted Cash Flow and Project Evaluation and Review Techniques, and link them up with their true predecessors, the Kings and Princes and Prime Ministers and Generals, the Barons and Cardinals and Courtiers, who have been trying to cope with the same problems for the past two or three thousand years.

XXVII The principle of self-interest

You might think that if you take a man on, give him a guarantee of employment, a fair salary and a well-defined job, you can assume from then onwards that he will work for the good of the corporation which is employing him. Perhaps there are some who do. But on the whole it is safer to assume that, while the good of the corporation will always be an important consideration, it will not be his first loyalty: that is reserved for himself, for his present status and rewards and his future career. And it is only too possible for them to come into conflict with it.

A firm which pays its department heads according to the number of staff in their department, for instance, is obviously tempting them all to increase their staff at every possible opportunity, and yet there are firms which do, in practice, use this as a salary yardstick without any intention of so helping to solve the national unemployment problem. On the other hand the converse of this – some scheme like paying managers ten per cent of the salary of every post they abolish, so long as they continue to meet their targets – is almost unheard of, although just as logical. Another example is firms which give the responsibility for authorising new projects to someone who will get the blame if it fails, whereas someone else will get the credit if it succeeds. It is a system designed to squash all originality, enterprise, and daring. If on the other hand the man who gets the blame will also get the credit, these qualities have a chance. [...]

The principle at the root of this is [...]: the self interest of individuals must be harnessed to the good of the state, or the corporation. It is easy enough at the lower levels, when you can simply say that the more productive a worker is, the better the corporation is served. In the same way, salesmen's bonuses and commissions are constructed with painstaking and elaborate ingenuity to encourage them to sell hardest the goods which the company is most anxious to get rid of. But at the higher managerial levels it can be very difficult, as it becomes progressively easier for people to invert the process, to pursue their own interests while deftly harnessing the good of the corporation to them by subtle sophistries. By all means assume that any given manager is always working exclusively for the general good of the whole corporation; but construct the system so that he is penalised if he isn't.

To arrange the internal structure of the corporation so that every manager's ego is pulling at full power in exactly the direction the corporation wants to go is quite an achievement. Even so, it is not enough: it produces high efficiency, but not necessarily internal unity. For that, every group's influence must be in proportion to its importance; formal representation must run along the lines of real power, power as it is now and not as it was, historically, when the institutions of state – the departments and committees and boards – were first set up. The new growth area of the organisation – say the office copying group of a photographic firm, the monolithic circuit group of an electronics company, the numerical control group of a machine-tool manufacturer – does not only need pay and encouragement in proportion to its success, it also needs political power, it needs its voice to be heard in the highest councils of the realm. It will have criticisms and grievances which need airing – usually about excessive budget, status and importance given to other less-booming but longer-entrenched departments, and insufficient attention and respect given to its own aspirations and ideas – and if they are not heard and met, or at least satisfactorily answered, they are liable to turn inward in resentment, revolt, and even secession: it is a reformation situation. It happened in England in the nineteenth century, when the political power lay, as the constituency boundaries were drawn, along the lines of the rural landowning classes, whereas more and more of the nation's prosperity depended on the urban manufacturing and industrial classes. Not surprisingly they felt that since they were contributing so much to the nation's wealth and greatness, they should have proportionate say in how it was employed. The great battles over the Reform Bill and the repeal of the Corn Laws were a symptom of influence and importance being out of line: the unreformed parliament gave disproportionate weight to the countryside as against the towns, to the landowner as against the industrialist, and the Corn Laws were seen as protecting the income of the unproductive landowning minority at the expense of dearer bread (and therefore a need for higher wages) for the labouring urban majority. The Reform Act of 1832 was the acknowledgement of the arrival of the new political force, the repeal of the Corn Laws in 1846 was proof of its strength.

The chief difficulty is that it is often only in retrospect that the ultimate importance for a growing group can be gauged. At the time, you do not know if it is going to get any bigger, you suspect that improved competitive products will halt its progress or that it is just coming up to a plateau where demand levels out, in which case promotion and status-raising could prove an embarrassment. One of the first lessons of authority is that it is ten times easier to withhold than to withdraw. Political privileges, legal rights, welfare benefits – a state can hold these back from its people for many years: but once grant them and to take them away again is to risk a revolution. [...]

The problem of down-grading or removing an honest, loyal and hardworking executive is always a thorny one; logic cries out for it, nature rebels against it. You can say to the man, "You have done good and faithful service, your value is great, but this is not the job for you," and he may even believe you, but he knows all his colleagues and subordinates will know he has had the push. Many states have found a solution, or a partial solution, in an honours system. A peerage, a knighthood, an order of the legion of honour, or (under Louis XIV) the privilege of handing the sovereign his breeches at the levee, these are ways of demonstrating to everyone that this man remains in high personal esteem with the government, even though he has been passed over, removed or down-graded in terms of function. And the honours can also be used lower down the scale as a mark of favour for a rising young courtier who cannot yet be given the seniority his talents deserve. It is fascinating to watch the honours system developing inside the corporations: the development of a mass of small privileges and distinctions which of themselves convey no extra authority, carry no extra salary, and involve no extra function, and yet are avidly sought and jealously guarded by nearly all the executives. Titles (Manager, Vice-President, Director) are the obvious one – to be allowed to use a better-sounding one gives as much kick as a pay rise. Size of office is another, so is quality of furnishings; then there is the authority to order a tray of tea or coffee in the office, and the quality of the china when it arrives. There are the orders of dining (works canteen, staff restaurant, senior managers' mess, board dining room) and parking (general car park, reserved car park, board car park) and a wealth of other distinctions that start with Name On Door, and progress through Secretary in Separate Office to the higher distinctions like Drink Cabinet and Personal Chauffeur. But although the system has developed with such wealth and complexity, most corporations are very shy about exploiting it. They tend to make these privileges the automatic accompaniment of certain levels of job, and to be slightly sheepish about their principles of segregation. But the time must soon come when the whole system is seen not as an invidious chore of the Personnel Department but, as it has been in so many states, a powerful weapon in the hand of the chief executive. Then these distinctions, while still automatic at certain levels, can be awarded below that level for special incentive, reward or compensation. […] Of course the award must seem to be the personal wish of the chief executive and not the impersonal decision of a committee; and of course it must not be asked to do too much, to act as the equivalent of promotion, as an adequate substitute for a pay rise. It is a lubricant, not a fuel. But if the corporation is going to make frequent mechanical adjustments to keep the weight of employees' opinions in proportion with the weight of their responsibilities, then without regular lubrication there is liable to be constant friction and a great deal too much heat generated.

8

UNDERSTANDING POWER IN ORGANIZATIONS

Jeffrey Pfeffer

Source: Edited from *Managing with Power*. 1992. Harvard.

Norton Long, a political scientist, wrote, "People will readily admit that governments are organizations. The converse – that organizations are governments – is equally true but rarely considered" (Long, 1962: 110). But organizations, particularly large ones, are like governments in that they are fundamentally political entities. To understand them, one needs to understand organizational politics, just as to understand governments, one needs to understand governmental politics. Ours is an era in which people tend to shy away from this task. As I browse through bookstores, I am struck by the incursion of "New Age" thinking, even in the business sections. New Age can be defined, I suppose, in many ways, but what strikes me about it are two elements: (1) a self-absorption and self-focus, which looks toward the individual in isolation; and (2) a belief that conflict is largely the result of misunderstanding, and if people only had more communication, more tolerance, and more patience, many (or all) social problems would disappear. These themes appear in books on topics ranging from making marriages work to making organizations work. A focus on individual self-actualization is useful, but a focus on sheer self-reliance is not likely to encourage one to try to get things done with and through other people – to be a manager or a leader. "Excellence can be achieved in a solitary field without the need to exercise leadership" (Nixon, 1982: 5).

[...]

One can be quite content, quite happy, quite fulfilled as an organizational hermit, but one's influence is limited and the potential to accomplish great things, which requires interdependent action, is almost extinguished. If we are suspicious of the politics of large organizations, we may conclude that smaller organizations are a better alternative. There is, in fact, evidence that the average size of establishments in the United States is decreasing. This is not just because we have become more of a service economy and less of a manufacturing economy; even within manufacturing, the average size of establishments and firms is shrinking. The largest corporations have shed thousands, indeed hundreds of thousands of employees – not only middle managers, but also production workers, staff of all kinds, and employees who performed tasks that are now contracted out. Managers and employees who were stymied by the struggles over power and influence that emerge from interdependence and differences in points of view have moved to a world of smaller, simpler organizations, with less internal interdependence and less internal diversity, which are, as a consequence, less political. Of course, such structural changes only increase interdependence among organizations, even as they decrease interdependence and conflict within these organizations.

I see in this movement a parallel to what I have seen in the management of our human resources. Many corporations today solve their personnel problems by getting rid of the personnel. The rationale seems to be that if we can't effectively manage and motivate employees, then let's turn the task over to another organization. We can use leased employees or contract workers, or workers from temporary help agencies, and let those organizations solve our problems of turnover, compensation, selection, and training.

It is an appealing solution, consistent with the emphasis on the individual, which has always been strong in U.S. culture, and which has grown in recent years. How can we trust large organizations when they have broken compacts of long-term employment? Better to seek security and certainty within oneself, in one's own competencies and abilities, and in the control of one's own activities.

There is, however, one problem with this approach to dealing with organizational power and influence. It is not clear that by ignoring the social realities of power and influence we can make them go away, or that by trying to build simpler, less interdependent social structures we succeed in building organizations that are more effective or that have greater survival value. Although it is certainly true that large organizations sometimes disappear, (Hannan and Freeman 1989) it is also true that smaller organizations disappear at a much higher rate and have much worse survival properties. By trying to ignore issues of power and influence in organizations, we lose our chance to understand these critical social processes and to train managers to cope with them.

By pretending that power and influence don't exist, or at least shouldn't exist, we contribute to what I and some others [...] see [...] as the major problem facing many corporations today, particularly in the United States – the almost trained or produced incapacity of anyone except the highest-level managers to take action and get things accomplished. As I teach in corporate executive programs, and as I compare experiences with colleagues who do likewise, I hear the same story over and over again. In these programs ideas are presented to fairly senior executives, who then work in groups on the implications of these ideas for their firms. There is real strength in the experience and knowledge of these executives, and they often come up with insightful recommendations and ideas for improving their organizations. Perhaps they discover the wide differences in effectiveness that exist in different units and share suggestions about how to improve performance. Perhaps they come to understand more comprehensively the markets and technologies of their organizations, and develop strategies for both internally oriented and externally oriented changes to enhance effectiveness. It really doesn't matter, because the most frequently heard comment at such sessions is, "My boss should be here." And when they go back to their offices, after the stimulation of the week, few managers have either the ability or the determination to engineer the changes they discussed with such insight.

I recall talking to a store manager for a large supermarket chain with a significant share of the northern California grocery market. He managed a store that did in excess of $20 million in sales annually, which by the standards of the average organization makes him a manager with quite a bit of responsibility – or so one would think. In this organization, however, as in many others, the responsibilities of middle-level managers are strictly limited. A question arose as to whether the store should participate in putting its name on a monument sign for the shopping center in which the store was located. The cost was about $8,000 (slightly less than four hours' sales in that store). An analysis was done, showing how many additional shoppers would need to be attracted to pay back this small investment, and what percentage this was of the traffic count passing by the center. The store manager wanted the sign. But, of course, he could not spend even this much money without the approval of his superiors. It was the president of the northern California division who decided, after a long meeting, that the expenditure was not necessary.

There are many lessons that one might learn from this example. It could be seen as the result of a plague of excessive centralization, or as an instance of a human resource management policy that certainly was more "top down" than "bottom up". But what was particularly interesting was the response of the manager – who, by the way, is held accountable for this store's profits even as he is given almost no discretion to do anything about them. When I asked him about the decision, he said, "Well, I guess that's why the folks at headquarters get the big money; they must know something we don't." Was he going to push for his idea, his very modest proposal? Of course no, he said. One gets along by just biding one's time, going along with whatever directives come down from the upper management.

I have seen this situation repeated in various forms over and over again. I talk to senior executives who claim their organizations take no initiative, and to high-level managers who say they can't or won't engage in efforts to change the corporations they work for, even when they know such changes are important, if not essential, to the success and survival of these organizations. There are politics involved in innovation and change. And unless and until we are willing to come to terms with organizational power and influence, and admit that the skills of getting things done are as important as the skills of figuring out what to do, our organizations will fall further and further behind. The problem is, in most cases, not an absence of insight or organizational intelligence. Instead the problem is one of passivity: [...]

In this country – and in most other democracies – power has such a bad name that many good people persuade themselves they want nothing to do with it. The ethical and spiritual apprehensions are understandable. But one cannot abjure power. Power, as we are now speaking of it ... is simply the capacity to bring about certain intended consequences in the behavior of others. ... In our democratic society we make grants of power to people for specified purposes. If for ideological or temperamental reasons they refuse to exercise the power granted, we must turn to others. ... To say a leader is preoccupied with power is like saying that a tennis player is preoccupied with making shots his opponent cannot return. Of course leaders are preoccupied with power! The significant questions are: What means do they use to gain it? How do they exercise it? To what ends do they exercise it?

(Gardner, 1990: 55–57).

[...]

Our ambivalence about power

That we are ambivalent about power is undeniable. Rosabeth Kanter, noting that power was critical for effective managerial behavior, nevertheless wrote, "Power is America's last dirty word. It is easier to talk about money – and much easier to talk about sex – than it is to talk about power." (Kanter, 1979: 65). [...] The concepts of power and organizational politics are related; most authors, myself included, define organizational politics as the exercise or use of power, with power being defined as a potential force. [...] [W]e know that power and politics exist, and we even grudgingly admit that they are necessary to individual success, but we nevertheless don't like them.

This ambivalence toward, if not outright disdain for, the development and use of power in organizations stems from more than one source. First, there is the issue of ends and means – we often don't like to consider the methods that are necessary to get things accomplished. [...] We are also ambivalent about ends and means because the same strategies and processes that may produce outcomes we desire can also be used to produce results that we consider undesirable. Second, some fundamental lessons we learn in school really hinder our appreciation of power and influence. Finally, in a related point, the perspective from which we judge organizational decisions often does not do justice to the realities of the social world. [...]

There is no doubt that power and influence can be acquired and exercised for evil purposes. Of course, most medicines can kill if taken in the wrong amount, thousands die each year in automobile accidents, and nuclear power can either provide energy or mass destruction. We do not abandon chemicals, cars, or even atomic power because of the dangers associated with them; instead we consider danger an incentive to get training and information that will help us to use these forces productively. Yet few people are willing to approach the potential risks and advantages of power with the same pragmatism. People prefer to avoid discussions of power, apparently on the assumption that, "If we don't think about it, it won't exist." I take a different view. [...]

The means to any end are merely mechanisms for accomplishing something. The something can be grand, grotesque, or, for most of us, I suspect, somewhere in between. The end may not always justify the means, but neither should it automatically be used to discredit the means. Power and political processes in organizations can be used to accomplish great things. They are not always used in this fashion, but that does not mean we should reject them out of hand. It is interesting that when we use power ourselves, we see it as a good force and wish we had more. When others use it against us, particularly when it is used to thwart our goals or ambitions, we see it as an evil. A more sophisticated and realistic view would see it for what it is – an important social process that is often required to get things accomplished in interdependent systems.

[...]

Lessons to be unlearned – Our ambivalence about power also comes from lessons we learn in school. The first lesson is that life is a matter of individual effort, ability, and achievement. After all, in school, if you have mastered the intricacies of cost accounting, or calculus, or electrical engineering, and the people sitting on either side of you haven't, their failure will not affect your performance – unless, that is, you had intended to copy from their papers. In the classroom setting, interdependence is minimized. It is you versus the material, and as long as you have mastered the material, you have achieved what is expected. Cooperation may even be considered cheating.

Such is not the case in organizations. If you know your organization's strategy but your colleagues do not, you will have difficulty accomplishing anything. The private knowledge and private skill that are so useful in the classroom are insufficient in organizations. Individual success in organizations is quite frequently a matter of working with and through other people, and organizational success is often a function of how successfully individuals can coordinate their activities. Most situations in organizations resemble football more than golf, which is why companies often scan resumés to find not only evidence of individual achievement but also signs that the person is skilled at working as part of a team. In achieving success in organizations, "power transforms individual interests into coordinated activities that accomplish valuable ends" (Zaleznick and Kets de Vries, 1975: 109).

The second lesson we learn in school, which may be even more difficult to unlearn, is that there are right and wrong answers. We are taught how to solve problems, and for each problem, that there is a right answer, or at least one approach that is more correct than another. The right answer is, of course, what the instructor says it is, or what is in the back of the book, or what is hidden away in the instructor's manual. Life appears as a series of "eureka" problems, so-called because once you are shown the correct approach or answer, it is immediately self-evident that the answer is, in fact, correct.

[...]

In the world in which we all live, things are seldom clearcut or obvious. Not only do we lack a book or an instructor to provide quick feedback on the quality of our approach, but the problems we face often have multiple dimensions – which yield multiple methods of evaluation. The consequences of our decisions are often known only long after the fact, and even then with some ambiguity.

An alternative perspective on decision-making

Let me offer an alternative way of thinking about the decision-making process. There are three important things to remember about decisions. First, a decision by itself changes nothing. You can decide to launch a new product, hire a job candidate, build a new plant, change your performance evaluation system, and so forth, but the decision will not put itself into effect. As a prosaic personal example, recall how many times you or your friends "decided" to quit smoking, to get more exercise, to relax more, to eat healthier foods, or to lose weight. Such resolutions often fizzle out before producing any results. Thus, in addition to knowledge of decision science, we need to know something about "implementation science." Second, at the moment a decision is made, we cannot possibly know whether it is good or bad. Decision quality, when measured by results, can only be known as the consequences of the decision become known. We must wait for the decision to be implemented and for its consequences to become clear.

The third, and perhaps most important, observation is that we almost invariably spend more time living with the consequences of our decisions than we do in making them. It may be an organizational decision, such as whether to acquire a company, change the compensation system, fight a union-organizing campaign; or a personal decision, such as where to go to school, which job to choose, what subject to major in, or whom to marry.

In any case, it is likely that the effects of the decision will be with us longer than it took us to make the decision, regardless of how much time and effort we invested. Indeed, this simple point has led several social psychologists to describe people as rationalizing (as contrasted with rational) animals (Aronson, 1972). The match between our attitudes and our behavior, for instance, often derives from our adjusting our attitudes after the fact to conform to our past actions and their consequences (Festinger, 1957).

If decisions by themselves change nothing, if, at the time a decision is made, we cannot know its consequences, and if we spend, in any event, more time living with our decisions than we do in making them, then it seems evident that the emphasis in much management training and practice has been misplaced. Rather than spending inordinate amounts of time and effort in the decision-making process, it would seem at least as useful to spend time implementing decisions and dealing with their ramifications. In this sense, good managers are not only good analytic decision makers; more important, they are skilled in managing the consequences of their decisions. "Few successful leaders spend much time fretting about decisions once they are past. [...] The only way he can give adequate attention to the decisions he has to make tomorrow is to put those of yesterday firmly behind him" (Nixon, 1982: 329).

[...]

The point is that decisions in the world of organizations are not like decisions made in school. There, once you have written down an answer and turned in the test, the game is over. This is not the case in organizational life. The important actions may not be the original choices, but rather what happens subsequently, and what actions are taken to make things work out. This is a significant point because it means that we need to be somewhat less concerned about the quality of the decision at the time we make it (which, after all, we can't really know anyway), and more concerned with adapting our new decisions and actions to the information we learn as events unfold. Just as Honda emerged as a leader in many American markets more by accident and trial-and-error learning than by design, it is critical that organizational members develop the fortitude to continue when confronted by adversity, and the insight about how to turn situations around. The most important skill may be managing the consequences of decisions. And, in organizations in which it is often difficult to take any action, the critical ability may be the capacity to have things implemented.

Ways of getting things done

Why is implementation difficult in so many organizations, and why does it appear that the ability to get decisions implemented is becoming increasingly rare? One way of thinking about this issue, and of examining the role of power and influence in the implementation process, is to consider some possible ways of getting things done.

One way of getting things to happen is through hierarchical authority. Many people think power is merely the exercise of formal authority, but it is considerably more than that, as we will see. Everyone who works in an organization has seen the exercise of hierarchical authority. Those at higher levels have the power to hire and fire, to measure and reward behavior, and to provide direction to those who are under their aegis. Hierarchical direction is usually seen as legitimate, because the variation in formal authority comes to be taken for granted as a part of organizational life. Thus the phrase, "the boss wants . . ." or "the president wants . . ." is seldom questioned or challenged. [...]

There are three problems with hierarchy as a way of getting things done. First, and perhaps not so important, is that it is badly out of fashion. In an era of rising education and the democratization of all decision processes, in an era in which participative management is advocated in numerous places, (Bradford and Cohen, 1984; Pasmore, 1988) and particularly in a country in which incidents such as the Vietnam War and Watergate have led many people to mistrust the institutions of authority, implementation by order or command is problematic. [...]

A second, more serious problem with authority derives from the fact that virtually all of us work in positions in which, in order to accomplish our job and objectives, we need the cooperation of others who do not fall within our direct chain of command. We depend, in other words, on people outside our purview of authority, whom we could not command, reward, or punish even if we wanted to. Perhaps, as a line manager in a product division, we need the cooperation of people in human resources for hiring, people in finance for evaluating new product opportunities, people in distribution and sales for getting the product sold and delivered, and people in market research for determining product features and marketing and pricing strategy. Even the authority of a chief executive is not absolute, since there are groups outside the focal organization that control the ability to get things done. To sell overseas airline routes to other domestic airlines requires the cooperation of the Transportation and Justice Departments, as well as the acquiescence of foreign governments. To market a drug or medical device requires the approval of the Food and Drug Administration; to export products overseas, one may need both financing and export licenses. The hierarchical authority of all executives and administrators is limited, and for most of us, it is quite limited compared to the scope of what we need in order to do our jobs effectively.

There is a third problem with implementation accomplished solely or primarily through hierarchical authority: what happens if the person at the apex of the pyramid, the one whose orders are being followed, is incorrect? When authority is vested in a single individual, the organization can face grave difficulties if that person's insight or leadership begins to fail. [...]

Another way of getting things done is by developing a strongly shared vision or organizational culture. If people share a common set of goals, a common perspective on what to do and how to accomplish it, and a common vocabulary that allows them to coordinate their behavior, then command and hierarchical authority are of much less importance. People will be able to work cooperatively without waiting for orders from the upper levels of the company. Managing through a shared vision and with a strong organizational culture has been a very popular prescription for organizations (Davis, 1984; Deal and Kennedy, 1982; Peters and Waterman, 1982). A number of articles and books tell how to build commitment and shared vision and how to socialize individuals, particularly at the time of entry, so that they share a language, values, and premises about what needs to be done and how to do it (O'Reilly, 1989; Pascale, 1985).

Without denying the efficacy and importance of vision and culture, it is important to recognize that implementation accomplished through them can have problems. First, building a shared conception of the world takes time and effort. There are instances when the organization is in crisis or confronts situations in which there is simply not sufficient time to develop shared premises about how to respond. For this very reason, the military services rely not only on techniques that build loyalty and *esprit de corps*, (Dombusch, 1955) but also on a hierarchical chain of command and a tradition of obeying orders.

Second, there is the problem of how, in a strong culture, new ideas that are inconsistent with that culture can penetrate. A strong culture really constitutes an organizational paradigm, which prescribes how to look at things, what are appropriate methods and techniques for solving problems, and what are the important issues and problems (Brown, 1978).

[...]

There is a third process of implementation in organizations – namely, the use of power and influence. With power and influence the emphasis is on method rather than structure. It is possible to wield power and influence without necessarily having or using formal authority. Nor is it necessary to rely on a strong organizational culture and the homogeneity that this often implies. Of course, the process of implementation through power and influence is not without problems of its own. What is important is to see power and influence as one of a set of ways of getting things done – not the only way, but an important way.

From the preceding discussion we can see that implementation is becoming more difficult because: (1) changing social norms and greater interdependence within organizations have made traditional, formal authority less effective than it once was, and (2) developing a common vision is increasingly difficult in organizations composed of heterogeneous members – heterogeneous in terms of race and ethnicity, gender, and even language and culture. At the same time, our ambivalence about power, and the fact that training in its use is far from widespread, mean that members of organizations are often unable to supplement their formal authority with the "unofficial" processes of power and influence. As a result their organizations suffer, and promising projects fail to get off the ground. This is why learning how to manage with power is so important.

[...]

Power is defined [...] as the potential ability to influence behavior, to change the course of events, to overcome resistance, and to get people to do things that they would not otherwise do. (Emerson, 1962; Kanter, 1979; Pfeffer, 1981). Politics and influence are the processes, the actions, the behaviors through which this potential power is utilized and realized.

What does it mean, to manage with power?

First, it means recognizing that in almost every organization, there are varying interests. This suggests that one of the first things we need to do it to diagnose the political landscape and figure out what the relevant interests are, and what important political subdivisions characterize the organization. It is essential that we do not assume that everyone necessarily is going to be our friend, or agree with us, or even that preferences are uniformly distributed. There are clusters of interests within organizations, and we need to understand where these are and to whom they belong.

Next, it means figuring out what point of view these various individuals and subunits have on issues of concern to us. It also means understanding why they have the perspective that they do. It is all too easy to assume that those with a different perspective are somehow not as smart as we are, not as informed, not as perceptive. If that is our belief, we are likely to do several things, each of which is disastrous. First, we may act contemptuously toward those who disagree with us – after all, if they aren't as competent or as insightful as we are, why should we take them seriously? It is rarely difficult to get along with those who resemble us in character and opinions. The real secret of success in organizations is the ability to get those who differ from us, and whom we don't necessarily like, to do what needs to be done. Second, if we think people are misinformed, we are likely to try to "inform" them, or to try to convince them with facts and analysis. Sometimes this will work, but often it will not, for their disagreement may not be based on a lack of information; it may, instead, arise from a difference perspective on what our information means. Diagnosing the point of view of interest groups as well as the basis for their positions will assist us in negotiating with them in predicting their response to various initiatives.

Third, managing with power means understanding that to get things done, you need power – more power than those whose opposition you must overcome – and thus it is imperative to understand where power comes from and how these sources of power can be developed. We are sometimes reluctant to think very purposefully or strategically about acquiring and using power. We are prone to believe that if we do our best, work hard, be nice, and so forth, things will work out for the best. I don't mean to imply that one should not, in general, work hard, try to make good decisions, and be nice, but that these and similar platitudes are often not very useful in helping us get things accomplished in our organizations. We need to understand power and try to get it. We must be willing to do things to build our sources of power, or else we will be less effective than we might wish to be.

Fourth, managing with power means understanding the strategies and tactics through which power is developed and used in organizations, including the importance of timing, the use of structure, the social psychology of commitment and other forms of interpersonal influence. If nothing else, such an understanding will help us become astute observers of the behavior of others. The more we understand power and its manifestations, the better will be our clinical skills. More fundamentally, we need to understand strategies and tactics of using power so that we can consider the range of approaches available to us, and use what is likely to be effective.

Again, as in the case of building sources of power, we often try not to think about these things, and we avoid being strategic or purposeful about employing our power. This is a mistake. Although we may have various qualms, there will be others who do not. Knowledge without power is of remarkably little use. And power without the skill to employ it effectively is likely to be wasted.

Managing with power means more than knowing the ideas discussed in this article. It means being […] willing to do something with that knowledge. It requires political savvy to get things done, and the willingness to force the issue. […]

Getting things done requires power. The problem is that we would prefer to see the world as a kind of grand morality play, with the good guys, and the bad ones easily identified. Obtaining power is not always an attractive process, nor is its use. [...]We are troubled by the issue of means and ends. We are perplexed by the fact that "bad" people sometimes do great and wonderful things, and that "good" people sometimes do "bad" things, or often, nothing at all. Every day, managers in public and private organizations acquire and use power to get things done. Some of these things may be, in retrospect, mistakes, although often that depends heavily on your point of view. Any reader who always does the correct thing that pleases everyone should immediately contact me – we will get very wealthy together. Mistakes and opposition are inevitable. What is not inevitable is passivity, not trying, not seeking to accomplish things.

In many domains of activity we have become so obsessed with not upsetting anybody, and with not making mistakes, that we settle for doing nothing. [...]Analysis and forethought are, obviously, fine. What is not so fine is paralysis or inaction, which arise because we have little skill in overcoming the opposition that inevitably accompanies change, and little interest in doing so.

[...]

It is easy and often comfortable to feel powerless – to say, "I don't know what to do, I don't have the power to get it done, and besides, I can't really stomach the struggle that may be involved." It is easy, and now quite common, to say, when confronted with some mistake in your organization, "It's not really my responsibility, I can't do anything about it anyway, and if the company wants to do that, well that's why the senior executives get the big money – it's their responsibility." Such a response excuses us from trying to do things; in not trying to overcome opposition, we will make fewer enemies and are less likely to embarrass ourselves. It is, however, a prescription for both organizational and personal failure. This is why power and influence are not the organization's last dirty secret, but the secret of success for both individuals and their organizations. Innovation and change in almost any arena requires the skill to develop power, and the willingness to employ it to get things accomplished. Or, in the words of a local radio newscaster, "If you don't like the news, go out and make some of your own."

References

Aronson, Elliot. *The Social Animal* (San Francisco, CA: W. H. Freeman, 1972).

Bradford, D. L. and Cohen, A. R. *Managing for Excellence* (New York, NY: John Wiley, 1984).

Brown, R. H. "Bureaucracy as Praxis: Toward a Political Phenomenology of Formal Organizaions", *Administrative Science Quarterly, 23* (1978): 365–382.

Davis, S. *Managing Corporate Culture* (Cambridge, MA: Ballinger, 1984).

Deal, T. and Kennedy, A. A. *Corporate Cultures* (Reading, MA: Addison-Wesley, 1982).

Dombusch, S. M. "The Military Academy as an Assimilating Institution," *Social Forces 33* (1955): 7, 16–221.

Emerson, R. M. "Power-Dependence Relations," *American Sociological Review*, 27 (1962): 31–41.

Festinger, L. *A Theory of Cognitive Dissonance* (Stanford, CA: Stanford University Press, 1957).

Gardner, J. W. *On Leadership* (New York, NY: Free Press, 1990).

Hannan, M. T. and Freeman, J. *Organizational Ecology* (Cambridge, MA: Harvard University Press, 1989).

Kanter, R. M. "Power Failure in Management Circuits," *Harvard Business Review, 57* (July/August 1979).

Long, N. E. "The Administrative Organization as a Political System," in S. Mailick and E.H. Van Ness, eds, *Concepts and Issues in Administrative Behavior* (Englewood Cliffs, NJ: Prentice-Hall, 1962).

Nixon, R. M. *Leaders* (New York, NY: Warner Books, 1982).

O'Reilly, C. "Corporations, Culture, and Commitment: Motivation and Social Control in Organizations," *California Management Review, 31* (1989): 9–25.

Pascale, R. T. "The Paradox of 'Corporate Culture': Reconciling Ourselves to Socialization," *California Management Review, 26* (1985): 26–41

Pasmore, W. A. *Designing Effective Organizations: The Sociological Systems Perspective* (New York, NY: John Wiley, 1988).

Peters, T. J. and Waterman, R. H. *In Search of Excellence* (New York, NY: Harper and Row, 1982).

Pfeffer, J. *Power in Organizations* (Marshfield, MA: Pitman Publishing, 1981).

Zaleznick, A. and Kets de Vries, M. F.R. *Power and the Corporate Mind* (Boston, MA: Houghton Mifflin, 1975).

9

THE DIALECTIC OF SOCIAL EXCHANGE
Theorizing corporate-social enterprise collaboration

MariaLaura Di Domenico, Paul Tracey and Helen Haugh

Source: Edited from *Organization Studies*, 2009, 30 (8), pp. 887–907.

Introduction

Organizational scholars have become increasingly interested in inter-organizational collaboration. Much of this work has focused on collaboration between corporations, and the dynamics of managing co-operative relationships between organizations that may also be in competition (e.g. Dyer and Singh 1998; Powell *et al.* 1996). In this paper, however, we are concerned with a different form of collaboration: cross-sector collaboration between corporations and social enterprises.[1] These collaborations involve the formation of a political-economic arrangement that seeks to reconcile wealth creation with social justice, and the efficient functioning of markets with the welfare of communities. We believe this arrangement needs to be viewed through a different conceptual lens than same-sector collaborations because it brings together two contrasting organizational forms.

Despite their differences, social enterprises and corporations appear to have strong reasons to collaborate with one another. Social enterprises are defined broadly as non-profit organizations that pursue social objectives through the sale of goods or services (Pearce 2003). Non-profit organizations have been encouraged by governments and charitable foundations to move away from reliance on subsidy and donations and generate income through trading (Pharoah *et al.* 2004). As part of this process, many social enterprises have sought to build relationships with corporations in order to improve their viability as businesses (DTI 2005).

Corporations, on the other hand, have been placed under increasing pressure to be socially responsible in the wake of recent corporate scandals, increased regulation from governments, and rising expectations from consumers about

---

[1]Note that our focus is on collaborations forged by organizations from different economic, as opposed to industry, sectors.

corporate roles and responsibilities. For example, Brown and Dacin (1997) found that the extent to which a firm is perceived to be socially responsible significantly influences consumers' attitudes towards that firm's products. Many corporations have responded by seeking to forge relationships with social enterprises and other non-profit organizations (Tracey et al. 2005). Collaborations with social enterprises represent an alternative to independent corporate-social responsibility (CSR) initiatives, with the potential to improve their community knowledge and local legitimacy.[2]

While we focus primarily on the UK to illustrate our arguments, it is important to note that corporate-social enterprise collaboration is an international phenomenon. For example, the Bendigo Bank in Australia has a community banking programme which allows non-profit organizations to take ownership of a franchise in order to deliver financial services in places that are poorly served (Datamonitor 2005). Moreover, Brugmann and Prahalad (2007: 85) have noted that many Non-Governmental Organizations (NGOs) in developing countries are increasingly creating business ventures to achieve their social objectives, with this opening up the possibility of relationships with corporations on a commercial basis. These authors give the example of Grameen Phone, a joint venture between the telecommunications firm Telenor and the Grameen Bank, involving the sale of mobile phones through the bank's network of credit groups in Bangladesh. We thus consider that our theorising has broad applicability.

Given the increasing support for corporate-social enterprise collaboration internationally, we believe that it is important to consider their forms, the social processes involved in their creation, and the outcomes for both partners. However, we propose that the main perspectives currently used to conceptualize inter-organizational collaboration are not well suited for understanding the emergence of new political-economic arrangements of this sort. We therefore build an alternative theoretical framework which develops social exchange theory (SET) through the lens of dialectical theory.

The crux of our argument is that corporate-social enterprise collaborations are shaped by (1) the value that each member of the collaboration attributes to the inputs of their partner, (2) the competing practices and priorities intrinsic to the corporation and the social enterprise, and (3) the expected benefits of the collaboration to each partner. More specifically, we suggest that social enterprises' exchange value is rooted in their local knowledge, social capital and social legitimacy, while corporations' exchange value is rooted in their commercial knowledge, financial capital and market legitimacy. However, differences in corporations' and social enterprises' goals, ownership structures, governance mechanisms and lines of accountability may lead to a series of tensions. For a synthesized state of collaboration to emerge and the partnership sustained, we posit that the antithetical forces inherent within the relationship must be resolved.

[...]

---

[2]In this chapter we are concerned with external CSR initiatives involving relationship building with local stakeholders. We recognise that CSR is much broader than this and may include a range of internal practices.

Towards the dialectic of social exchange: A theoretical approach to the study of corporate-social enterprise collaboration

The focus of our framework is on *dyadic* exchanges in a given partnership. This can be contrasted with 'generalized' social exchanges, which involve interactions between three or more actors and which entail quite different social processes (Das and Teng 2002). Moreover, we consider only collaborations that are bound by normative obligations, involve repeated interactions, and are based on reciprocal exchange of resources; unreciprocated surrender of resources between organizations – such as charitable donations or gifts – is excluded from our analysis.

Social exchange theory

SET is well established in the social sciences (Ekeh 1974; Blau 1964; Homans 1961) and has recently received renewed attention in management studies (e.g. Muthusamy and White 2005). The theory views interpersonal interactions from an exchange perspective in which social costs and benefits are 'traded' in relationships governed by normative rules and agreements. [...W]e extend SET beyond the micro-level by applying it to exchanges between organizations.

Although SET is often referred to as a coherent set of ideas, it is more appropriate to consider it as an interrelated set of social exchange *theories*. SET draws most notably on two theoretical strands. One strand, pioneered by Homans (1961), is heavily influenced by psychological-behaviorist ideas. The other strand, pioneered by Blau (1964), has its roots in economics, assuming that individuals engage in social exchange because of the need or desire to acquire intrinsic or extrinsic rewards that they are unable to obtain by themselves. Our framework is aligned with Blau's socio-economic perspective, which more appropriately lends itself to collaboration between organizations.

When each organization in a dyadic collaboration holds resources (whether economic, political or social) that are deemed valuable by the other partner, the norm of reciprocity becomes established as fundamental to their interaction. Reciprocity assumes that exchange is guided by an expectation of return or behaviour in kind. This implies that actors engage in actions and/or interactions in order to achieve their goals after considering strategically the options available to them (Heath 1976). However, the way that each partner interacts and is able to influence strategic objectives is shaped by power relationships between key decision-makers (Cook and Emerson 1978). Collaboration is thus based on mutually beneficial patterns of co-operation that affect and are affected by the access that participants have to resources, their choices between alternative courses of action or reaction, and anticipated outcomes. Of particular interest, therefore, is the way in which the partners attempt to achieve balance in their exchange relationships.

Corporate-social enterprise collaborations, like all collaborations, involve both economic and social exchange. Indeed, according to Blau (1964), social elements of the exchange may involve benefits to either party which are either extrinsic and hold economic value, such as information and knowledge, or intrinsic and without overt economic value, such as support or friendship. In addition, intangible elements of knowledge, skills, and expertise may be exchanged (Muthusamy and White 2005).

The dialectic of social exchange

SET has been criticized for its failure to acknowledge that mutual exchange relationships can 'develop dialectically into complex, emergent structures in which concealment, manipulation and domination are pervasive' (Zeitz 1980: 86). Zeitz suggests that the traditional assumptions embedded within SET about the mutual benefits of exchange, the voluntary nature of exchange engagement and decision-making, and the awareness by both parties of the potential costs and payoffs of the exchange, may be pertinent to partnerships during the formative stages of relationships, but the applicability of such assumptions is likely to deteriorate over time as inequalities emerge and the interaction increases or decreases in its appeal to either party. We seek to address these issues within our framework by taking account of the dynamic nature of inter-organizational relations. Specifically, we consider that dialectical theory provides insights into the development of relationships between organizational forms that contain elements of contradiction, and that it can be incorporated logically into SET to create a new framework for the analysis of corporate-social enterprise collaborations.

Dialectical analysis has a long and diverse tradition in philosophy. Its use in the modern world is usually attributed to Kant, but it is most commonly associated with the writings of Hegel and Marx. Dialectical theory has been interpreted in many different ways, but organizational scholars have tended to draw upon a Marxian interpretation of the dialectic (see, for example, Seo and Creed 2002; Benson 1977; Lourenco and Glidewell 1975) and this is the approach adopted in this paper. From this perspective, dialectics refer to social processes that involve aspects of 'conflict, paradox, [and] mutual interaction' (Zeitz 1980: 73).

A core element of the Marxian dialectic is the 'law of the negation of the negation' which posits that where there is a collision of two opposites, one opposite negates the other and is in turn negated by higher order historical or social processes which allow aspects of both negated positions to be preserved. This is sometimes represented as the three stages of thesis, antithesis and synthesis (Edgley 2006) in which the dialectic is viewed as a sequence: 'the parties to… conflict relate as thesis and antithesis and resolve into the form of synthesis, which not only subsumes aspects of both thesis and antithesis but creates new patterns or structures' (Lourenco and Glidewell 1975: 490). In other words, a Marxian view of dialectical analysis focuses upon 'the transformation through which one set of arrangements gives way to another' (Benson 1977: 3).

This interpretation of dialectical theory is strongly refuted by some political philosophers, who consider it a distortion of Hegelian dialectical thought. Indeed, while the thesis-antithesis-synthesis triad is often attributed to Hegel, the only time that he actually referred to it was in the preface to *'The Phenomenology of Mind'* (1807). In fact, this view of dialectics was initially popularized by Chalybäus (1837) and only later adopted by Marx in his analysis of class structure and conflict (see, for example, *The Poverty of Philosophy*, 1995; orig. 1847). While this 'Hegel myth' (Kaufmann 1951) is dismissed by some scholars as 'Marxism superimposed on Hegel' (Mueller 1958: 413), it nevertheless captures the essence of Marx's interpretation of Hegel's ideas.

More broadly, Marxian interpretations of dialectical theory have had a significant influence upon organization studies, allowing scholars to shed light on important organizational phenomena. For example, McGuire (1988: 122) adopts a Marxian dialectical perspective to study inter-organizational networks showing that network relations are underpinned not only by resource dependence and desire for 'efficiency', but also reflect 'the domination of particular ideologies' and the need to balance the interests of network members. These ideologies, she argued, have a significant bearing on the dialectical process of network formation and, ultimately, the nature of any synthesis. In another important contribution, Lourenco and Glidewell's (1975) longitudinal study of the interactions between a local television station and its company headquarters adopts a Marxian dialectical analysis to examine the relationships between conflict and social control. They conclude that conflict resolution (i.e. synthesis) requires the 'mutual balancing' of multiple bases of social power.

We recognize that these studies, as well as the collaborations with which we are concerned, depart from both Marx and Hegel in an important respect: they are voluntary arrangements in which the partners *choose* to participate. In contrast, Marx and Hegel considered that dialectical forces were inexorable. Nevertheless, we contend that dialectical theory is very relevant to our analysis. Thus, dialectical forces infuse inter-organizational exchanges, whereby actions create tensions that stimulate reactions and renewed collaborative measures. These may result in the creation of new organizational arrangements which incorporate reconciled ideological standpoints or partnership dissonance resulting from the repeated collision of structural forces.

In organization studies, scholars have used the dialectic principally as a way of conceptualizing power and its reproduction within organizations (e.g. Benson 1977). Relations *between* organizations have received less attention from proponents of dialectical thought. We posit that conceptualizing power dynamics through dialectics is relevant to inter-organizational collaboration in general, and corporate-social enterprise partnerships in particular, because of the differing attributes that each partner offers the collaboration. More specifically, incorporating the dialectic into a social exchange framework allows the nature and goals of each partner and the dynamics within and between the partners to be analysed over the life of the partnership. Before applying our framework, however, we provide a more detailed account of social enterprise.

Social enterprise as an emerging organizational form

As noted in the Introduction, we define a social enterprise as a non-profit venture which aims to achieve a given social purpose through strategies which generate income from commercial activity.[3] While social enterprises, like corporations, participate in markets through the sale of goods and services, they adhere to very different structures and practices than corporations. Specifically: they hold wealth in trust for community benefit, they democratically involve stakeholders in organizational governance, and they seek to be accountable to the constituencies they serve (Pearce 2003). Thus social enterprises differ from private enterprises in terms of their social goals, ownership structures, governance and accountability, and from traditional non-profit organizations in their pursuit of commercial activity rather than reliance on grants, donations or membership fees (Di Maggio and Anheier 1990).

In other words, social enterprises endeavour to combine the private sector's capacity for wealth creation with an ethos of community participation: they are a hybrid organizational form that straddles both markets and civil society (Giddens 1998). [...]

[...A]lthough corporatism and material consumption have become pervasive in all market-based economies, social enterprise represents an alternative strategy, within a market framework, capable of undermining the profit-maximizing interests of business (Pearce 2003). Social enterprises may therefore be part of a broader progression, or even a new stage, in the evolution of capitalism.

At present, social enterprise remains a relatively small component of the UK economy. To increase their role and contribution, social enterprises need to demonstrate that they can create both commercial and social value. Thus far, the evidence is at best mixed. Indeed, the most comprehensive study of UK social enterprise paints a picture of 'limited achievement, set against high policy expectations', and describes a sector characterized by high failure rates, heavy reliance on public sector funding and low-quality entrepreneurship (Amin *et al.* 2002: 116).

As noted, this limited track record of commercial success has been a key motivation for social enterprises to collaborate with corporations. As well as accessing the skills and resources needed to build successful businesses, many social enterprises consider that partnering with corporations will augment their legitimacy (Kendall 2000). Changes to social policy and funding regimes constitute an additional incentive: statutory funding available to non-profit organizations has become increasingly scarce, and much of the remaining funding is awarded on condition that recipients achieve financial sustainability by the end of the grant or contract (Amin *et al.* 2002). [...] The upshot is that many social enterprises have come to view collaborations with corporations as a key element of organizational

---

[3]Social enterprise is, of course, a contested term. See Pharoah *et al.* (2004: 2–3) for an overview of the key areas of contention.

strategy. In the next section of the paper we apply our framework to this form of collaboration.

The attribution of exchange value in corporate-social enterprise collaboration

As social enterprise is a relatively new phenomenon it is likely that, in a given collaboration, the corporation will be larger and more established than the social enterprise. However, whilst we recognise the importance of scale and financial resources, we focus on the aims and priorities intrinsic to each partner as the key modifying influences upon inter-organizational dynamics. We conceptualize these with respect to the exchange value arising from tangible and intangible assets that each partner brings to the collaboration.

The collaborative relationship that emerges from the social exchange process is necessarily different for each partner, but nevertheless draws upon elements of both. While the extent to which the relationship is more closely aligned with the priorities of either partner is likely to depend upon the collaboration's centrality to organizational objectives, the core of our argument is that each party's relative position within the partnership is contingent upon the value placed on their contribution.

Traditional relationships between corporations and non-profit organizations have tended to be based on philanthropy and characterized by the overwhelming dominance of the corporation (Husted 2003). However, as more social enterprises have been created, Tracey *et al.* (2005) have referred to exchanges between social enterprises and corporations that are characterized by mutual advantage and relative equity. From this perspective, the position of the social enterprise within the partnership is enhanced because its exchange value increases; i.e. it is perceived as an exponent of social capital[4] and local knowledge, and not only as a mechanism for delivering CSR objectives.

Thus the basis of a social enterprise's exchange value is its embeddedness among local stakeholders, providing a level of community legitimacy that few corporations are able to achieve independently. This means that partnering with a social enterprise may have a positive effect on the reputation and perceived trustworthiness of the corporation. Moreover, partnerships with social enterprises offer corporations the potential for effective resource allocation and longer-term project sustainability that is largely absent in philanthropy-based relationships between corporations and non-profit organizations (Husted 2003). For example, local social capital might deliver commercial benefits in terms of improved local knowledge, greater local awareness, and increased local demand. Thus corporations are likely to prefer collaborations with social enterprises to one-way philanthropic exchanges with non-profit organizations or independent CSR initiatives.

The exchange value of corporations, on the other hand, stems from their capacity for wealth creation in general, and their commercial and financial

---

[4]Following Coleman (1993), we define social capital as the social relationships, norms and values that facilitate individual and collective action.

competencies in particular. Corporations also have the potential to provide knowledge and infrastructure, such as technological, accounting and marketing expertise, which many social enterprises have found difficult to develop in-house. Moreover, given the lack of awareness about social enterprise as an organizational form (Bank of England 2003), corporations' legitimacy among key actors in market transactions, such as financial institutions and other corporations, further augments their exchange value. Thus collaborations with corporations offer social enterprises the possibility to decrease their reliance on contributed income, and to develop earned income strategies through commercial activity.

In sum, the exchange value of local knowledge, social capital and social legitimacy is an asset that has the potential to be drawn upon by the social enterprise in partnership creation, development and maturation. At the same time, the exchange value of commercial knowledge, financial capital and market legitimacy is an asset that has the potential to be drawn upon by the corporation in partnership creation, development and maturation. If the respective exchange values of the partners are considered to be sufficiently high, collaboration may lead to benefits for both parties.

As outlined earlier, social enterprises differ in their goals and practices from corporations. While exchanges between organizations in the same sector may involve goal equity, this is less likely in partnerships between social enterprises and corporations. Indeed, partner selection is critical in these collaborations and a significant proportion is unlikely to move beyond 'courtship' (Kanter 1994). Specifically, due to their central goal of achieving social objectives, we suggest that social enterprises will not collaborate with organizations whose goals and values fundamentally conflict with their social aims, regardless of the potential economic gains. Corporations, on the other hand, will only collaborate with a social enterprise if the partnership is likely to bring commercial benefits such as new customers or enhanced reputation, regardless of the potential social capital and local legitimacy it would yield.

For those that proceed beyond courtship, however, the differences between the social enterprise and the corporation make this form of collaboration distinctive. Thus the initial *thesis* stage of the collaboration occurs during the early phases of the relationship, and involves establishing whether the exchange values of the partners are sufficiently high to justify formally establishing the partnership. There are a number of examples of collaborations that are at this stage in partnership evolution.

For instance, 'Power Factory' is a joint venture between Arts Factory, a social enterprise based in Wales, and United Utilities, a multinational energy company. The collaboration consists of a wind farm with eight turbines. As well as stimulating local employment opportunities through the generation of 'green' electricity, income generated from the project funds Arts Factory's community initiatives. Arts Factory also gains commercial experience from collaborating with a successful MNC. For United Utilities, the collaboration, and in particular the community legitimacy of Arts Factory, allowed local hostilities to the wind farm to be overcome, and has become an important part of its CSR profile (DTI 2005: 32–33).

[...]

Managing dialectical forces in corporate-social enterprise collaboration: Competing morphologies as modifying influences upon inter-organizational dynamics

Following the thesis stage of the partnership, we argue that temporal maturity of the collaboration will give rise to conflict, or *antithesis*, due to the differing goals and practices of the partners. This is likely to cause partnership dissonance, an exchange state upon which we elaborate later in this section. Despite some areas of organizational convergence due to the hybrid nature of the social enterprise and its engagement in trading activities, tensions are likely to arise from the dialectical forces which exist *a priori* between partners.

To identify these tensions we rely upon Benson's (1977: 10) notion of organizational morphology – 'the officially enforced and conventionally accepted view of the organization'. Benson suggests that organizations have four morphological components, and that analyzing each of them is crucial to dialectical analysis. The four components are: (1) the paradigm commitments of the organization; (2) the officially recognized and legitimate structural arrangements of the organization; (3) the constitution (i.e. bases of participation and involvement) of the organization; and (4) organization–environment linkages.

We considered the organizational morphologies of corporations and social enterprises in relation to Benson's components, and concluded that the core contradictions underpinning collaborations between them are: (1) the profit goals and market logic of the corporation, and the social goals and community logic of the social enterprise; (2) the for-profit ownership structure of corporations in which profits are distributed to owners, and the non-profit ownership structure of social enterprises in which profits are invested for social purposes; (3) the corporation's hierarchical governance structure, and the social enterprise's democratic/participative governance structure; and (4) the corporation's need to be accountable to its shareholders, and the social enterprise's need to be accountable to a broad range of stakeholders of which the community is most important. We explore each of these contradictions, and the tensions they engender, in the next part of this section. (See Table 9.1 for a summary.)

Contradiction 1: Goals and Logic. As noted, corporations and social enterprises have different primary goals. Specifically, the objective of corporations, in the Anglo-American world at least, is to maximize wealth for their owners. Profit, turnover, market share, and (in the case of limited companies) share price are the main measures used to indicate performance. In contrast, social enterprises engage in commercial activity to create a sustainable venture through which their social objectives can be achieved, rather than to create surplus value. Success is measured in social outcomes as well as commercial performance. Consequently, collaborations between corporations and social enterprises are likely to be characterized by tensions with respect to the core goals of the exchange, with corporations viewing strategic decision-making within the partnership from a market logic (i.e. in terms of market demand) and social enterprises viewing strategic decision-making from a social/community logic (i.e. in terms of community need).

Contradiction 2: Ownership. The different ownership structures of corporations and social enterprises constitute a second contradiction, and lead to different assumptions about how profits should be used. Most notably, tensions may result from disagreements about how to invest returns. Social enterprises may pursue the collaboration as a route to achieve further growth and avoid dependency on grants, but nevertheless remain committed to investing surpluses for a social or community benefit. Indeed, the non-profit structure of social enterprises imposes legal responsibilities upon them to ring fence profits for their social missions. For corporations, which have a fiduciary duty to act in owners' interests, it may be more rational to invest in activities such as marketing or recruitment with a view to stimulating further growth, rather than potentially loss-making community initiatives. Differences in approaches to partnership development and investment may therefore stem from inherent structural contradictions between corporations and social enterprises.

Contradiction 3: Governance. In the relationship's early stages, the collaboration's nature and strategic direction are liable to be determined by those in senior positions in each organization. This presents particular challenges for social enterprises, as community involvement is central to the way they function. Clearly, this contrasts with the internally-oriented and often hierarchical governance mechanisms employed by corporations. From the social enterprise's perspective, the effort and resources required to ensure that participative principles of governance are maintained within the collaboration may be a source of frustration and reduce the incentive to partner with a corporation. From the corporation's perspective, the protracted nature of decision-making and the pressure to engage with external stakeholders may be a source of frustration and reduce the incentive to partner with a social enterprise.

Contradiction 4: Accountability. For social enterprises, the concept of horizontal accountability – the notion that the community 'has a legitimate right to know what benefits or dis-benefits an organization is producing' (Pearce 2003: 40) – is a key priority. Consequently a complex set of mechanisms and procedures for reporting social performance have been developed within the social enterprise sector (Paton 2003). Corporations, on the other hand, are required to be accountable primarily to their shareholders; the General Meeting is the statutory mechanism for shareholders to challenge directors on their decision-making and the financial performance of the company. Thus differing stakeholder priorities and expectations are also a source of tension: social enterprises are liable to be concerned with accounting for social value to community stakeholders, while corporations are liable to be concerned with accounting for financial value to shareholders.

Thus, as corporate-social enterprise partnerships develop and mature, the contradictions and tensions outlined above are likely to constrain the collaborative process, leading to partnership dissonance. Even when the partnership continues to yield benefits for both partners, tensions are likely to increase over time, which may lead to the collaboration being abandoned. An example of partnership

TABLE 9.1 Sources of tension inherent in corporate–social enterprise collaboration

		Sources of tension	
Morphology	Contradiction	Corporation	Social enterprise
Paradigm commitments	Goals and logic	Driven primarily by commercial objectives. Seeks to maximise the organization's value for for the benefit of shareholders. Is market focused, i.e. responds to demand or potential demand for its products or services.	Driven primarily by social objectives. Seeks to achieve sustainability to through trading, holding wealth in trust for community benefit. Is community focused; i.e. responds to gaps in the availability of products and services. Serves a defined social/community need, even where this may not be economically advantageous (e.g. in 'deprived' communities with low levels of disposable income).
Legitimate structural arrangements	Ownership	Depending on its size, can trade as a sole proprietorship, a partnership, a company limited by guarantee, or a public limited company. Surpluses distributed to owners and/or reinvested into the enterprise in order to build competitive advantage.	Assumes a variety of legal structures (e.g. company limited by guarantee, industrial and provident society, community interest company). Some are also registered charities. Surpluses must (by law) be used to achieve social/ community objectives or reinvested in the enterprise.

Constitution	Governance	Shareholders elect the board of directors to act on their behalf. Directors responsible for the strategic direction of the enterprise. Governance mechanisms relatively clear.	Members of the community (either the local community or a community of interest) elect board of directors to act on their behalf. Directors/trustees responsible for the strategic direction of the enterprise, but are expected to involve stakeholders (and in particular community members) in governance. This can make governance issues. This can make governance very complex, when serving multiple constituencies.
Organization–environment linkages	Accountability	Operates primarily in the interests of their owners – the actions and decisions of organizational members taken broadly with a view to their interests. Accounting for financial performance is paramount.	Operates primarily in the interests of their community – the actions and decisions of organizational members taken broadly with a view to their interests. Accounting for social performance is paramount.

dissonance which led to partnership break-up can be seen in the case of the former UK social enterprise Recycle-IT. It generated revenue by acquiring disused computers from companies, refurbishing them, and selling them on at affordable prices to charities and low-income families.

Recycle-IT entered into a collaboration with Business Development Group (BDG), a business consultancy firm, which agreed to invest capital and personnel in the business and to take seats on Recycle-IT's board. However, the relationship later broke down. This was attributed in part to a lack of forthcoming finance from BDG and to different ideas on how Recycle-IT should be run. Most notably, there were disagreements about how commercially focused the enterprise ought to be, and whether it needed to be more aggressive in its marketing and sourcing of computers. As the relationship between the partners deteriorated, the profitability of Recycle-IT declined sharply, and following the dissolution of the partnership it was placed into receivership. Although there were other factors that influenced the closure of this social enterprise, the failure of its collaboration with BDG because of the inability of partners to reconcile tensions was a contributing factor (Stothart 2006).

Although partnership dissonance may lead to break-up, this is not inevitable – the partners may seek to persevere despite the destabilising effects of the exchange. Specifically, the social enterprise is unlikely to abandon the partnership where this would either jeopardise its long-term economic sustainability, or impede its ability to attain its social goals. The decision-making process for the corporate partner is less complex because their core priorities are more clearly defined: any decision to dissolve the partnership will be based upon the commercial advantages of the exchange, and the implications for the reputation of the firm. This is particularly pertinent during partnership maturity, as there may be an expectation of greater returns in order to counterbalance the opportunity and set-up costs that accompany the initiation and formation stages.

Reconciling dialectical forces in corporate-social enterprise collaboration: the emergence of a new political-economic arrangement

The nature of the tensions that we have outlined means that partnership dissonance is liable to be a common outcome of corporate-social enterprise partnerships. However, where both partners can reconcile these tensions, we believe that this will allow for value synthesis in a dialectic sense, and the emergence of a new organizational form (see Figure 9.1). Moreover, we suggest that a synthesized state of collaboration needs to emerge if a given corporate-social enterprise partnership is to be sustainable.

For synthesis to occur, both the corporation and the social enterprise need to operate according to a set of values which are substantively different from those that guide their respective behaviours outside the parameters of the collaboration. However, we contend that synthesis also requires a two-way transfer of resources

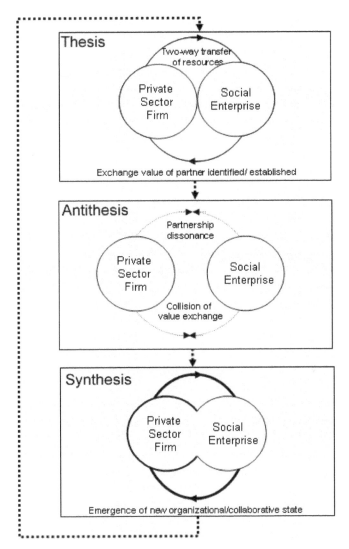

FIGURE 9.1 Evolution of corporate-social enterprise collaboration

and a high level of exchange equity between partners. Collaborations must therefore involve negotiated exchanges for mutual benefit rather than a one-way transfer of resources.

From our perspective, synthesis is most easily achieved through a process of harmonizing organizational goals and practices. However, it is difficult to predict the specific morphology that synthesized collaborations may take. Indeed we suspect that there may be variance in the morphologies of collaboration which reach this stage, contingent upon the nature of participating organizations and the context in which collaborations take place.

One possibility is that partners will seek to resolve tensions by compromising on each morphological component. For example, with regard to paradigm commitments, partners may agree specific areas where social objectives take priority and those where commercial objectives take priority. With regard to structural arrangements, partners may decide to divide surpluses evenly between community and business investments. With regard to constitution, partners may develop mechanisms which allow for community consultation on some issues, but managerial discretion on others. Finally, with regard to organization–environment linkages, partners may agree to account equally for social and financial performance. Another possibility is that partners will concede ground on one or more morphological components in return for concessions in others. For example, a social enterprise may agree to prioritize the commercial outcomes of a given collaboration in return for high levels of community involvement. Alternatively, a corporation may agree to prioritize the social outcomes of the collaboration in return for control of how it is managed.

Notwithstanding these uncertainties concerning the resolution of tensions, our general argument is that synthesis results in a new kind of political-economic arrangement that reconciles the welfare of markets with the welfare of communities. Crucially, this involves the creation of both economic *and* social value. In other words, the collaboration achieves financial returns on investment sufficient to provide an incentive for the corporation's continued involvement, and also achieves identifiable social outcomes in line with the aims of the social enterprise.

Although examples of this kind of socio-political arrangement are rare, a synthesized state of collaboration that appears to be consistent with our arguments is the collaboration between Ben & Jerry's, a US-based ice-cream retailer, and the Cresco Trust, a social enterprise based in Northern Ireland whose remit is to provide training for young people who have been marginalized from mainstream labour markets (DTI 2005). The collaboration involves Cresco operating two Ben & Jerry's franchises under its 'PartnerShop initiative', in which Ben & Jerry's waives its standard franchise fee for non-profit organizations. During the thesis stage, Cresco reasoned that it would benefit from a proven business model to generate surpluses and to train young people. Ben & Jerry's reasoned that it would benefit reputationally from collaborating with a social-purpose organization, and financially from a share of the outlets' profits.

However, the modest commercial performance of the first PartnerShop meant that as the relationship matured it experienced partnership dissonance. The first PartnerShop, which was located in Londonderry, a city with relatively low income levels and consumer demand, prioritized youth training over sales and this impacted on profitability. Cresco responded by making two adaptations to its model: (1) it switched to a mixed labour pool with experienced retail staff working alongside young people with minimal work experience, and (2) it opened a second outlet in Belfast, a city with higher levels of disposable income and a more developed retail sector. These changes resulted in significantly improved commercial performance and enhanced the relationship between the partners; Ben & Jerry's was enthused by the commercial and reputational benefits it accrued, while Cresco was able to generate surpluses while maintaining its core mission. This strategic adaptation of the collaboration's original goals thus allowed the partnership to progress towards synthesis: Cresco achieved its social goals in a way that was consistent with its corporate partner's commercial logic.

[...]

The relative scarcity of corporate-social enterprise collaborations reaching synthesis is perhaps due to the comparatively small scale and relative infancy of the social enterprise sector. An alternative explanation is that the dialectical processes involved in these collaborations are so strong that synthesis is unlikely. Moreover, where it does occur, synthesis may not be an equitable process and, in line with the isomorphic pressures described by Di Maggio and Powell (1983), the resulting goals, priorities and modes of operation of the collaboration may more closely resemble those of the corporation; as the social enterprise aims to build its legitimacy, it may seek to imitate the corporation. Under these circumstances synthesis would not result in the novel kind of political-economic arrangement that we have described, but rather an arrangement which is not significantly different from the corporate form (see Figure 9.1).

Conclusions

We have suggested that corporate-social enterprise collaboration is important because it has the potential to generate a new type of political-economic arrangement that seeks to reconcile community welfare with wealth creation. In examining this arrangement, we have proposed a conceptual framework that draws upon SET whilst embracing dialectical change processes. Through our analysis, we argue that newly formed collaborations fall within the first stage of the dialectic process, where the *thesis* is that of exchanging assets and resources perceived as mutually advantageous. Some partnerships may progress to the second *antithesis* stage, where dialectical tensions lead to conflict between partners. The final *synthesis* stage involves a reconciliation of these tensions and the creation of a new set of inter-organizational arrangements. Given the emergent nature of social enterprise it is unlikely that many corporate-social enterprise partnerships will have reached synthesis. This final stage, if achieved, may lead to a new thesis.

Although presented as linear, this process is indeed more intricate than suggested by our framework; the thesis stage may be accompanied by antithetical elements due to the complexity of the participating organizations and the collaboration itself. However, antithetical elements are unlikely to form a solid oppositional front in the collaboration's early stages unless there are ideological forces that prevent its development in the first instance. Once the partnership has been formed, the risk that participating organizations will create destructive opposing forces increases, but the formation of weaker 'criss-crossing lines of conflict' (Dahrendorf 1959) is more likely to characterise relations between the actors than partnership meltdown. Ultimately, however, a synthesized state of collaboration needs to emerge for the collaboration to be sustainable.

We believe that our framework represents an important step in understanding corporate-social enterprise collaboration. Clearly, however, further work is needed to examine our framework and its assumptions. More specifically, our analysis raises a number of questions for future research. First, on what basis do social enterprises and corporations choose potential partners? We have suggested that exchange value constitutes the central criterion, but there may be other factors. For example, the role of networks, social ties or geographical proximity may constitute an equally important set of motivations.

Second, we have outlined a series of dialectical tensions in our framework. This raises the question: which of these tensions has the greatest impact on the collaboration, and upon what factors is the influence of particular tensions contingent? The nature of these tensions is likely to impact on governance structures and accountability processes. But what are these strategies and structures, and what are their implications for each partner and for the collaboration?

Third, given the differing organizational morphologies of social enterprises and corporations, can the partners resolve tensions without undermining either their position in the partnership or the distinctive characteristics of their respective organizational forms? In other words, is synthesis possible within these collaborations? If it is, how is it manifest, and does it correspond to a new kind of political-economic arrangement that is able both to generate wealth and achieve meaningful social outcomes, as we have suggested?

Finally, while we have emphasized that corporate-social enterprise collaboration is an international phenomenon, we have focused our arguments on the UK context. We are acutely aware that, because there are profound distinctions between both corporations and social enterprises in different countries (Pearce 2003), such partnerships are liable to vary considerably between national contexts. Further research examining how corporate-social enterprise collaboration manifests itself in different national contexts would make a significant contribution to current knowledge.

References

Amin, Ash, Angus Cameron, and Ray Hudson 2002 *Placing the social economy*. Abingdon: Routledge.

Bank of England 2003 The financing of social enterprises. London: Bank of England.

Benson, J. Kenneth 1977 'Organizations: A dialectical view'. *Administrative Science Quarterly* 22: 1-21.

Blau, Peter 1964 Exchange and power in social life. New York: Wiley.

Boschee, Jerr 2001 *The social enterprise sourcebook*. Minneapolis, MN: Northland Institute.

Brown, Tom, and Peter A. Dacin 1997 'The company and the product: Corporate associations and consumer product responses'. *Journal of Marketing* 61: 68-84.

Brugmann, Jeb, and Coimbatore Krishnarao Prahalad 2007 'Cocreating business's new social compact'. *Harvard Business Review* 85/2: 80-90.

Chalybäus, Heinrich Moritz 1837 Historische Entwickelung der speculativen Philosophie von Kant bis Hegel. Dresden.

Coleman, James 1993 'The design of organizations and the right to act'. *Sociological Forum* 8: 527-46.

Cook, Karen, and Richard Emerson 1978 'Power, equity and commitment in exchange networks'. *American Sociological Review* 43: 721-39.

Dahrendorf, Ralf 1959 *Class and class conflict in industrial society*. Stanford, CA: Stanford University Press.

Das, T. K., and Bing-Sheng Teng 2002 'Alliance constellations: A social exchange perspective'. *Academy of Management Review* 27: 445–456.

Datamonitor 2005 'Bendigo Bank case study: Growth through community involvement'. Dublin: Datamonitor.

Di Maggio, Paul, and Helmut Anheier 1990 'The sociology of nonprofit organizations and sectors'. *Annual Review of Sociology* 16: 137–159.

Di Maggio, Paul, and Walter Powell 1983 'The iron cage revisited: Institutional isomorphism and collective rationality in organizational fields'. *American Sociological Review* 48: 147–60.

DTI 2005 Match winners: A guide to commercial collaborations between social enterprise and private sector business. London: Department of Trade and Industry in collaboration with the Community Action Network.

Dyer, Jeffrey, and Harbir Singh 1998 'The relational view: Competitive strategy and sources of interorganisational competitive advantage'. *Academy of Management Review* 23: 660–79.

Edgley, R. 2006 'Dialectical materialism' in *A dictionary of Marxist thought*. T. Bottomore (ed.), 142–3. Oxford: Blackwell.

Ekeh, Peter 1974 *Social exchange theory: The two traditions*. Cambridge, MA: Harvard University Press.

Giddens, Anthony 1998 *The third way: The renewal of social democracy*. Cambridge: Polity Press.

Heath, Anthony 1976 *Rational choice and social exchange: A critique of exchange theory*. Cambridge: Cambridge University Press.

Hegel, Georg W. F. 1807 *The phenomenology of mind*. Translated by J. B. Bailey. New York: Dover Publications.

Holmstrom, Bengt 1982 'Moral hazard in teams'. *Bell Journal of Economics* 13: 324–342.

Homans, George 1961 *Social Behavior*. New York: Harcourt Brace and World.

Husted, Bryan 2003 'Governance choices for corporate social responsibility: To contribute, collaborate or internalize?' *Long Range Planning* 36: 481–498.

Kanter, Rosabeth Moss 1994 'Collaborative advantage: The art of alliances'. *Harvard Business Review* 72: 96–108.

Kaufmann, Walter A. 1951 'The Hegel myth and its method'. *Philosophical Review* 60: 486–489.

Kendall, Jeremy 2000 'The mainstreaming of the third sector into public policy in England: Whys and wherefores'. *Policy and Politics* 28: 541–562.

Lourenco, Susan, and John Glidewell 1975 'A dialectical analysis of organisational conflict'. *Administrative Science Quarterly* 20: 489–508.

Marx, Karl 1995; orig. 1847 *The poverty of philosophy*. Translated by H. Quelch. NY: Prometheus Books.

McGuire, Jean 1988 'A dialectical analysis of interorganisational networks'. *Journal of Management* 14: 109–124.

Mueller, Gustav E. 1958 'The Hegel legend of "thesis-antithesis-synthesis"'. *Journal of the History of Ideas* 19: 411–414.

Muthusamy, Senthil, and Margaret White 2005 'Learning and knowledge transfer in strategic alliances: A social exchange view'. *Organization Studies* 26: 415–441.

Paton, Rob 2003 Managing and measuring social enterprises. London: Sage.

Pearce, John 2003 *Social enterprise in anytown*. London: Calouste Gulbenkian Foundation.

Pharoah, Cathy, Duncan Scott, and Andrew Fisher 2004 *Social enterprise in the balance*. Glasgow: Charities Aid Foundation.

Powell, Walter W., Kenneth W. Koput, and Laurel Smith-Doerr 1996 'Interorganizational collaboration and the locus of innovation: Networks of learning in biotechnology'. *Administrative Science Quarterly* 41: 116–145.

Seo, Myeong-Gu, and Douglas Creed 2002 'Institutional contradictions, praxis, and institutional change: A dialectical perspective'. *Academy of Management Review* 27: 222–248.

Stothart, Chloe 2006 'Why the computer recycler burned out'. *Social Enterprise Magazine*. 21 April.

Tracey, Paul, Nelson Philips, and Helen Haugh 2005 'Beyond philanthropy: Community enterprise as a basis for corporate citizenship'. *Journal of Business Ethics* 58: 327–344.

Zeitz, Gerald 1980 'Interorganizational dialectics'. *Administrative Science Quarterly* 25: 72–88.

PART III

Cultural diversity

Introduction

Nik Winchester

In this section we turn to the issue of culture. The concept of culture arrives in the social sciences with a myriad of definitions and a series of critical debates (of varying intensity). Its passage into the field of organizational behaviour and business studies in general has alighted on two distinct streams of thought. First the concept of a national culture, that there is a certain commonality within a nation state that affects both individuals, and, to a certain degree, organizational behaviour (not forgetting the interaction between individuals and organizations); indeed it has been claimed that national culture might be a source of competitive advantage. The second focuses on the organization with the claim that the organization displays certain types of practices, norms, values, etc. that make them distinct and once again (and emphasised in early debates on this issue) might give an organization an edge over its competitors.

One of the challenges in approaching culture is coming up with an acceptable definition. Some argue that it concerns the deepest level of human experience, our deepest sources of behaviour which profoundly affect our ways of being in the world, e.g. our values by which we orient our lives. Others argue that the concept should be restricted to the symbols displayed (e.g. company logos, modes of dress) and explicit practices operative within an organizational domain (as you will see in the reading by Schein some argue that these two levels are inextricably linked). Whatever their emphasis, however, there is a general acceptance of a degree of commonality within a domain which shapes and influences behaviour. Whether these are values, ethics, norms, symbols, logos, practice or language, culture envelops action.

The literature on culture is extensive and the four articles selected for this reader are designed to give you a flavour of theories and applications in current debates.

The first article offers a critical tour of one of the most influential accounts of national culture within the business studies discipline. Geert Hofstede's account of national culture described culture across four dimensions (subsequently developed to five). This analysis was based upon a survey of IBM offices across the world and has generated a vast series of secondary work both confirmatory and critical; making it, perhaps, the key battleground of national culture studies. The first article presented here, written by Brendan McSweeney, is one of the most influential broadsides in the recent and ongoing debates. In this article McSweeney takes issue with virtually all aspects of Hofstede's work on culture and offers a critical challenge for those who want to follow Hofstede's approach to and account of national culture.

From the critical we move to exposition with an account of a classic discussion of organizational culture presented by one of the founders of organizational culture research, Edgar H. Schein. This chapter offers an introduction and summary of Schein's influential levels of culture framework in which we see an intimate relation between the basic underlying assumptions, espoused values and artefacts that constitute the culture of an organization. The article also presents a challenge to us as researchers and scholars of organizational culture by reminding us that although the artefacts of culture are most visible, they are also the most difficult to interpret. We should be cautious in making claims concerning the fundamental assumptions of a culture by virtue of those features we can most readily access.

The third article can be presented as a critical appreciation of Schein's comments on the status and meaning of espoused values. It is also a useful corrective to taking these statements at face value. The theme parks of the Disney corporation present a carefully managed set of experiences emphasising the culture of Disney as a family-friendly values-driven organization. Indeed they describe themselves to potential employees as being able to 'add a little magic to the lives of our employees'[1]. The article by Jane Kuenz offers a different view by analysing the experience of employees at Walt Disney World in Florida and their somewhat different view of the Disney experience. In the course of this discussion we are reminded that what an organization presents to the world, and its potential employees, might be somewhat different from its practices and indeed those experiencing the culture first hand as its 'cast members'.

The concept of culture enables us to identify similarities within groups as well as differences between them. What happens when these cultural differences meet and what challenges does it raise? A cross-national collaboration or cross-national work-group needs to function effectively as a team if it is to deliver results. However, team members from different cultures may have, for example, different values or beliefs, which are displayed in different work practices and interaction within a team; an inability to recognise such differences may lead to inefficiency, if not outright failure. In the final article of this section Jeanne Brett, Kristin Behfar and Mary C. Kern explore cultural issues generated by multi-cultural teams and attendant management challenges. Managing cultural difference is not simply a

---

[1]http://corporate.disney.go.com/careers/perks.html

matter of reaching mutual understanding but requires purposive management intervention at appropriate points. However, it is worth noting that one of their strategies, 'Exit', suggests that sometimes the issues generated by cultural difference cannot be overcome and it may be better to remove an individual from a team rather than struggle on, ultimately undermining the team as a whole.

As with other themes in the reader the literature on culture is both extensive and surrounded by critical exchange. In the articles presented here you will discover the broad parameters of some of these debates and insight into points of controversy. Culture, it appears, has become entrenched in our understanding of organizational behaviour and the contexts in which it operates and debates continue to flourish. However, as a final concluding note, the vision of what we share should be tempered with an appreciation of what makes us, and the organizations we operate within, different.

10

HOFSTEDE'S MODEL OF NATIONAL CULTURAL DIFFERENCES AND THEIR CONSEQUENCES
A triumph of faith – a failure of analysis

Brendan McSweeney

Source: Edited from *Human Relations*, 2002, 55 (1), pp. 89–118.

Hofstede's model

Hofstede's main research on *national* culture is principally described in *Culture's consequences* (1980a, 1984). On a few occasions he has added to his model, but he has never acknowledged any significant errors or weaknesses in that research. Indeed many of his subsequent publications are robust, at times aggressive, defences of his 1980 methods and findings: [...]

Hofstede's primary data were extracted from a pre-existing bank of employee attitude surveys undertaken around 1967 and 1973 within IBM subsidiaries in 66 countries. In retrospect, some of the survey questions seemed to Hofstede to be pertinent to understanding the respondents' 'values' which he defines as 'broad tendencies to prefer certain states of affairs over others' and which are for him the 'core element in culture' (1991: 35). He statistically analysed the answers to these survey questions. That analysis, together with some additional data and 'theoretical reasoning' (p. 54), revealed, he states, that there are four central and 'largely independent' (1983: 78) bi-polar dimensions of a national culture and that 40 out of the 66 countries in which the IBM subsidiaries were located could be given a comparative score on each of these four dimensions (1980a, 1983, 1991). Hofstede defines these dimensions as follows. *Power Distance*: 'the extent to which the less powerful members of organizations and institutions (like the family) expect and accept that power is distributed unequally' (Hofstede, 1991: 28; Hofstede and Peterson, 2000: 401). *Uncertainty Avoidance*: 'intolerance for uncertainty and ambiguity' (Hofstede, 1991: 113; Hofstede and Peterson, 2000: 401). *Individualism versus Collectivism*: 'the extent to which individuals are integrated into groups' (Hofstede, 1991: 51; Hofstede and Peterson, 2000: 401). *Masculinity versus Femininity*: 'assertiveness and competitiveness versus modesty and caring' (Hofstede, 1991: 82–3, 1998b; Hofstede and Peterson, 2000: 401).

[...]

Hofstede's findings

[...]

Hofstede's use of questionnaires

Hofstede, and many of his devotees, make much of the scale of the IBM survey – 117,000 questionnaires administered in 66 countries (Hofstede, 1980a: 54, 1983: 77, 1998a: 480; Hofstede *et al.*, 1990: 287, for instance). Using a large number of respondents does not of itself guarantee representativeness (Bryman, 1988), but in any event a closer examination of the number of questionnaires used by Hofstede reveals that the average number per country was small, and that for some countries it was minuscule.

Two surveys were undertaken – around 1968–9 and repeated around 1971–3. The figure of 117,000 questionnaires is the combined number for *both* surveys. Furthermore not all the questionnaires were used – although the survey covered 66 countries, the data from only 40 countries were used in characterizing national cultures.

In only six of the included countries (Belgium, France, Great Britain, Germany, Japan and Sweden) were the numbers of respondents more than 1000 in both surveys. In 15 countries (Chile, Columbia, Greece, Hong Kong, Iran, Ireland, Israel, New Zealand, Pakistan, Peru, Philippines, Singapore, Taiwan, Thailand and Turkey) the numbers were less than 200. The first survey in Pakistan was of 37 IBM employees, the second of 70 employees (Hofstede, 1980a: 73). The only surveys in Hong Kong and Singapore were of 88, 71 and 58 respondents respectively (1980a: 411). In response to criticisms of the small number of respondents in some countries (Goodstein, 1981), Hofstede (1981) stated that:

> ... if a sample is really homogeneous with regard to the criteria under study, there is very little to gain in reliability over an absolute sample size of 50. ... I could therefore have done my research on 40 (countries) – 50 (respondents per country) – 2 (survey rounds) – or 4000 respondents in total – and obtained almost equally reliable results. (p. 65)

The crucial condition in this claim is: the homogeneity of the population, so that a sample of 50, indeed even 1, would be representative of that population (Mead, 1962). Later I argue that such a condition cannot validly be deemed to have been satisfied by the IBM surveys analysed by Hofstede. For the moment I observe that were an academic to claim that she or he had been able to compare the 'intelligence' of the populations of two particular nations on the basis of the examination results of, say, 88 and 58 students, his or her views would rightly be scorned. Even if the notion of measuring 'intelligence' were not deemed problematic, few, if any, would regard the students in any class in any university to be representative of the entire population of their respective nations. So why should a claim to have measured national cultures absolutely or comparatively from the responses of similarly minute proportions of national populations be regarded as any more valid?

The scale problem of Hofstede's research is radically compounded by the narrowness of the population surveyed. Although he speaks of 'national samples' (1980a, 1999), the respondents were exclusively from a single company – IBM. Furthermore, although the surveys (which were undertaken within IBM for quite different reasons) covered all employees, the data used by Hofstede to construct national cultural comparisons were largely limited to responses from marketing-plus-sales employees (1980a). He argues as follows.

Those surveyed were similar in every respect other than nationality. As the respondents all worked for IBM they shared a single monopolistic 'organizational culture' common between and within every IBM subsidiary. As they were matched on an 'occupational' basis, each matched group also shared a common 'occupational culture'. Thus, he states that:

> The only thing that can account for systematic and consistent differences between national groups within such a homogeneous multinational population is nationality itself ... Comparing IBM subsidiaries therefore shows national culture with unusual clarity. (1991: 252)

This article now examines crucial assumptions upon which this conclusion is based. These assumptions are 'crucial' in the sense that *each* is a necessary condition for his identification claims. The failure of even one would invalidate his identification assertions. It is argued that they are *all* flawed.

Assumption 1: Three discrete components

The cultures carried by each respondent are effectively assumed to be exclusively three non-interacting and durable cultures: the 'organizational', an 'occupational', and the 'national'. As the respondents were all from the 'same' organization and were matched by Hofstede on an occupational basis, *Assumption 1* allows him to conclude that the response differences show 'national culture with unusual clarity' (1991: 252). There is, he assumes, only one IBM culture – not cultures – which, as it were, possesses all employees and every occupation has a common worldwide occupational culture (p. 181). Every IBM employee – whether in, say, a long-established Texan plant or a then, recently established, Turkish branch, it is claimed, was a bearer of the same single organizational culture and he assumes that every member of the same occupational category in (or indeed outside) IBM shared the same occupational culture – every German 'laboratory clerk' (1980a: 79), had the same laboratory clerks' culture as every other German laboratory clerk which was also the same occupational culture as that of every Bangladeshi laboratory clerk, and so forth; otherwise, he could not have attributed the response differences to national cultures.

[...]

However, about 10 years after the initial publication of his analysis of the IBM survey data, Hofstede had begun to belatedly acknowledge that there *is* cultural variety within and between units of the same organization (e.g. 1991: 193, 1998a: 11). Research projects which he directed on *organizational cultures* revealed, he states, 'considerable differences' (1991: 182). An inevitable implication of this changed characterization of organizational culture is that during the IBM survey periods there were cultural differences both within each IBM national unit and between them (1991: 253) and not cultural uniformity as Hofstede had originally claimed and trumpeted as a distinctive virtue of his research. An acknowledgement that organizations possibly have multiple cultures and not a single culture might seem to contradict a crucial part of *Assumption 1* and thus undermine Hofstede's national culture mapping claims.

However, in parallel with his belated acknowledgement of cultural heterogeneity in organizations, Hofstede redefined 'organizational culture' in terms – which if accepted – would not invalidate *Assumption 1* and would therefore leave his national culture identification claims undisturbed. How? He states that 'national cultures and organizational cultures are phenomena of a different order' (1991: 182). Whilst national cultures are characterized, he says, by core [phenomenological] values – which his questionnaire analysis sought to identify – 'the core of an organization's culture' is, he states, not shared 'values', but, 'shared perceptions of daily practices' (1991: 182–3). Thus he concludes that the cultural heterogeneity within IBM did not affect his cross-subsidiary comparison of values, as organizational culture does not contain/reflect values (1999: 38).

[...]

Hofstede's initial supposition of a single world-wide IBM culture and his later assertion that organizational cultures are value-free practices has allowed him to claim that by occupationally matching the IBM responses he was able to isolate the differences caused by national cultures. His earlier and later notions of organizational culture were criticized earlier. His notion of uniform world-wide *occupational* cultures also rests upon highly contestable suppositions, specifically on a deterministic model of permanently imprinted socialization. Such cultures (and indeed national culture also) are, he claims, 'programmed into' carriers in pre-adulthood. 'Values', he states:

> ... are acquired in one's early youth, mainly in the family and in the neighbourhood, and later at school. By the time a child is 10 years old, most of its basic values have been programmed into its mind. [...] For occupational values the place of socialization is the school or university, and the time is in between childhood and adulthood. (Hofstede, 1991: 182; see also Hofstede *et al.*, 1990: 312; Hofstede and Peterson, 2000: 405).

Hofstede's supposition of continuity – the notion that national and occupational cultures are permanent and completed consequences of early 'socialization' – has few supporters. [...] And yet the continuity assumption is crucial for Hofstede's analysis. Without it, the mere matching of respondents on an occupational basis could not be deemed to isolate national cultural values.

There are problems even *within* his deterministic notion of permanent programming of 'occupational cultures'. It wrongly implies that: (a) members of each organizational occupation regardless of country will have attended the same type of courses – yet someone in, say, marketing in IBM was just as likely to have studied zoology, or anthropology, or French, as 'marketing' itself; (b) the fundamental contents of the pertinent third-level courses are the same, regardless of country, and yet we are all aware that even within single countries there is not uniformity of course content; (c) occupational 'socialization' only occurs pre-work: at 'school or university' (1991: 182) – thus excluding occupational socialization at the work place, or in parallel with work in, for example, the vast number of post-experience courses; and (d) respondents regardless of age or length of service had never changed occupations outside or within IBM.

As the social and the institutional are defined as consequences of national culture, Hofstede's model is closed to the idea that values might be, or might also be, the consequences of the social/institutional (cf. Whitley, 1992; McSweeney, 1994; Djelic, 1998). Thus, the possibility that the views of members of particular occupational groupings in a country, say US accountants, might be influenced by – amongst many other factors – the short-termism of the US capital market compared with the possible effects of the longer-termism of the German capital market on German accountants is ignored, so maintaining the convenient, but fantastic, assumption that throughout the world, members of the same occupation, regardless of diverse entry requirements, regulations, social status, structure and number of trade associations or professional bodies, each share an identical world-wide occupational culture. National cultures are said to influence occupational contexts and practices, but somehow that national diversity is not assumed to create national differences in occupational or organizational cultures.

Assumption 2: The national is identifiable in the micro-local

This assumption underlies Hofstede's claims in two ways – depending on which definition of the sharedness of national culture he relies on. National culture is said to be carried by all individuals in a nation (1980a: 38) or a 'central tendency' (1991: 253).

Assumption 2: Version 1 (the national is uniform)

When Hofstede relies on *[the existence of a common individual national culture]* he is presupposing the existence of that which he purports to have 'found' (1980b: 44). Only by presupposing national uniformity (of culture or whatever else) may a general conclusion be based on local sites of analysis. But how could this be known? As Maurice Farber (1950) states:

There has been a tendency in some . . . circles . . . to minimise this problem, apparently on the theoretical ground that every member of [or organization in] a nation necessarily exhibits the national character, so that it matters little which particular individuals one studies. *To simplify, it is as if all members of a nation were envisaged as having been immersed in the homogeneous fluid of national culture, with the soaked up fluid readily identifiable by trained observer.*

(p. 37, emphasis added)

The circularity of Hofstede's reasoning is evident from the effect of not presupposing national uniformity. Without that supposition there are no valid grounds for treating the minuscule local as representative of the national. Instead there is a huge and unbridged conceptual chasm between the micro-local (IBM) and the national. To *assume* national uniformity, as Hofstede does, is not appropriate for a study which purports to have *found* it.

Assumption 2: Version 2 (an average tendency is the average tendency)

In Hofstede's cultural triad, occupational and organizational cultures are defined as uniform. If Hofstede were epistemologically consistent, he would also define the third component as homogeneous [...]; that is, each individual within a country would share the same national culture. [...] If a national culture were common to all national individuals (and survey responses could identify those cultures) then there would not have been significant intra-country differences in individuals' responses. But the IBM survey responses *within* each country were characterized by radical differences. Hofstede acknowledges this. Relying on his second definition of national culture he states that there was only an 'average' or 'central' 'tendency' (1991: 253). Although, for example, some Japanese respondents 'scored more individualist' than did some American respondents, each of the diverse responses were nationally averaged and then held to be representative of the cultural differences between the countries. Highly varied responses were converted into single national IBM responses and those averaged responses – when compared with other nationally classified data – were then labelled the respective national cultural differences.

Within a very heterogeneous set of data there is, in principle, always an 'average tendency'. If it is supposed that there are national cultures then it can be legitimately argued that national cultures as 'central tendencies' exist. But Hofstede maintains not merely that in each country there is a national cultural central tendency, but that he identified such national tendencies, or differences between them, from data from some respondents in a single micro-location.

If somehow the average tendency of IBM employee responses is assumed to be nationally representative then, with equal plausibility – or rather equal implausibility – it must also be assumed that this would be the same as the average tendency in every other company, tennis club, knitting club, political

party, massage parlour, socialist party, and fascist party within the same country.
[...]

But there are no valid reasons for assuming that the IBM responses somehow reflected 'the' national average. This argument would be correct even if a 'typical' (whatever that might be and however it might be identified) national company or sports club, or whatever had been surveyed. But in any event IBM subsidiaries had many nationally atypical characteristics. These include: the company's selective recruitment only from the 'middle classes' (Hofstede, 1980a: 56) – 'the crisp young white-shirted men who move softly among [the computers] like priests' (*Time* magazine cited in Alexander, 1990: 309); the frequent international training of employees; the technologically advanced and unusual characteristics of its products during the survey periods – which were before the development of the 'personal computer'; the 'frequent personal contacts' between subsidiary and international headquarters staff (Hofstede, 1980a: 55); its tight internationally centralized control; its US ownership during a period in which foreign direct investment was comparatively new and controversial; and 'the relatively young and inexperienced managers [that is in comparison with those in other companies in the same countries] due to fast company growth in the 1960s' (Hofstede, 1980a: 56). Furthermore, IBM employees most likely diverged from the general population more in some nations than in others. Each IBM unit surveyed was not, contrary to Hofstede's claim, 'atypical in the same way from one country to another' (1980a: 39). For instance, during the time the survey(s) were undertaken, working for a non-family owned firm or the public sector would have been much more unusual in Ireland or Taiwan for example than in, say, Britain, or the USA and working for high-technology business would have been more unusual in Third World nations such as El Salvador and Bangladesh than in industrialized nations such as West Germany and the United States (Whitley, 1992; Lytle *et al.*, 1995). As Lytle *et al.* (1995) state: 'Hofstede's (1980) data ... was representative of a very limited segment of the overall national population' (p. 197).

Hofstede's research can legitimately be called a cross-national opinion comparison only in the sense that data *from* organizations in different countries were compared. He fails to satisfactorily justify his claim that *an* average tendency based on questionnaire responses from some employees in a single organization is also *the* national average tendency. His generalization to the national from the micro-local is unwarranted.
[...]

Assumption [3]: It's the same in any circumstances within a nation

The [third] core assumption in Hofstede's analysis is that national culture is situationally non-specific. Although the sub-title of *Culture's consequences* (1980a) is 'International differences in work-related values' – Hofstede claims that 'data obtained within a single MNC [IBM] does have the power to uncover the secrets of entire national cultures' (1980b: 44). He does not claim to have identified national cultural differences that are specific to workplaces, but to have compared and hierarchically located differences between national cultures that are *pervasive* (1991: 15). Within each country there is a single national culture, not merely a single national work-place culture. On what grounds does Hofstede make this claim? Again, I suggest, that the apparent *derivation* of a national generalization from situationally specific data is in fact a *presupposition*. The conclusion is not the end but the beginning.

The IBM data analysed were situationally restricted in four ways: (i) the analysed surveys were confined to certain categories of IBM employees – thus excluding blue-collar workers, the non-employed, the retired, the unemployed, full-time students, the self-employed, and others; (ii) the questions were almost exclusively about workplace issues; (iii) the surveys were administered only within the formal workplace – 'the front-room' in Goffman's language; and (iv) the surveys were not repeated in non-work place locations for (a) the same respondents and/or (b) others.

Hofstede's claim of entire-national and not merely national-work-place validity is simply a result of his *presupposition* that national cultures are not situationally specific within a nation. A claim that should have been explored and/or tested is conveniently, but inappropriately, presumed. As Sorge (1983) states: '[a] large power distance in the enterprise [one of Hofstede's dimensions of national culture], for instance, does not necessarily imply a corresponding large power distance in the family, such as between father and children' (p. 628). Triandis (1994) succinctly illustrates this argument with an example: 'I may be very individualistic, but when my university gives me the job to represent it at a meeting, I act collectivistically in that setting' (p. 45).

In summary, the validity of the identification claims face two profound problems. First, the *generalizations* about national level culture from an analysis of *sub*-national populations necessarily relies on the unproven and unprovable supposition that within each nation there is a uniform national culture and on the widely contested assertion that micro-local data from a section of IBM employees are representative of that supposed national uniformity. Second, the *elusiveness* of culture. It was argued that what Hofstede 'identified' is not national culture, but an averaging of situationally specific opinions from which dimensions or aspects of national culture are unjustifiably inferred. Even if we heroically assume that the answers to a narrow set of questions administered in constrained circumstances are 'manifestations' of a determining national culture, it requires an equally contestable act of faith to claim that the underlying national culture or cultural differences can be discerned through the explicit and recordable. Hofstede's claim to have empirically measured national culture differences relies on crucial but unwarranted assumptions.

[…]

The plausibility of systematically causal national cultures

The failure of Hofstede's stories – once unpacked – to show a causal link between his dimensions of a particular national culture and a specific national action is not surprising, given the earlier critique of his construction of his national cultural cameos. But, in any event, how credible is the notion of systematically causal national cultures?

[…]

Other cultural influences

Even if the causes of social actions/institutions within a nation are restricted to that which is cultural, why should it be assumed that only the national culture is influential? Hofstede acknowledges that within nations there are other cultures, or what he calls 'sub-cultures' (Hofstede, 1980a, 1991). But Hofstede is inconsistent in his conception of culture. Whilst national culture is treated as constitutive, other types of cultures are acknowledged to exist but allowed little, if any, influence. Any constitutive interplay between different levels and types of culture is precluded.

Non-cultural causation

Hofstede's reliance on a single explanatory variable effectively closes his model not only to the possible effects of non-national cultures but also to the possible influence of the non-cultural.

Why should the idea of national–cultural–causation be privileged over administrative, coercive, or other means of social action (Archer, 1989)? As Maurice Farber (1950) argues:

> Would it be meaningful, for example, to talk of the religiosity of the Spaniards without description of the officially monopolistic position of the church in Spain, or of the irreligiosity of the Russians without considering the attitude of the Soviet government towards religion? (p. 313)

The radical decline in church attendance in post-Franco Spain and the considerable increase in post-Soviet Russia does not support the idea of an enduring national culture driving social action, but rather the influence of other historical specificities of which the demise of coercive regimes is but one illustration. As subjects, or citizens, or partners, or employees or whatever, we take our positions within relations of power and within our understanding of those relations (Kondo, 1990: 301).

Some on-going, and changed actions, may even have simple physical explanations. Cosco (1997) records that:

Wotherspoon and Satzwich (1993) ... describe a ... study that determined that aboriginal Canadian people do not value cars, televisions, and other such material goods. This was considered to be a cultural phenomenon. However, Wotherspoon and Satzwich point out that it may simply be the lousy roads and reception band in their area that have rendered the commodities valueless. (p. 19)

National heterogeneity

If, as suggested earlier, non-national cultures and/or non-cultural forces operate within nations then national uniformity cannot be presumed. The extent of uniformity of actions, structures, institutions, and so forth, within a nation is an open question. Indeed, there is an extensive literature which has 'found' national *diversity*. As Philip Bock (1999) unhesitatingly states 'we must conclude that the uniformity assumption is false' (p. 111). [...] The prefixing of the name of a country to something to imply national uniformity is grossly over-used (Archer, 1989; Kondo, 1990; Shearing and Ericson, 1991).

'Nations' may fissure, coalesce, combine, be combined, expand, or contract (Connor, 1978). A recent example of the first type was the breakup of Yugoslavia, and a contemporary example of the latter type has been the 'integration' of Hong Kong into the People's Republic of China. What are the implications of these changes for Hofstede's claims? When nations fissure, the only possible conclusion consistent with Hofstede's methodology is that his national culture characterization of the former nation must also be that of each of the multiple new nations. For instance, although Hofstede depicted Yugoslavia as having a high level of Collectivism, a strong degree of Uncertainty Avoidance, and being very Feminine (1980a: 222, 165, 279), it violently disintegrated into a number of separate states. And we are now, consistent with his claims, supposed to believe that the national cultures of each of these states; Serbia, Croatia, Kosovo, Bosnia, and so forth, are identical to each other. Such an idea beggars belief, but if it is not true, then what was really identified/measured as Yugoslavian 'nation culture' – indeed of every nation – by Hofstede? A statistical myth, I suggest.

The occurrence, or the possibility of, converse situations also destabilizes Hofstede's analysis. If a 'nation' fuses with, or is deemed to have been reunited with another nation then – consistent with Hofstede's assumption that what is true of a part is true of the whole – the national culture of the enlarged nation must be defined as that of the former part(s). An example is the supposed national culture of China. Following the [re]integration of Hong Kong into China are we to believe that what was measured in the IBM subsidiary in Hong Kong is also true for the entire Chinese nation? The IBM unit in Taiwan was also surveyed. There were some radical differences between the national culture dimensions measurements for each of these 'nations' and none of the four dimensional scores were similar (1980a: 105, 165, 222, 279, 315–16, 324; see also Paik *et al.*, 1996).

If prior to Hong Kong's (re)integration with the rest of China, Taiwan had been reunited into China then Hofstede's description of Taiwanese culture, and not that of Hong Kong, would be taken, consistent with his national generalization assumption, as characterizing the culture of China as a whole. If Taiwan is subsequently (voluntarily or forcibly) reintegrated into China, which Hofstedeian depiction of China's national culture – that of Hong Kong or Taiwan – should his devotees choose? Which would describe what Hofstede calls 'the Chinese mind' (1991: 162)? The potential instability of the object of analysis is ill matched with Hofstede's claims to have achieved measurement precision.

Concluding remarks

Perhaps when first published Hofstede's national culture claims contributed to the challenge to wholly universalistic notions of management, although it should be recalled that during *and* preceding that time a range of scholarly texts on international cultural differences and similarities were also published including six volumes of the *Handbook of cross-cultural psychology* (Triandis, 1980). Why Hofstede's work should have achieved and retained eminence within parts of the management disciplines is not considered in this article. Although the management literature includes work as good as the best in other social science disciplines, the on-going unquestioning acceptance of Hofstede's national culture research by his evangelized entourage suggests that in parts of the management disciplines the criteria for acceptable evidence are far too loose.

Perhaps the quantity of data and the 'sophistication' of their statistical analysis impress some. But fallacious assumptions necessarily lead to inaccurate empirical descriptions regardless of the quantity of data and statistical manipulation used. A parallel can be seen with Samuel George Morton's *Crania Americana* (1839, in Smith, 1998) which empirically 'demonstrated' that racial hierarchy is a function of differences in mental capacity. Morton had access to the largest collection of human skulls in the world. The cranial cavity of a skull provides an accurate measure of the brain it once contained. Using one-eighth-inch diameter lead pellets he measured the size of the cranial cavities and thus brain sizes. He classified the results by 'race' and his 'hard and irrefutable data' demonstrated that there was indeed a hierarchy of mental capacity – with 'Caucasians' at the top and 'Blacks' at the bottom (Gould, 1981; Smith, 1998). But the conclusions drawn from apparently precise measurements and comparisons rested on a number of invalid assumptions; for example, that brain size is equivalent to mental capacity. Similarly, as this article has sought to show, Hofstede's apparently sophisticated analysis of extensive data necessarily relies on a number of profoundly flawed assumptions to measure the 'software of the mind' as did Morton's measurement of the hardware, as it were, of the mind. Hofstede's claims are excessive and unbalanced; excessive because they claim far more in terms of identifiable characteristics and consequences than is justified; unbalanced, because there is too great a desire to 'prove' his *a priori* convictions rather than evaluate the adequacy of his 'findings'.

The limited characterization of culture in Hofstede's work, its confinement within the territory of states, and its methodological flaws mean that it is a restricter not an enhancer of understanding particularities. The identification claims are fundamentally flawed and the attribution of national level actions/institutions to national cultures is an easy but impoverishing move. We may think about national culture, we may believe in national culture, but Hofstede has not demonstrated that national culture is how we think. If the aim is understanding then we need to know more about the richness and diversity of national practices and institutions – rather than merely assuming their 'uniformity' and that they have an already known national cultural cause. Both outside and within the management disciplines there are rich considerations of the characteristics of individuals, organizations, societies, nations and regions. Intense reviews and debates about the conceptualization, interaction and effects of 'agency' and 'structure' are now readily available. Extreme, singular, theories, such as Hofstede's model of national culture are profoundly problematic. His conflation and uni-level analysis precludes consideration of interplay between macroscopic and microscopic cultural levels and between the cultural and the non-cultural (whatever we choose to call it). Instead of seeking an explanation for assumed national uniformity from the conceptual lacuna that is the essentialist notion of national culture, we need to engage with and use theories of action which can cope with change, power, variety, multiple influences – including the non-national – and the complexity and situational variability of the individual subject.

References

Alexander, J.C. The promise of a cultural sociology: Technological discourse and the sacred and profane information machine. In J.C. Alexander and S. Seidman (Eds), *Culture and society: Contemporary debates*. Cambridge: Cambridge University Press, 1990.

Archer, M.S. *Culture and agency: The place of culture in social theory*. Cambridge: Cambridge University Press, 1989.

Bock, P.K. *Rethinking psychological anthropology*, 2nd edn. Prospect Heights, IL: Waveland, 1999.

Bryman, A. *Quantity and quality in social research*. Abingdon: Routledge, 1988.

Connor, W. A nation is a nation, is an ethnic group is a . . . *Ethnic and Racial Studies*, 1978, *1*(4), 379–88.

Cosco, G. Untitled mimeo, Department of Accounting and Management Information Systems, University of Alberta, 1997.

Djelic, M. *Exporting the American model: The postwar transformation of European business*. Oxford: Oxford University Press, 1998.

Farber, M.L. The problem of national character: A methodological analysis. *The Journal of Psychology*, 1950, *30*, 307–16.

Goodstein, L.D. Commentary: Do American theories apply abroad? *Organizational Dynamics*, 1981, Summer, 49–54.

Gould, S.J. *The mismeasure of man*. London: Penguin, 1981.

Hofstede, G. *Culture's consequences: International differences in work-related values*. Beverly Hills, CA: Sage, 1980a.

Hofstede, G. Motivation, leadership and organization: Do American theories apply abroad? *Organizational Dynamics*, 1980b, Summer, 42–63.

Hofstede, G. Do American theories apply abroad? A reply to Goodstein and Hunt. *Organizational Dynamics*, 1981, Summer, 63–8.

Hofstede, G. The cultural relativity of organizational practices and theories. *Journal of International Business Studies*, 1983, Fall, 75–90.

Hofstede, G. *Culture's consequences: International differences in work-related values*, abridged version. London: Sage, 1984.

Hofstede, G. *Cultures and organizations: Software of the mind*. London: McGraw-Hill, 1991.

Hofstede, G. Attitudes, values and organizational culture: Disentangling the concepts. *Organization Studies*, 1998a, *19*(3), 477–92.

Hofstede, G. and Associates *Masculinity and femininity: The taboo dimension of national cultures*. Thousand Oaks, CA: Sage, 1998b.

Hofstede, G. The universal and the specific in 21st-century global management. *Organizational Dynamics*, 1999, Summer, 34–43.

Hofstede, G., Neuijen, B., Ohayv, D. and Sanders, G. Measuring organizational cultures: A qualitative and quantitative study across twenty cases. *Administrative Science Quarterly*, 1990, *35*, 286–316.

Hofstede, G. and Peterson, M.F. National values and organizational practices. In N.M. Ashkanasy, C.P.M. Wilderom and M.F. Peterson (Eds), *Handbook of organizational culture and climate*. London: Sage, 2000, pp. 401–5.

Kondo, D.K. *Crafting selves: Power, gender, and discourses of identity in a Japanese workplace*. Chicago, IL: University of Chicago Press, 1990.

Lytle, A.L., Brett, J.M., Barsness, Z.I., Tinsley, C.H. and Janssens, M.A. Paradigm for confirmatory cross-cultural research in organizational behaviour. *Research in Organizational Behaviour*, 1995, *17*, 167–214.

McSweeney, B. Management by accounting. In A.G. Hopwood and P. Miller (Eds), *Accounting as social and institutional practice*. Cambridge: Cambridge University Press, 1994, pp. 237–68.

Mead, M. National character. In S. Tax (Ed.), *Anthropology today*. Chicago, IL: University of Chicago Press, 1962.

Paik, Y., Vance, C.M. and Stage, H.D. The extent of divergence in human resource practice across three Chinese national cultures: Hong Kong, Taiwan and Singapore. *Human Resource Management Journal*, 1996, *6*(2), 20–31.

Shearing, C.D. and Ericson, R.V. Culture as figurative action. *The British Journal of Sociology*, 1991, *42*(4), 481–506.

Smith, M.J. *Social science in question*. London: Sage, 1998.

Sorge, A. Review of 'Culture's consequences: International differences in work-related values'. *Administrative Science Quarterly*, 1983, December, 625–9.

Triandis, H.C. (Ed.) *Handbook of cross-cultural psychology*, 6 vols. Boston, MA: Allyn & Bacon, 1980.

Triandis, H.C. Theoretical and methodological approaches to the study of collectivism and individualism. In U. Kim, H.C. Triandis, C. Kagitcibasi, S-C. Choi and G. Yoon (Eds), *Individualism and collectivism: Theory, methods and applications*. London: Sage, 1994, pp. 41–51.

Whitley, R. The social construction of organizations and markets: The comparative analysis of business recipes. In M. Reed and M. Hughes (Eds), *Rethinking organization*. London: Sage, 1992.

Wotherspoon, T. and Satzwich, V. *First nations: Race, class, and gender relations*. Scarborough: Nelson Canada, 1993.

11

THE LEVELS OF CULTURE

Edgar Schein

Source: *Organizational Culture and Leadership*. 2004. Jossey-Bass.

The purpose of this chapter is to show that culture can be analyzed at several different levels, with the term *level* meaning the degree to which the cultural phenomenon is visible to the observer. Some of the confusion surrounding the definition of what culture really is results from not differentiating the levels at which it manifests itself. These levels range from the very tangible overt manifestations that one can see and feel to the deeply embedded, unconscious, basic assumptions that I am defining as the essence of culture. In between these layers are various espoused beliefs, values, norms, and rules of behaviour that members of the culture use as a way of depicting the culture to themselves and others.

Many other culture researchers prefer the term *basic values* to describe the concept of the deepest levels. I prefer *basic assumptions* because these tend to be taken for granted by group members and are treated as non-negotiable. Values are open to discussion and people can agree to disagree about them. Basic assumptions are so taken for granted that someone who does not hold them is viewed as a "foreigner" or as "crazy" and is automatically dismissed.

The major levels of culture analysis are shown in Figure 11.1.

Artifacts

At the surface is the level of artifacts, which includes all the phenomena that one sees, hears, and feels when one encounters a new group with an unfamiliar culture. Artifacts include the visible products of the group, such as the architecture of its physical environment; its language; its technology and products; its artistic creations; its style, as embodied in clothing, manners of address, emotional displays, and myths and stories told about the organization; its published lists of values; its observable rituals and ceremonies; and so on.

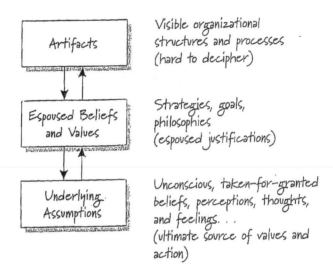

The "climate" of the group is an artifact of the deeper cultural levels, as is the visible behaviour of its members. Artifacts also include, for purposes of cultural analysis, the organizational processes by which such behaviour is made routine, and structural elements such as charters, formal descriptions of how the organization works, and organization charts.

The most important point to be made about this level of the culture is that it is both easy to observe and very difficult to decipher. The Egyptians and the Mayans both built highly-visible pyramids, but the meaning of pyramids in each culture was very different – tombs in one, temples as well as tombs in the other. In other words, observers can describe what they see and feel, but cannot reconstruct from that alone what those things mean in the given group, or whether they even reflect important underlying assumptions.

On the other hand, one school of thought argues that one's own response to physical artifacts such as buildings and office layouts can lead to the identification of major images and root metaphors that reflect the deepest level of the culture (Gagliardi, 1990). This kind of immediate insight would be especially relevant if the organization one is experiencing is in the same larger culture as the researcher. The problem is that symbols are ambiguous, and one can only test one's insight into what something may mean if one has also experienced the culture at the deeper levels of values and assumptions.

It is especially dangerous to try to infer the deeper assumptions from artifacts alone, because one's interpretations will inevitably be projections of one's own feelings and reactions. For example, when one sees a very informal, loose organization, one may interpret that as inefficient if one's own background is based on the assumption that informality means playing around and not working.

Or, alternatively, if one sees a very formal organization, one may interpret that to be a sign of lack of innovative capacity, if one's own experience is based on the assumption that formality means bureaucracy and formalization.

Every facet of a group's life produces artifacts, creating the problem of classification. In reading cultural descriptions, one often notes that different observers choose to report on different sorts of artifacts, leading to non-comparable descriptions. Anthropologists have developed classification systems, but these tend to be so vast and detailed that cultural essence becomes difficult to discern.

If the observer lives in the group long enough, the meanings of artifacts gradually become clear. If, however, one wants to achieve this level of understanding more quickly, one can attempt to analyze the espoused values, norms, and rules that provide the day-to-day operating principles by which the members of the group guide their behaviour. This kind of inquiry takes us to the next level of cultural analysis.

Espoused beliefs and values

All group learning ultimately reflects someone's original beliefs and values, their sense of what ought to be, as distinct from what is. When a group is first created or when it faces a new task, issue, or problem, the first solution proposed to deal with it reflects some individual's own assumptions about what is right or wrong, what will work or not work. Those individuals who prevail, who can influence the group to adopt a certain approach to the problem, will later be identified as leaders or founders, but the group does not yet have any *shared* knowledge as a group because it has not yet taken a common action in reference to whatever it is supposed to do. Whatever is proposed will only be perceived as what the leader wants. Until the group has taken some joint action and together observed the outcome of that action, there is not as yet a shared basis for determining whether what the leader wants will turn out to be valid.

For example, in a young business, if sales begin to decline a manager may say "We must increase advertising" because of her belief that advertising always increases sales. The group, never having experienced this situation before, will hear that assertion as a statement of that manager's beliefs and values: "She believes that when one is in trouble it is a good thing to increase advertising." What the leader initially proposes, therefore, cannot have any status other than a value to be questioned, debated, challenged, and tested.

If the manager convinces the group to act on her belief, and if the solution works, and if the group has a shared perception of that success, then the perceived value that advertising is good gradually becomes transformed: first into a shared value or belief, and ultimately into a shared assumption (if actions based on it continue to be successful). If this transformation process occurs, group members will tend to forget that originally they were not sure and that the proposed course of action was at an earlier time just a proposal to be debated and confronted.

Not all beliefs and values undergo such transformation. First of all, the solution based on a given value may not work reliably. Only those beliefs and values that can be empirically tested and that continue to work reliably in solving the group's problems will become transformed into assumptions. Second, certain value domains – those dealing with the less controllable elements of the environment or with aesthetic or moral matters – may not be testable at all. In such cases, consensus through social validation is still possible, but it is not automatic.

By *social validation* I mean that certain values are confirmed only by the shared social experience of a group. For example, any given culture cannot prove that its religion and moral system are superior to another culture's religion and moral system, but if the members reinforce each other's beliefs and values, they come to be taken for granted. Those who fail to accept such beliefs and values run the risk of "excommunication" – of being thrown out of the group. Such beliefs and values typically involve the group's internal relations; the test of whether they work or not is how comfortable and anxiety-free members are when they abide by them. Social validation also applies to those broader values that are not testable, such as ethics and aesthetics.

In these realms the group learns that certain beliefs and values, as initially promulgated by prophets, founders, and leaders, "work" in the sense of reducing uncertainty in critical areas of the group's functioning. And, as they continue to work, they gradually become transformed into non-discussible assumptions supported by articulated sets of beliefs, norms, and operational rules of behaviour. The derived beliefs and moral and ethical rules remain conscious and are explicitly articulate because they serve the normative or moral function of guiding members of the group in how to deal with certain key situations, and in training new members how to behave. A set of beliefs and values that become embodied in an ideology or organizational philosophy thus can serve as a guide and as a way of dealing with the uncertainty of intrinsically uncontrollable or difficult events. An example of such an ideology is Hewlett-Packard's *The HP Way* (Packard, 1995).

Beliefs and values at this conscious level will predict much of the behaviour that can be observed at the artifacts level. But if those beliefs and values are not based on prior learning, they may also reflect only what Argyris and Schön (1978) have called "espoused theories", which predict well enough what people will *say* in a variety of situations but which may be out of line with what they will actually *do* in situations in which those beliefs and values should, in fact, be operating. Thus, a company may say that it values people and that it has high quality standards for its products, but its record in that regard may contradict what it says.

If the espoused beliefs and values are reasonably congruent with the underlying assumptions, then the articulation of those values into a philosophy of operating can be helpful in bringing the group together, serving as a source of identity and core mission. But in analyzing beliefs and values one must discriminate carefully between those that are congruent with underlying assumptions and those that are, in effect, either rationalizations or only aspirations for the future. Often such lists of beliefs and values are so abstract that they can be mutually contradictory, as when a company claims to be *equally* concerned about stockholders, employees, and customers, or when it claims both highest quality and lowest cost. Espoused beliefs and values often leave large areas of behaviour unexplained, leaving us with a feeling that we understand a piece of the culture but still do not have the culture as such in hand. To get at that deeper level of understanding, to decipher the pattern, and to predict future behaviour correctly, we have to understand more fully the category of basic underlying assumptions.

Basic underlying assumptions

When a solution to a problem works repeatedly, it comes to be taken for granted. What was once a hypothesis, supported only by a hunch or a value, gradually comes to be treated as a reality. We come to believe that nature really works this way. Basic assumptions, in this sense, are different from what some anthropologists called "dominant value orientations" in that such dominant orientations reflect the *preferred* solution among several basic alternatives, but all the alternatives are still visible in the culture, and any given member of the culture could, from time to time, behave according to variant as well as dominant orientations (Kluckhohn and Strodtbeck, 1961). [...]

Basic assumptions, like theories-in-use, tend to be non-confrontable and non-debatable, and hence are extremely difficult to change. To learn something new in this realm requires us to resurrect, re-examine, and possibly change some of the more stable portions of our cognitive structure – a process that Argyris and others have called "double-loop learning", or "frame breaking" (Argyris *et al.*, 1985; Bartunek, 1984). Such learning is intrinsically difficult because the re-examination of basic assumptions temporarily destabilizes our cognitive and interpersonal world, releasing large quantities of basic anxiety.

Rather than tolerating such anxiety levels, we tend to want to perceive the events around us as congruent with our assumptions, even if that means distorting, denying, projecting, or in other ways falsifying to ourselves what may be going on around us. It is in this psychological process that culture has its ultimate power. Culture as a set of basic assumptions defines for us what to pay attention to, what things mean, how to react emotionally to what is going on, and what actions to take in various kinds of situations. Once we have developed an integrated set of such assumptions – a "thought world" or "mental map" – we will be maximally comfortable with others who share the same set of assumptions and very uncomfortable and vulnerable in situations where different assumptions operate, because either we will not understand what is going on, or, worse, we will misperceive and misinterpret the actions of others (Douglas, 1986).

The human mind needs cognitive stability; therefore, any challenge or questioning of a basic assumption will release anxiety and defensiveness. In this sense, the shared basic assumptions that make up the culture of a group can be thought of at both the individual and the group level as psychological cognitive defense mechanisms that permit the group to continue to function. Recognizing this connection is important when one thinks about changing aspects of a group's culture, for it is no easier to do that than to change an individual's pattern of defense mechanisms. We can also think of culture at this level as the group's DNA, so if new learning or growth is required, the genes have to be there to make such growth possible and the autoimmune system has to be neutralized to sustain new growth. In any case the two keys to successful culture change are (1) the management of the large amounts of anxiety that accompany any relearning at this level and (2) the assessment of whether the genetic potential for the new learning is even present.

To illustrate how unconscious assumptions can distort data, consider the following example. If we assume, on the basis of past experience or education, that other people will take advantage of us whenever they have an opportunity, we expect to be taken advantage of and we then interpret the behaviour of others in a way that coincides with those expectations. We observe people sitting in a seemingly idle posture at their desk and interpret their behaviour as "loafing" rather than "thinking out an important problem". We perceive absence from work as "shirking" rather than "doing work at home".

If this is not only a personal assumption but also one that is shared and thus part of the culture of an organization, we will discuss with others what to do about our "lazy" workforce and institute tight controls to ensure that people are at their desks and busy. If employees suggest that they do some of their work at home, we will be uncomfortable and probably deny the request because we will figure that at home they would loaf (Bailyn, 1992; Perin, 1991).

In contrast, if we assume that everyone is highly motivated and competent, we will act in accordance with that assumption by encouraging people to work at their own pace and in their own way. If someone is discovered to be unproductive in such an organization, we will make the assumption that there is a mismatch between the person and the job assignment, not that the person is lazy or incompetent. If the employee wants to work at home, we will perceive that as evidence of his wanting to be productive even if circumstances required him to be at home.

In both cases there is the potential for distortion, in that the cynical manager will not perceive how highly motivated some of the subordinates really are, and the idealistic manager will not perceive that there are subordinates who are lazy and who are taking advantage of the situation. As McGregor noted many decades ago, such assumptions about "human nature" become the basis of management and control systems that perpetuate themselves because if people are treated consistently in terms of certain basic assumptions, they come eventually to behave according to those assumptions in order to make their world stable and predictable (McGregor, 1960).

Unconscious assumptions sometimes lead to ridiculously tragic situations, as illustrated by a common problem experienced by American supervisors in some Asian countries. A manager who comes from an American pragmatic tradition assumes and takes it for granted that *solving* a problem always has the highest priority. When that manager encounters a subordinate who comes from a different cultural tradition, in which good relationships and protecting the superior's "face" are assumed to have top priority, the following scenario has often resulted.

The manager proposes a solution to a given problem. The subordinate knows that the solution will not work, but his unconscious assumption requires that he remain silent because to tell the boss that the proposed solution is wrong is a threat to the boss's face. It would not even occur to the subordinate to do anything other than remain silent or, if the boss were to inquire what the subordinate thought, to even reassure the boss that they should go ahead and take the action.

The action is taken, the results are negative, and the boss, somewhat surprised and puzzled, asks the subordinate what he would have done. When the subordinate reports that he would have done something different, the boss quite legitimately asks why the subordinate did not speak up sooner. The question puts the subordinate into an impossible double bind because the answer itself is a threat to the boss's face. He cannot possibly explain his behaviour without committing the very sin he was trying to avoid in the first place – namely, embarrassing the boss. He may even lie at this point and argue that what the boss did was right and only "bad luck" or uncontrollable circumstances prevented it from succeeding.

From the point of view of the subordinate, the boss's behaviour is incomprehensible because it shows lack of self-pride, possibly causing the subordinate to lose respect for that boss. To the boss, the subordinate's behaviour is equally incomprehensible. He cannot develop any sensible explanation of his subordinate's behaviour that is not cynically colored by the assumption that the subordinate at some level just does not care about effective performance and therefore must be got rid of. It never occurs to the boss that another assumption – such as "one never embarrasses a superior" – is operating, and that, to the subordinate, that assumption is even more powerful than "one gets the job done".

If assumptions such as these operate only in an individual and represent her idiosyncratic experience, they can be corrected more easily because the person will detect that she is alone in holding a given assumption. The power of culture comes about through the fact that the assumptions are shared and, therefore, mutually reinforced. In these instances probably only a third party or some cross-cultural education could help to find common ground whereby both parties could bring their implicit assumptions to the surface. And even after they have surfaced, such assumptions would still operate, forcing the boss and the subordinate to invent a whole new communication mechanism that would permit each to remain congruent with his or her culture – for example, agreeing that, *before* any decision is made and before the boss has stuck his neck out, the subordinate will be asked for suggestions and for factual data that would not be face threatening. Note that the solution has to keep each cultural assumption intact. One cannot in these instances simply declare one or the other cultural assumption "wrong". One has to find a third assumption to allow them both to retain their integrity.

I have dwelled on this long example to illustrate the potency of implicit, unconscious assumptions and to show that such assumptions often deal with fundamental aspects of life – the nature of time and space, human nature and human activities, the nature of truth and how one discovers it, the correct way for the individual and the group to relate to each other, the relative importance of work, family, and self-development, the proper role of men and women, and the nature of the family. These assumptions form the core cultural content.

We do not develop new assumptions about each of these areas in every group or organization we join. Members of any new group will bring their own cultural learning from prior groups, from their education, and from their socialization into occupational communities, but as the new group develops its own shared history, it will develop modified or brand-new assumptions in critical areas of its experience. It is those new assumptions that make up the culture of that particular group.

Any group's culture can be studied at these three levels – the level of its artifacts, the level of its espoused beliefs and values, and the level of its basic underlying assumptions. If one does not decipher the pattern of basic assumptions that may be operating, one will not know how to interpret the artifacts correctly or how much credence to give to the articulated values. In other words, the essence of a culture lies in the pattern of basic underlying assumptions, and once one understands those, one can easily understand the other more surface levels and deal appropriately with them.

Summary and conclusions

Though the essence of a group's culture is its pattern of shared, basic taken-for-granted assumptions, the culture will manifest itself at the level of observable artifacts and shared espoused beliefs and values. In analyzing cultures, it is important to recognize that artifacts are easy to observe but difficult to decipher and that espoused beliefs and values may only reflect rationalizations or aspirations. To understand a group's culture, one must attempt to get at its shared basic assumptions and one must understand the learning process by which such basic assumptions come to be.

Leadership is originally the source of the beliefs and values that get a group moving in dealing with its internal and external problems. If what leaders propose works, and continues to work, what once were only the leader's assumptions gradually come to be shared assumptions. Once a set of shared basic assumptions is formed by this process, it can function as a cognitive defense mechanism both for the individual members and for the group as a whole. In other words, individuals and groups seek stability and meaning. Once achieved, it is easier to distort new data by denial, projection, rationalization, or various other defense mechanisms than to change the basic assumption. As we will see, culture change, in the sense of changing basic assumptions is, therefore, difficult, time-consuming, and highly anxiety-provoking – a point that is especially relevant for the leader who sets out to change the culture of the organization.

The most central issue for leaders, therefore, is how to get at the deeper levels of a culture, how to assess the functionality of the assumptions made at that level, and how to deal with the anxiety that is unleashed when those levels are challenged.

References

Argyris, C., Putnam, R. and Smith, D.M. (1985). *Action Science*. San Francisco, CA: Jossey Bass.

Argyris, C., and Schön, D.A. (1978). *Organizational Learning*. Reading, MA: Addison-Wesley.

Bailyn, L. (1992). Changing the conditions of work: Implications for career development. In D.H. Montross and C.J. Shinkman (Eds), *Career development in the 1990s: Theory and practice*. Springfield, IL: Thomas.

Bartunek, J. (1984). Changing interpretative scheme and organizational restructuring: The example of a religious order. *Administrative Science Quarterly*, 29, 355–372.

Douglas, M. (1986). *How institutions think*. Syracuse, NY: Syracuse University Press.

Gagliardi, P. (Ed.) (1990). *Symbols and artifacts: Views of the corporate landscape*. New York: Walter de Gruyter.

Kluckhohn, F.R. and Strodtbeck, F.L. (1961). *Variations in value orientations*. New York: Harper Collins.

McGregor, D.M. (1960). *The human side of enterprise*. New York: McGraw-Hill.

Packard, D. (1995). *The HP Way*. New York: HarperCollins.

Perin, C. (1991). The moral fabric of the office. In S. Bacharach, S.R. Barley, and P.S. Tolbert (Eds), *Research in the sociology of organizations* (special volume on the professions). Greenwich, CT: JAI Press.

12

WORKING AT THE RAT

Jane Kuenz

Source: Edited from *Inside the Mouse: Work and play at Disney World, The Project on Disney*, 1995, pp. 110–66. Duke University Press.

Team Disney

> We have our own security, our own fire department, our own doctors. It's like a town. It's like an army post. – Pam

When Disney's employees arrive every day for work, they enter the world of "property". They are "on property", a phrase conjoining the language of theatre with that of real estate. This property extends for almost 28,000 acres – "forty-three square miles of fun", the brochures proclaim. It crosses county lines and encompasses two municipalities, Bay Lake and Lake Buena Vista, both governed by residents, usually Disney employees living in the area, in conjunction with the Reedy Creek Improvement District, a.k.a. Walt Disney Co. Officially recognized as a quasi-governmental body largely independent of state and local authority, this entity is endowed with powers to tax and to regulate such things as its own zoning, fire protection, liquor sales, water and sewage, roads and bridges.

[...]

If the production of magic depends on creating this isolated place and elaborating its architecture, it also presumes not providing a position for those within to see, as it were, the lie of the land. Again, a lot of this is practical, the result of the ever more refined divisions and subdivisions of workers throughout the park. The collective paranoia inculcated in Disney workers from the get go – manifested in the suspicion that there is always another rule one can be found breaking – and which results in their feeling that they are always expected to perform the frequently irritating role of "Disney cast member", is a function of both the tight control that the company exercises over its dominions and a segmented and hierarchical system of relations between management and labor and within labor itself. For better or worse, probably worse, Disney's corporate structure is the model for work in the new world order, its repetitive and service-based jobs subject to the authority not of one head, but a system of specialized functional units, each with its own set of chiefs, all working earnestly at their one task, the left hand oblivious to the right – the CIA model, where one room collects weather data, another trade statistics, while upstairs someone else coordinates so that conclusions can be drawn and the troops sent in. This is a work in which all social planning has been replaced – as every attraction at EPCOT'S Future World predicts and hopes it will be – by corporate planning, every advance in social coordination conforming to and confirming the logic of the company's needs.

The divisions of the work force intended by this system include the distinctions between full- and part-time workers and those who fall between those categories. Almost everyone aspires to be 'permed' – Permanent Full Time – at which point down pour the manna of Disney benefits. "You have better insurance than your parents", says a twentyish man. Everyone agrees: Disney's benefits are great if you can get them. Anyone who's been full time for three months is automatically eligible, but the trick is becoming full time, and even that is no guarantee of permanent employment. Many workers simply hope to be rehired every year. One performer spoke of the annual jitters among her crowd: "Even now people are starting to sweat for no other reason than they've gotten a part and maintained a certain type of lifestyle and they could literally say to you, 'Thank you, you have two weeks'." Short of full time, one might instead be designated Casual Regular, which is part time but "regular", that is, ongoing, not seasonal, with some but not all benefits. This is apparently also known by the oxymoronic "Permanent Temporary". For seasonal work, there are the CTS (Casual Temporary Seasonal), the worst of the lot: long hours, though never officially full time; temporary, but with no assurance of rehire in the following season. The brunt of the entry-level jobs, many of the characters and musicians, sales persons, hotel and restaurant staff, reservationists, etc. are staffed by CTS. Many return year after year, hoping to get back their old job; others hang on in whatever capacity they can, hoping to move up to full time. During the summer, up to half of the park's employees may be CTS; many others – the high school crowd – are Casual Regular.

The dividing and subdividing of Disney workers and their jobs continues in their placement: they can work on property or off, on stage or backstage; they may be assigned to a department (e.g. Entertainment or Retail), which is further divided by park (Magic Kingdom or MGM), by area (Frontierland or Future World), and by attraction ("The Living Seas" or "30,000 Leagues"). Then they are given a specific position within the attraction, shop, or restaurant. Some workers are rooted in one area all day while others may canvass several areas in the course of it. The life-sized Disney characters – Minnie, Mickey, *et al.* – may do breakfast stints on the *Empress Lilly* and afternoon atmosphere sets in several areas of the Magic Kingdom, or EPCOT, or MGM. A spieler, one who spiels prewritten scripts, however, cannot leave his or her attraction and wander up and down Main Street. In other words, some workers are identified more by what they do, others by where they are, although all are subject to both and to strict rules about who can appear where wearing what. Being found out of place or time or otherwise out of costume is grounds for automatic dismissal.

The relentless categorizing and subdividing of employees by place, type, and amount of work has the effect of encouraging workers' identification with their area, their immediate group, rather than with other people in the park who might be doing similar things but in different places. The "Pirates of the Caribbean" people hang out with other "Pirates of the Caribbean" people. Chip sticks with Dale. While Disney sponsors what appears to be an extensive network of intramural sports, clubs, and workshops for its employees to meet and mingle (including the Rush Limbaugh Society and the Alliance, a gay and lesbian organization, the latter apparently the stronger), most of the people I spoke with had very little contact with anyone in the park outside of those they worked with every day. As a server in a park hotel puts it, "You have to be identified with your area, and because of that you tend to stick with those people. I don't know anyone in the hotels who runs around with someone in the park." In other words, labor at Disney is themed along with everything else; one is not just a restaurant server, but a server in a particularly themed restaurant in a themed area of one of the parks. One's identification is not with other servers or even with restaurant workers generally – much less with CTS generally – but with the restaurant itself.

It's in the reified space of Disney themed work that one loses sense of where one is standing and in relation to whom. Here, any chance of collective perspective is appropriated by Disney under the rubric of corporate "community" and subsequently disabused of any liberatory potential. This project is boldly announced at Team Disney, the company's corporate offices in Florida. Disney's notion of community is well known; it is cited by employees as one of the initial attractions of the job, and consists of several implied or stated commitments: promoting from within, thus giving every employee the opportunity to advance, and, as a corollary, giving each employee a valid and equal voice in the doings of the company – the sign of "equality" being an informal familiarity among employees regardless of rank. In practice, however, the relationship among these elements engenders the contradictions that render suspect any community they were intended to promote; certainly they work at cross-purposes for the bulk of Disney's workers, for whom "community" specifically excludes their perspective as it invites, and indeed requires, confusing the personal and the corporate.

For example, internal promotion at Walt Disney World is usually in the form of the promotion of someone to the position of lead. Leads are hourly workers selected from among their peers, sometimes with seniority, sometimes not, to work as the first line of supervision. They are not supervisors or management, however, and, while they earn more per hour than the others in the area, they aren't salaried either. They are given a high profile in Disney self-promotional materials – where a leadship is cited as the first stepping stone to upper management: they've already topped out on their wage scale and have probably been passed over for a promotion to supervisor, much less to area manager. That is, they have to do most of the difficult work of actually supervising workers, with few of the rewards. Many workers feel that very few employees advance into real supervisory positions, and the ones that do move up at all become leads and stop there. As one attractions operator put it, "If you're a lead, you're not really going anywhere. It's kind of giving you power but not." Among the park's performers and artists, there is a vague belief that leads are the lesser talents who have risen to their level of incompetence, that they are leads because they're not as good at playing or improvising: "There were certain people who could make up a sentence on the spot." Those who could not were "the bad spielers, the ones that sound like they're reading it ... More than likely if you weren't a good spieler, you were a lead".

While supervisors and executives are frequent objects of contempt or hostility ("You're not people of course"), workers' relations to leads are more complex. Some find them helpful mediators: leads are supposed to bridge relations between workers and supervisors. There is a sense, however, that leads are simultaneously discouraged from cultivating any genuine relationship with other employees either below or above them. In certain off-the-clock Disney watering holes – the Big Bamboo in Kissimee, for example, where outdated Disney IDs decorate the wall like so many mounted trophies – Disney employees gather but not together:

> You'd see that the people who were going out together weren't the leads. They weren't going out with you. They were staying away from us. You didn't really understand why. The leads would have their own little pack. The supervisors would have their own little pack. And nobody interacted in between. If you were a lead that hung out with your operators, you were not favored by the supervisors because the supervisors thought you should be with your leads. You needed to separate yourself.

Other workers feel the leads' precarious position relative to supervisors and workers makes difficult if not impossible the kind of community the company says it tries to create. In fact, the word used most often by workers to describe "community" at Disney was the rather less gracious "clique". The uniformity of this particular designation was surprising; the same term was used with equal ease and spontaneity by both the formerly embittered and the currently endeared:

> They treat you like a dog. They treat you like low life. If you're not in a clique, you're out of it. It takes a while to establish that clique. What defines a clique? If you're going to be a brownnoser. That's how you start being.

> It's very cliquey. If you have a role in one of the primary shows, you're probably going to be doing shows for a lifetime. It's a group of people, and it's very hard to infiltrate. I don't care if you were the better dancer than me, I was there, and you're not getting in.

> You can see somebody new. They're in awe. They're welcomed in, but if they don't fit the criteria of your particular group, they become outcasts very fast. There's a very big turnover.

In extreme cases like Karen's, group acceptance is a function in part of the length of time a person works in an area, but is made structurally impossible by the circumstances of employment. Karen responded to an ad for a behind-the-scenes job, was hired in May, told she'd be considered for full time in three months, then promptly let go in September: "They let about twenty of us go at the same time. After that you'll see an ad in the paper for Disney. All of a sudden it shows up again." Since she and the twenty others who came in with her were hired with the intention of being kept on for only three months, there was no way for her to ever break into one of the groups that would help her secure promotion and consideration for a full time position:

> We're outcasts. I was outcast for at least two months. That very last month was when I was getting to know people. They don't want any part of you then. Just get your hours in and bye bye, and that's it. It's an invitation-only type thing.

For Karen, any possibility of achieving community with her fellow workers, much less the company itself, is cut short from the start. For the rest, identification with each other and the perspective on their work it might afford them have been replaced by Disney with a model of community whose interrelations are always one-way. In that model, cliquishness, coupled with everyone's hope of becoming full time and getting benefits, transforms the otherwise admirable goal of "promoting from within" into unhealthy competition, sycophancy, and mutual distrust. With few exceptions, every Disney worker I spoke with said that favoritism was the primary route to promotion up the ranks. They were sure that Disney's commitment to equal opportunity, Walt's bootstraps ethos, was self-evidently absurd, that in order not just to stay on – many of these, after all, are people who do not have a job guaranteed from one year to the next – but to move into a higher position, they had to be favored by someone above them, which usually requires them to be obsequious, not make problems, not complain:

> You've got to keep your mouth shut. You can't tell them your opinion. You have to do everything they say. The Disney way. Never say anything negative. Everything's positive. There's never a no. You never say I don't know. If you don't know something you find out fast, even on your own after work.

> They look for someone who can follow the rules, be a team player, never rock the boat no matter what the circumstances.

> If you made waves, you were a problem. It is very difficult to break in once they know you'll stick up for what you believe in.

They tend to put into higher positions the younger ones. It's very seldom that an older person my age is in those manager jobs. Because the younger ones are more malleable, pliable, and the older ones can see through the bullshit. We're not as easy to make believe something is true that isn't.

That workers lower on a company's scale of value believe blatant sycophancy and problem avoidance are the keys to survival is not inconsistent with the experience of people similarly situated elsewhere, even in the "professions"; consider, for example, the tenuous situation of the lowly assistant professor who daily negotiates the line between self-promotion and self-abasement. What made Disney workers bitter was the gap between their expectations for opportunity with Disney and the eventual reality. When the pixie dust finally cleared, they were not impressed: "That's not what Disney stood for to me. I always thought it was, you know, equal, start at the bottom and work your way up."

Internal promotion contributes to and complicates this cliquishness and consequent favoritism in part because leads are always selected from within the area where they will operate as leads. While supervisors might migrate, no one is made a lead then sent to another area: "They don't bring anybody new in to be a lead. Nobody from the Space Mountain Ride is going to come in and be a lead somewhere else. It's always your same family." Leads are significant to the company to the extent that they *know* their area and the people in them. This is the source of both the respect and contempt given leads. One worker, a sometime Minnie Mouse, puts it in classic Disney-speak: "Leads are someone that wore a head once and forgot what it was like to wear a head. Leads were someone that they put in a polyester costume and they forgot where they came from." If there's anger in her voice, it's double-edged: She is put out with the lead, the person who used to do the kind of work she still does – prance around in a heavy costume all day "wearing a head" – and who apparently has forgotten its difficulties once in the polyester lead costume. But she's also angry with the company that uses the leads' knowledge of worker culture for its own ends:

> To be a better lead, you better tell on someone else or find out what's going on. They'll actually put you out of your polyester and back into a head with me to sit around a while then you'll know what's going on, what this one's saying about the other. Sometimes you'll be coming straight down to the zoo, so you have twenty-five minutes of talk time, so people sit around and they talk. Here you are a lead, you're back in costume now. Sometimes [everyone else] doesn't know you're the lead inside the costume. So now you know what's going on. Next week you're a lead again … It's like Judas.

In other words, they're spying. There's a lot of this going on at Disney World, though one hesitates to call it spying since everyone knows they're being spied on, except perhaps the guests, many of whom, if they knew, would approve anyway because that knowledge would augment the sense of safety so many of them claim to feel in the park and which appears to be premised on their not caring about a number of things. Besides the kind described above, spying takes several forms at Disney: there are "foxes", those who spy on guests (their name consistent with Disney's menagerie of animal names) and those who spy on employees, the even more aptly named "shoppers". Both dress like tourists. Foxes carry cameras; they keep the peace and hope to curtail some of the shoplifting which, along with counterfeiting and full-fledged armed robbery, appear to constitute the bulk of Disney World crime. Shoppers roam the parks acting nasty to see if, like visitors at Buckingham Palace, they can aggravate employees enough to make them step out of character. Or they simply observe how workers interact with other guests; that is, they "shop" them:

> I was shopped one day. She gave me a good report because I'm always friendly to people. I had no idea who she was and still don't know. They come in. They buy two or three things. Disney gives them the money. They pretend they're from Idaho or some damn place, figure no one's ever been there.

One might be tempted by their name to think that shoppers monitor only the shops and resort areas, but they are not so restricted. Shoppers can test anyone in the park regardless of what they do. From an employee's perspective, the effect is to transform all guests into potential *surveillantes*. The name "shopper", by the way, is indicative of Disney's perception of its guests: it's not that there are guests, some of whom shop; all Disney guests are shoppers, either now or in the future.

[…]

Both the actual spying and the expectation that it is always potentially present affect worker habits in predictable ways. If the shopper is known, then one may act out accordingly. One performer says, "There are some people who start doing acting backflips when [they know shoppers] are out more so than otherwise, because it is a scary thing." But most shoppers are not identified, and so one is stuck mechanically reproducing the same commodified Disney charm: "You feel like you're a robot after a while. It's a strain sometimes. It's very stressful, but you just have to."

It's in this context – the surveillance, the status of leads relative to those above and below them, and the culture of mutually generating suspicion and dependence effected by both – that we need to read the cheery familiarity and sense of equality Disney claims to foster between workers and management, but in fact enforces as a matter of policy, a very different thing. For example, everyone goes by first name. Everyone is encouraged to air problems on an area bulletin board, where complaints will be picked up and addressed at larger meetings. Anyone with an idea for how to improve the parks or the work done in them can leave their idea at another drop-off known simply as "I Have an Idea", after which, they will presumably receive credit and compensation for their contribution. But the last is a farce: technically, Disney owns any idea its workers have on property, a fact they attest to when they sign, sometimes unwittingly, a statement to that effect when they turn in their idea. And the efficacy of the second varies with employee status and area: Permanent full timers brag about their complaint session while the more contingent among them fear a trick wherein the meetings serve to isolate not the problems people are having, but the people calling them to management's attention.

[...]

Shiny happy people

At one end of the hole under Disney's Magic Kingdom, under the "Carousel", backstage, lies the "zoo". Here, mice and bears, the whole Disney menagerie, gather between their public appearances to kill time without being seen. They must arrive early for their shift to pick up and put on the heavy costumes they negotiate above ground for $5.60 an hour. Inside the huge heads, the heat of a Florida afternoon builds. Some say it gets as high as 130 degrees Fahrenheit. All peripheral vision is cut off. Some of the heads are so unwieldy or the body of its wearer so small that a metal brace is worn on the shoulders with a post extending down the back and up into the head to keep it aloft. Without this, a child's overzealous hug might throw the characters off balance and send them, like grotesque babies, following the head to the ground. The working conditions are so bad that the characters are supposed to go above ground for only 20 to 25 minutes at a time, though in peak seasons they may stay longer. Even then, it is not unusual for the characters to pass out on stage. If you know what to look for you can see them around the park as they wait for a lead to scurry them back to the "zoo", where they can finally remove the head. Leaning against replicas of eighteenth-century lampposts or propped against a float's lit backboard, their inhuman heads flashing a permanent smile, they wait, half conscious, hand raised from the elbow, waving absently to no one in particular.

Apparently the costumes alone can make wearers sick or, in conjunction with drugs and the Florida heat, can be so painful that wearers are more susceptible to heat exhaustion. Disney has an elaborate roster of height requirements for each kind of costume character: the costumes are built to the specifications of a particular body height and type, although not – as is the case for some performers in MGM Studios – to specific bodies. The bears, for example, require not just height, but strength because of the brace supporting the head. Problems arise when, in the crunch of the summer season, people (usually women, teenagers, and some younger kids) are put into costumes they are not equipped physically to handle:

> When you put a head on, it's supposed to fit on your shoulders. That's why there are height requirements for each individual costume. I have found kids that were 5' given costumes that should have been given to someone

who was 5'4". So to hold that costume on, they strap the brace on you to make the shoulders stick out. This is how they're walking around for anywhere from 25 to 45 minutes. I've seen children being hurt by it. They are tired; they're fatigued; their backs, their necks are hurting. And if you were to say "I can't wear this costume", then you can be sure you won't be working there for very long. Your hours would be cut, or you're just not one of the favorites.

It sounds crazy. The gummy bears costumes do not fit somebody that was 4'10" and they were putting 4'10" people in them. It was still too large and too heavy for the shoulders of someone with that frame. I played Sunny Gummy and Scruffy – that's the little mean gummy. The heads dig into your collar bones. When you're dancing or even if you're on the moving float, you are in pain. That's metal. There's no way out of it, and there's no relief when you're in it.

It's unclear how many of the Disney characters pass out on a given summer day, though everyone is sure that they do. One man reports that during the summer a goodly part of his job is devoted to driving around retrieving characters where they fall. One day he picked up three at one stop – Donald, Mickey, and Goofy: "All of them had passed out within five minutes of each other. They were just lined up on the sidewalk". This is in EPCOT which, unlike the Magic Kingdom with its system of underground tunnels, has a backstage behind the facades of the park's various attractions and to which the characters can escape if they have to. If they are in the Magic Kingdom, however, or on a parade float, they must simply ride it out to wait until they've recovered enough to walk to a tunnel entrance in costume and under their own steam. This can get a bit dicey. Passing out is sometimes prefaced by (and probably directly caused by) throwing up inside the head, which cannot be removed until out of public view:

You're never to be seen in a costume without your head, ever. It was automatic dismissal. It's frightening because you can die on your own regurgitation when you can't keep out of it. I'll never forget Dumbo – it was coming out of the mouth during the parade. You have a little screen over the mouth. It was horrible. And I made $4.55 an hour.

[...]

The cardinal rule among Disney costume characters is never to be seen out of character and specifically out of the head or, alternatively, never to let the costume be seen as a costume. Costumes must be black bagged when the characters travel to do work in town or out of the park: "Everything is black bagged ... God forbid if that black bag has a tear in it that you didn't know about, and a nose is sticking out of there. You're in trouble". The characters must follow rules about how to and not to move. They can't back up, for example, for the obvious reason that they can see only whatever is straight in front of them and even then only at eye level. They also cannot feel anything around them because the costumes stick out from their body and distort their sense of space. Sometimes these conditions provide the occasion for delight, as when Minnie Mouse came undone on stage: "I'm walking by the railroad and my pantaloons were around my ankles. You don't feel it because you have so much on you. People were hysterical. Finally, a lead came out, 'Minnie, Minnie, your panties have fallen'." The fate of Winnie the Pooh, however, is also instructive:

> One time somebody dressed up as Winnie the Pooh backed up. When she backed up she hit a bush and the head popped off. The head popped off Winnie the Pooh, and all the kids see this girl walking around in a Winnie the Pooh costume. And she's fired on the spot because her job is to be the character. And she didn't follow the rules. She should have turned around and walked out. Instead she backed up.

Her job is to be the character, and it is on this injunction to "be" a Disney character that the rule not to lose one's head is grounded. Apparently losing her panties is in character for Minnie; Winnie, however, is fired immediately for losing her head, the same way Dumbo would be fired immediately for taking off the one he had just thrown up in because both actions destroy the park's magic, the illusion that the characters are real. One person I spoke with refused for an hour to acknowledge even that there were actual human people inside the Disney character costumes: "That's one of the things I really can't talk about. Not because I work there, but because it keeps it kind of sacred." "Snow White is Snow White", another explains. Thus, when she goes to receive an award at a local hospital, Disney officials will not allow her to publicly accept it out of costume. Instead, she must appear as Snow White so those either assembled for the occasion or made privy to it later will not be disillusioned by her transformation into a regular person.

[...]

For the bulk of the park's employees engaged in the repetitive, often mindless, if not idiotic tasks that together produce Disney's magic, the putting on of happy faces is daily work. "We have a hard time", says David, an attractions host, because

> you go out in public and be this Boy Scout for eight hours a day. When you come home, you're a mess. You're a maniac. You're angry. You're tired. You have to get rid of your anxieties. You start teaming up with people because you could all talk about the day's events. So you go out and get as drunk as you possibly can, pass out, and the next day get up and go to work. You're just like, "I can't take this anymore".

If reciting the same scripted spiel every fifteen minutes to a new, yet somehow ever more familiar audience is difficult, it is at least made bearable by Disney's rotation system. Ostensibly – and this is its advertised benefit – rotation exposes each employee to the work of those around him or her; this is, in fact, what it does, but only to the extent that the employee is kept going through the shift. Without rotation, says one, "you'd be just sick to death. They tap into a good thing there by moving you around. [...]" At a typical Disney attraction, rotation consists of a series of fifteen-minute or half-hour minishifts in which a worker is bumped from monitoring a line outside, to ushering crowds into a theatre ("Walk all the way to the end of the row please"), to spieling itself, and back again to the line. In other words, they're not really learning other aspects of the park or of the company's business, but how the particular machinery of their attraction works and how they can function interchangeably as cogs at various points in it. Guests don't register this, of course. What they sense is functionality in its pure and purely invisible form.

13

MANAGING MULTICULTURAL TEAMS

Jeanne Brett, Kristin Behfar and Mary Kern

Source: Edited from *Harvard Business Review*, 2006, 14 (1), November, pp. 84–91.

Teams whose members come from different nations and backgrounds place special demands on managers – especially when a feuding team looks to the boss for help with a conflict.

When a major international software developer needed to produce a new product quickly, the project manager assembled a team of employees from India and the United States. From the start the team members could not agree on a delivery date for the product. The Americans thought the work could be done in two to three weeks; the Indians predicted it would take two to three months. As time went on, the Indian team members proved reluctant to report setbacks in the production process, which the American team members would find out about only when work was due to be passed to them. Such conflicts, of course, may affect any team, but in this case they arose from cultural differences. As tensions mounted, conflict over delivery dates and feedback became personal, disrupting team members' communication about even mundane issues. The project manager decided he had to intervene – with the result that both the American and the Indian team members came to rely on him for direction regarding minute operational details that the team should have been able to handle itself. The manager became so bogged down by quotidian issues that the project careened hopelessly off even the most pessimistic schedule – and the team never learned to work together effectively.

Multicultural teams often generate frustrating management dilemmas. Cultural differences can create substantial obstacles to effective teamwork – but these may be subtle and difficult to recognize until significant damage has already been done. As in the case above, which the manager involved told us about, managers may create more problems than they resolve by intervening. The challenge in managing multicultural teams effectively is to recognize underlying cultural causes of conflict, and to intervene in ways that both get the team back on track and empower its members to deal with future challenges themselves.

We interviewed managers and members of multicultural teams from all over the world. These interviews, combined with our deep research on dispute resolution and teamwork, led us to conclude that the wrong kind of managerial intervention may sideline valuable members who should be participating or, worse, create resistance, resulting in poor team performance. We're not talking here about respecting differing national standards for doing business, such as accounting practices. We're referring to day-to-day working problems among team members that can keep multicultural teams from realizing the very gains they were set up to harvest, such as knowledge of different product markets, culturally sensitive customer service, and 24-hour work rotations.

The good news is that cultural challenges are manageable if managers and team members choose the right strategy and avoid imposing single-culture-based approaches on multicultural situations.

The challenges

People tend to assume that challenges on multicultural teams arise from differing styles of communication. But this is only one of the four categories that, according to our research, can create barriers to a team's ultimate success. These categories are direct versus indirect communication; trouble with accents and fluency; differing attitudes toward hierarchy and authority; and conflicting norms for decision making.

Direct versus indirect communication. Communication in Western cultures is typically direct and explicit. The meaning is on the surface, and a listener doesn't have to know much about the context or the speaker to interpret it. This is not true in many other cultures, where meaning is embedded in the way the message is presented. For example, Western negotiators get crucial information about the other party's preferences and priorities by asking direct questions, such as "Do you prefer option A or option B?" In cultures that use indirect communication, negotiators may have to infer preferences and priorities from changes – or the lack of them – in the other party's settlement proposal. In cross-cultural negotiations, the non-Westerner can understand the direct communications of the Westerner, but the Westerner has difficulty understanding the indirect communications of the non-Westerner.

An American manager who was leading a project to build an interface for a U.S. and Japanese customer-data system explained the problems her team was having this way: "In Japan, they want to talk and discuss. Then we take a break and they talk within the organization. They want to make sure that there's harmony in the rest of the organization. One of the hardest lessons for me was when I thought they were saying yes but they just meant 'I'm listening to you'."

The differences between direct and indirect communication can cause serious damage to relationships when team projects run into problems. When the American manager quoted above discovered that several flaws in the system would significantly disrupt company operations, she pointed this out in an e-mail to her American boss and the Japanese team members. Her boss appreciated the direct warnings; her Japanese colleagues were embarrassed, because she had violated their norms for uncovering and discussing problems. Their reaction was to provide her with less access to the people and information she needed to monitor progress. They would probably have responded better if she had pointed out the problems indirectly – for example, by asking them what would happen if a certain part of the system was not functioning properly, even though she knew full well that it was malfunctioning and also what the implications were.

As our research indicates is so often true, communication challenges create barriers to effective teamwork by reducing information sharing, creating interpersonal conflict, or both. In Japan, a typical response to direct confrontation is to isolate the norm violator. This American manager was isolated not just socially but also physically. She told us, "They literally put my office in a storage room, where I had desks stacked from floor to ceiling and I was the only person there. So they totally isolated me, which was a pretty loud signal to me that I was not a part of the inside circle and that they would communicate with me only as needed."

Her direct approach had been intended to solve a problem, and in one sense, it did, because her project was launched problem-free. But her norm violations exacerbated the challenges of working with her Japanese colleagues and limited her ability to uncover any other problems that might have derailed the project later on.

Trouble with accents and fluency. Although the language of international business is English, misunderstandings or deep frustration may occur because of non-native speakers' accents, lack of fluency, or problems with translation or usage. These may also influence perceptions of status or competence.

For example, a Latin American member of a multicultural consulting team lamented, "Many times I felt that because of the language difference, I didn't have the words to say some things that I was thinking. I noticed that when I went to these interviews with the U.S. guy, he would tend to lead the interviews, which was understandable but also disappointing, because we are at the same level. I had very good questions, but he would take the lead."

When we interviewed an American member of a U.S.–Japanese team that was assessing the potential expansion of a U.S. retail chain into Japan, she described one American teammate this way: "He was not interested in the Japanese consultants' feedback and felt that because they weren't as fluent as he was, they weren't intelligent enough and, therefore, could add no value." The team member described was responsible for assessing one aspect of the feasibility of expansion into Japan. Without input from the Japanese experts, he risked overestimating opportunities and underestimating challenges.

Non-fluent team members may well be the most expert on the team, but their difficulty in communicating knowledge makes it hard for the team to recognize and utilize their expertise. If teammates become frustrated or impatient with a lack of fluency, interpersonal conflicts can arise. Nonnative speakers may become less motivated to contribute, or anxious about their performance evaluations and future career prospects. The organization as a whole pays a greater price: Its investment in a multicultural team fails to pay off.

Some teams, we learned, use language differences to resolve (rather than create) tensions. A team of U.S. and Latin American buyers was negotiating with a team from a Korean supplier. The negotiations took place in Korea, but the discussions were conducted in English. Frequently the Koreans would caucus at the table by speaking Korean. The buyers, frustrated, would respond by appearing to caucus in Spanish – though they discussed only inconsequential current events and sports, in case any of the Koreans spoke Spanish. Members of the team who didn't speak Spanish pretended to participate, to the great amusement of their teammates. This approach proved effective: It conveyed to the Koreans in an appropriately indirect way that their caucuses in Korean were frustrating and annoying to the other side. As a result, both teams cut back on sidebar conversations.

Differing attitudes toward hierarchy and authority. A challenge inherent in multicultural teamwork is that, by design, teams have a rather flat structure. But team members from some cultures, in which people are treated differently according to their status in an organization, are uncomfortable on flat teams. If they defer to higher status team members, their behavior will be seen as appropriate when most of the team comes from a hierarchical culture; but they may damage their stature and credibility – and even face humiliation – if most of the team comes from an egalitarian culture.

One manager of Mexican heritage, who was working on a credit and underwriting team for a bank, told us, "In Mexican culture, you're always supposed to be humble. So whether you understand something or not, you're supposed to put it in the form of a question. You have to keep it open-ended, out of respect. I think that actually worked against me, because the Americans thought I really didn't know what I was talking about. So it made me feel like they thought I was wavering on my answer."

When, as a result of differing cultural norms, team members believe they've been treated disrespectfully, the whole project can blow up. In another Korean– U.S. negotiation, the American members of a due diligence team were having difficulty getting information from their Korean counterparts, so they complained directly to higher-level Korean management, nearly wrecking the deal. The higher-level managers were offended because hierarchy is strictly adhered to in Korean organizations and culture. It should have been their own lower-level people, not the U.S. team members, who came to them with a problem. And the Korean team members were mortified that their bosses had been involved before they themselves could brief them. The crisis was resolved only when high-level U.S. managers made a trip to Korea, conveying appropriate respect for their Korean counterparts.

Conflicting norms for decision making. Cultures differ enormously when it comes to decision making – particularly, how quickly decisions should be made and how much analysis is required beforehand. Not surprisingly, U.S. managers like to make decisions very quickly and with relatively little analysis by comparison with managers from other countries.

A Brazilian manager at an American company who was negotiating to buy Korean products destined for Latin America told us, "On the first day, we agreed on three points, and on the second day, the U.S.–Spanish side wanted to start with point four. But the Korean side wanted to go back and re-discuss points one through three. My boss almost had an attack."

What U.S. team members learn from an experience like this is that the American way simply cannot be imposed on other cultures. Managers from other cultures may, for example, decline to share information until they understand the full scope of a project. But they have learned that they can't simply ignore the desire of their American counterparts to make decisions quickly. What to do? The best solution seems to be to make minor concessions on process – to learn to adjust to and even respect another approach to decision making. For example, American managers have learned to keep their impatient bosses away from team meetings and give them frequent if brief updates.

A comparable lesson for managers from other cultures is to be explicit about what they need – saying, for example, "We have to see the big picture before we talk details."

Four strategies

The most successful teams and managers we interviewed used four strategies for dealing with these challenges: adaptation (acknowledging cultural gaps openly and working around them), structural intervention (changing the shape of the team), managerial intervention (setting norms early or bringing in a higher-level manager), and exit (removing a team member when other options have failed). There is no one right way to deal with a particular kind of multicultural problem; identifying the type of challenge is only the first step. The more crucial step is assessing the circumstances – or "enabling situational conditions" – under which the team is working. For example, does the project allow any flexibility for change, or do deadlines make that impossible? Are there additional resources available that might be tapped? Is the team permanent or temporary? Does the team's manager have the autonomy to make a decision about changing the team in some way? Once the situational conditions have been analyzed, the team's leader can identify an appropriate response [see Table 13.1 on page 161 "Identifying the right strategy"].

Adaptation. Some teams find ways to work with or around the challenges they face, adapting practices or attitudes without making changes to the group's membership or assignments. Adaptation works when team members are willing to acknowledge and name their cultural differences and to assume responsibility for figuring out how to live with them. It's often the best possible approach to a problem, because it typically involves less managerial time than other strategies; and because team members participate in solving the problem themselves, they learn from the process. When team members have this mind-set, they can be creative about protecting their own substantive differences while acceding to the processes of others.

An American software engineer located in Ireland who was working with an Israeli account management team from his own company told us how shocked he was by the Israelis' in-your-face style: "There were definitely different ways of approaching issues and discussing them. There is something pretty common to the Israeli culture: They like to argue. I tend to try to collaborate more, and it got very stressful for me until I figured out how to kind of merge the cultures."

The software engineer adapted. He imposed some structure on the Israelis that helped him maintain his own style of being thoroughly prepared; that accommodation enabled him to accept the Israeli style. He also noticed that team members weren't just confronting him; they confronted one another but were able to work together effectively nevertheless. He realized that the confrontation was not personal but cultural.

In another example, an American member of a postmerger consulting team was frustrated by the hierarchy of the French company his team was working with. He felt that a meeting with certain French managers who were not directly involved in the merger "wouldn't deliver any value to me or for purposes of the project," but said that he had come to understand that "it was very important to really involve all the people there" if the integration was ultimately to work.

A U.S. and U.K. multicultural team tried to use their differing approaches to decision making to reach a higher-quality decision. This approach, called fusion, is getting serious attention from political scientists and from government officials dealing with multicultural populations that want to protect their cultures rather than integrate or assimilate. If the team had relied exclusively on the Americans' "forge ahead" approach, it might not have recognized the pitfalls that lay ahead and might later have had to back up and start over. Meanwhile, the U.K. members would have been gritting their teeth and saying, "We told you things were moving too fast." If the team had used the "Let's think about this" U.K. approach, it might have wasted a lot of time trying to identify every pitfall, including the most unlikely, while the U.S. members chomped at the bit and muttered about analysis paralysis. The strength of this team was that some of its members were willing to forge ahead and some were willing to work through pitfalls. To accommodate them all, the team did both – moving not quite as fast as the U.S. members would have on their own and not quite as thoroughly as the U.K. members would have.

Structural intervention. A structural intervention is a deliberate reorganization or reassignment designed to reduce interpersonal friction or to remove a source of conflict for one or more groups. This approach can be extremely effective when obvious subgroups demarcate the team (for example, headquarters versus national subsidiaries) or if team members are proud, defensive, threatened, or clinging to negative stereotypes of one another.

TABLE 13.1 Identifying the right strategy

The most successful teams and managers we interviewed use four strategies for dealing with problems: adaptation (acknowledging cultural gaps openly and working around them), structural intervention (changing the shape of the team), managerial intervention (setting norms early or bringing in a higher-level manager), and exit (removing a team member when other options have failed). Adaptation is the ideal strategy because the team works effectively to solve its own problem with minimal input from management – and, most important, learns from the experience. The guide below can help you identify the right strategy once you have identified both the problem and the "enabling situational conditions" that apply to the team.

Representative problems	Enabling situational conditions	Strategy	Complicating factors
• Conflict arises from decision making differences • Misunderstanding or stonewalling arises from communication differences	• Team members can attribute a challenge to culture rather than personality • Higher-level managers are not available or the team would be embarrassed to involve them	**Adaptation**	• Team members must be exceptionally aware • Negotiating a common understanding takes time
• The team is affected by emotional tensions relating to fluency issues or prejudice • Team members are inhibited by perceived status differences among teammates	• The team can be subdivided to mix cultures or expertise • Tasks can be subdivided	**Structural intervention**	• If team members aren't carefully distributed, subgroups can strengthen pre-existing differences • Subgroup solutions have to fit back together
• Violations of hierarchy have resulted in loss of face • An absence of ground rules is causing conflict	• The problem has produced a high level of emotion • The team has reached a stalemate • A higher-level manager is able and willing to intervene	**Managerial intervention**	• The team becomes overly dependent on the manager • Team members may be sidelined or resistant
• A team member cannot adjust to the challenge on hand and has become unable to contribute to the project	• The team is permanent rather than temporary • Emotions are beyond the point of intervention • Too much face has been lost	**Exit**	• Talent and training costs are lost

A member of an investment research team scattered across continental Europe, the U.K., and the U.S. described for us how his manager resolved conflicts stemming from status differences and language tensions among the team's three "tribes." The manager started by having the team meet face-to-face twice a year, not to discuss mundane day-to-day problems (of which there were many) but to identify a set of values that the team would use to direct and evaluate its progress. At the first meeting, he realized that when he started to speak, everyone else "shut down," waiting to hear what he had to say. So he hired a consultant to run future meetings. The consultant didn't represent a hierarchical threat and was therefore able to get lots of participation from team members.

Another structural intervention might be to create smaller working groups of mixed cultures or mixed corporate identities in order to get at information that is not forthcoming from the team as a whole. The manager of the team that was evaluating retail opportunities in Japan used this approach. When she realized that the female Japanese consultants would not participate if the group got large, or if their male superior was present, she broke the team up into smaller groups to try to solve problems. She used this technique repeatedly and made a point of changing the subgroups' membership each time so that team members got to know and respect everyone else on the team.

The subgrouping technique involves risks, however. It buffers people who are not working well together or not participating in the larger group for one reason or another. Sooner or later the team will have to assemble the pieces that the subgroups have come up with, so this approach relies on another structural intervention: Someone must become a mediator in order to see that the various pieces fit together.

Managerial intervention. When a manager behaves like an arbitrator or a judge, making a final decision without team involvement, neither the manager nor the team gains much insight into why the team has stalemated. But it is possible for team members to use managerial intervention effectively to sort out problems.

When an American refinery-safety expert with significant experience through-out East Asia got stymied during a project in China, she called in her company's higher-level managers in Beijing to talk to the higher-level managers to whom the Chinese refinery's managers reported. Unlike the Western team members who breached etiquette by approaching the superiors of their Korean counterparts, the safety expert made sure to respect hierarchies in both organizations.

"Trying to resolve the issues," she told us, "the local management at the Chinese refinery would end up having conferences with our Beijing office and also with the upper management within the refinery. Eventually they understood that we weren't trying to insult them or their culture or to tell them they were bad in any way. We were trying to help. They eventually understood that there were significant fire and safety issues. But we actually had to go up some levels of management to get those resolved."

Managerial intervention to set norms early in a team's life can really help the team start out with effective processes. In one instance reported to us, a multicultural software development team's *lingua franca* was English, but some members, though they spoke grammatically correct English, had a very pronounced accent. In setting the ground rules for the team, the manager addressed the challenge directly, telling the members that they had been chosen for their task expertise, not their fluency in English, and that the team was going to have to work around language problems. As the project moved to the customer-services training stage, the manager advised the team members to acknowledge their accents up front. She said they should tell customers, "I realize I have an accent. If you don't understand what I'm saying, just stop me and ask questions."

Exit. Possibly because many of the teams we studied were project based, we found that leaving the team was an infrequent strategy for managing challenges. In short-term situations, unhappy team members often just waited out the project. When teams were permanent, producing products or services, the exit of one or more members was a strategy of last resort, but it was used – either voluntarily or after a formal request from management. Exit was likely when emotions were running high and too much face had been lost on both sides to salvage the situation.

An American member of a multicultural consulting team described the conflict between two senior consultants, one a Greek woman and the other a Polish man, over how to approach problems: "The woman from Greece would say, 'Here's the way I think we should do it.' It would be something that she was in control of. The guy from Poland would say, 'I think we should actually do it this way instead.' The woman would kind of turn red in the face, upset, and say, 'I just don't think that's the right way of doing it.' It would definitely switch from just professional differences to personal differences.

"The woman from Greece ended up leaving the firm. That was a direct result of probably all the different issues going on between these people. It really just wasn't a good fit. I've found that oftentimes when you're in consulting, you have to adapt to the culture, obviously, but you have to adapt just as much to the style of whoever is leading the project."

Though multicultural teams face challenges that are not directly attributable to cultural differences, such differences underlay whatever problem needed to be addressed in many of the teams we studied. Furthermore, while serious in their own right when they have a negative effect on team functioning, cultural challenges may also unmask fundamental managerial problems. Managers who intervene early and set norms; teams and managers who structure social interaction and work to engage everyone on the team; and teams that can see problems as stemming from culture, not personality, approach challenges with good humor and creativity. Managers who have to intervene when the team has reached a stalemate may be able to get the team moving again, but they seldom empower it to help itself the next time a stalemate occurs.

When frustrated team members take some time to think through challenges and possible solutions themselves, it can make a huge difference. Take, for example, this story about a financial services call center. The members of the call center team were all fluent Spanish-speakers, but some were North Americans and some were Latin Americans. Team performance, measured by calls answered per hour, was lagging. One Latin American was taking twice as long with her calls as the rest of the team. She was handling callers' questions appropriately, but she was also engaging in chitchat. When her teammates confronted her for being a free rider (they resented having to make up for her low call rate), she immediately acknowledged the problem, admitting that she did not know how to end the call politely – chitchat being normal in her culture. They rallied to help her: Using their technology, they would break into any of her calls that went overtime, excusing themselves to the customer, offering to take over the call, and saying that this employee was urgently needed to help out on a different call. The team's solution worked in the short run, and the employee got better at ending her calls in the long run.

In another case, the Indian manager of a multicultural team coordinating a companywide IT project found himself frustrated when he and a teammate from Singapore met with two Japanese members of the coordinating team to try to get the Japan section to deliver its part of the project. The Japanese members seemed to be saying yes, but in the Indian manager's view, their follow through was insufficient. He considered and rejected the idea of going up the hierarchy to the Japanese team members' boss, and decided instead to try to build consensus with the whole Japanese IT team, not just the two members on the coordinating team. He and his Singapore teammate put together an eBusiness road show, took it to Japan, invited the whole IT team to view it at a lunch meeting, and walked through success stories about other parts of the organization that had aligned with the company's larger business priorities. It was rather subtle, he told us, but it worked. The Japanese IT team wanted to be spotlighted in future eBusiness road shows. In the end, the whole team worked well together – and no higher level manager had to get involved.

PART IV

International management perspectives

Introduction

Dev Kumar Boojihawon

Doing business across borders is hard, but doing it while collaborating is even harder. In this section we look at the issue of international management of alliances. The rapid proliferation of alliances across national borders has become one of the flagrant features of the modern global economy. An international alliance can imply a collaborative relationship between two or more legally independent entities located in different countries. Such an alliance can be motivated by a joint effort to develop a new product or enter a new market. It can also support the offensive or defensive intents of the partners. Irrespective of the reasons for the alliances, their success is very much dependent on the continuous inter- and intra-organizational collaboration and negotiation between the alliance partners. This, however, is more easily said than done. Differing cultural backgrounds, and conflicting power and politicising partners increases the complexity of international alliances manifold, and continuously tests the strength of the alliance.

Incidentally, there exists a huge body of literature which tells us about difficulties and challenges that are experienced by international alliances, and many empirical findings suggest that many international alliances either fail or are taken over by one of the partners a few years following their start up. I do not intend to review this extensive literature in this section; instead I have selected four key articles that will give you a surface level understanding of how international alliances work and, in so doing, explore some of the complexities and intricacies that characterise the management of international alliances.

In the first article, Farok Contractor and Peter Lorange start by noting an "explosion" of alliances globally in the past two decades, which continues to grow. They emphasise that a shift has occurred in the way companies govern and organize themselves across borders, and therein interfirm cooperation has become a permanent and indispensable part of management. This paper is a reflective account of why and how international alliances have grown so rapidly as a global economic phenomenon, and analyses some of the underlying changes in the organization and the global economic environment that have accelerated this growth. Accordingly, they suggest a number of intertwined regulatory, economic and competitive factors which seem to favour the rapid formation of alliances today, and which are somewhat eased up by the reconceptualisation of the global economy as one which is knowledge-based. Indeed, a knowledge-based economy is driven by ideas – thought, design and organization – and promotes customisation, flexibility, quick response, and breaking down or reshuffling the constituent parts of the value chain to effectively create more, if not better, value. This understanding seems to fuel more fluid forms and mutations of alliances globally.

'Knowledge', however, can also be a serious impediment to the growth of international alliances. In fact, several theoretical perspectives, like the internalisation perspective argue that the more knowledge intensive the firm the lower its tendency to collaborate, and the transaction cost theory asserts that knowledge is 'sticky' by nature, that is it is deeply embedded in the functioning of an organization and often inexpressible except in forms that make it difficult to transfer between partners in a collaborative relationship. As such, the second paper, by Gary Hamel, focuses on finely analysing the determinants and processes of learning between partners in international alliances. Following the knowledge-based contention, his analysis is based on the contrast of a firm as a bundle of skills or portfolio of disciplines, 'core competencies', rather than a portfolio of product-market entities. In his view, global competitiveness is largely a function of the firm's pace, efficiency and extent of knowledge acquisition, and in this context, interfirm competition or cooperation becomes primarily concerned with the acquisition of skills. Hamel argues that we will know nothing of how successful alliances work if we focus merely on the contextual issues that drive such alliances. Instead, we need to understand the processes of knowledge acquisition and skills development and bundling in international alliances which seem to enhance or diminish partners' bases of global competitiveness.

The third paper, By Michael Hitt, Ho–Uk Lee and Emre Yucel, adopts an alternative view to the above papers and avers that success in international alliances demands more than 'what we know' and depends more on 'who we know' globally. Of essence to this paper is the concept of 'social capital' which emphasises the importance of relationships between firms in forming international alliances. Hitt and colleagues argue that global competition is increasingly characterised not by firms competing with individual competitors but with networks of firms. Firms in networks have many more resources they can access to enhance their ability to compete than do single firms operating independently. In this environment firms with social or relational capital have an advantage as proven by the experiences of guanxi (China), kankei (Japan), inmak (Korea) which provide a framework for business dealings and potential competitive advantage in many Asian countries. These networks constitute a web of social relationships and a continuous source of social capital where relationships provide a basis for the culture, business transactions, and value creation.

Relationships, however, need not matter only at the level of the firm but more importantly at the level of the people or teams involved in managing complex activities within international alliances. Such alliances can involve globally distributed organizations bringing people of different cultures and languages across heterogeneous locations together to collaborate on specific projects. In the fourth paper of this section, Pernille Bjørn and Ojelanki Ngwenyama take a functional view of how differences in shared meaning and breakdown in communication impact on the performance of two globally distributed virtual teams collaborating to undertake a complex activity. They also explore some of the difficulties of collaborating in such an environment and suggest the concepts of "shared meaning" – the background knowledge that guides actors in organizing and shaping their interpretation of events, and "translucence" – the triangulation of visibility, awareness and accountability as ways of overcoming some of the challenges of collaborative practice of virtual teams in international alliances.

As with other themes in the reader, the literature on the international management of collaborative alliances is both extensive and surrounded by pertinent debates. In the articles presented here you will discover the broad parameters, complexities and uncertainties of managing alliances globally. Globalisation, it appears, has an overarching impact on the global logic and performance of international alliances where much of the basis of a sound *entente* between partners seems to depend on whether they can start with a common global vision.

14

THE GROWTH OF ALLIANCES IN THE KNOWLEDGE-BASED ECONOMY

Farok Contractor and Peter Lorange

Source: Edited from *International Business Review*, 2002, Vol. 11, pp. 485–502.

1 Introduction

The "explosion" in alliances and other forms of interfirm cooperation is now at least a fifteen-year-old phenomenon. Far from a transient fad, or slowing down, as some observers predicted, the rate of alliance formation is indeed picking up. According to a Booz Allen and Hamilton report, the number of alliances grew at 25 percent per year in the period 1987–1997 (Harbison and Pekar, 1997). A recent Arthur Andersen survey, based on 323 questionnaire responses and over 400 interviews with senior executives, indicated that alliances were "...expected to account for 16 to 25 percent of median company value within five years and, astonishingly, more than 40 percent of market value for one-quarter of companies..." This report also cites a study of over 2000 alliances by Anand and Khanna (2000), of "abnormal returns" on stock market valuations following alliance announcements, which indicates that alliances already account for 6 to 16 percent of the total market capitalization of US firms. Even if one were to be sceptical of such numbers, there is little doubt that the alliance phenomenon is here not only to stay, but is set to grow rapidly.

Just fifteen years ago this was not so. Leading corporations, such as IBM and GE, prided themselves on internalized, hierarchical strategies based on competition, not cooperation. Alliances did not have a significant economic presence. They were primarily peripheral market entry strategies in socialist and developing nations, involving licensing and joint ventures mandated by host governments. Today, the former arch exponents of internalized control, such as IBM or GE, have alliances approaching or exceeding one thousand in number. The last benchmark survey of US Foreign Direct Investment (FDI) undertaken by the US Department of Commerce suggests that in the 1990s foreign licensing by US companies grew (at rates exceeding eleven percent per year) faster than both trade and FDI (Contractor, 1999).

Thus, from being an incidental emerging-market curiosity, alliances have indeed "revived" today (Oxley, 1999). Far from being driven by regulatory compulsion, alliances are now eagerly sought as a means of adding to firm value, more central to strategy (Lorange and Roos, 1992), more knowledge-intensive and more likely to involve competitors (Duysters, Kok, and Vaandrager, 2000). [...]

2 A globalizing economy with knowledge-based assets

In the twentieth century, mankind made a transition from a matter-based economy to one based on ideas — from an emphasis on natural resources to focusing on thought, design and organization. Accompanying this were two trends. First, services displaced manufacturing as the major component of economic activity. Second, manufactured items themselves were designed leaner — or more precisely, could produce larger quantities of output from the same, or a lighter, design.

By the end of the twentieth century, the de-materialization of the economy had advanced to the point where 79 percent of jobs, and 76 percent of the GNP in the USA were in the service sector (Survey of Current Business, 1995). Europe and Japan lagged only slightly behind. Emerging nations are also moving along a developmental path that seems to culminate with intangibles ultimately comprising the dominant portion of the economy. Several developing nations are already at or near the point where the service sector is worth more than half their economy (UNCTAD, 1992, 1995).

Since Tobin's Q Ratio (a company's market value divided by the replacement cost of its assets) (Tobin, 1969) was proposed, the ratio of market to book value of American companies doubled between 1973 and 1993 (*Economist*, 1999). Firms like Microsoft have most of their value in "knowledge capital," embedded in its personnel, its organization, patents, copyrights, brand value and so on (Lissack and Roos, 1999). In early 1999, the market-to-book ratio for Microsoft was over 25 compared to three for Ford. A study by Sveiby (1998) plots a long-term rising trend in the "market to book value" ratio over the course of the twentieth century. This is what one would expect, with the growing importance of intangible assets in company operations.

An economy based on ideas rather than material objects has several distinct characteristics. An economy of objects emphasizes mass production, internalized ownership, control and vertical integration. An economy based on knowledge favors customization, flexibility, rapid response and dis-internalization or deconstruction of the value chain. This favors alliances, as different pieces of the value chain under different ownership cooperate with each other.

But will the trend towards a growing emphasis on corporate knowledge necessarily continue to favor alliances? The knowledge-based economy today is very different from the conception of knowledge as a public good in traditional economics, where its use by one party did not diminish its use or value by another. In contrast, it is often argued today in internalization theory that the more knowledge-intensive the firm, the lower the propensity to form alliances — for fear of misappropriation of knowledge by allies who could become competitors (Dunning, 1980). Similarly, transaction costs theory suggests that corporate knowledge is sometimes so deeply embedded or "sticky" in the organization, and partially inarticulable, that its transfer to another ally firm is far from costless or instantaneous (Williamson, 1985) (Cohen and Levinthal, 1990) (Von Hippel, 1994). Thus the formation of alliances is impeded by (i) Fear of misappropriation and (ii) Cost of knowledge transfer.

However, these fears are today mitigated by two regulatory and environmental factors that favor alliances:

1 The global spread of the system of intellectual property protection under the aegis of TRIPS, a protocol of the World Trade Organization, which reduces the fear of misappropriation, and
2 greater articulation and codification of knowledge, which reduces the costs of its transfer to allies. The latter is aided by broad-based adaptation of information technology.

The remainder of this article will treat recent contextual and environmental changes that now favor the propensity to form alliances. These include:

1   Governmental policy changes (R):
1.1.   Further deregulation and economic liberalization (R)
1.2.   A move towards harmonization of standards and reciprocal acceptance of data (R)
1.3.   Spread of intellectual property laws and effective enforcement (R)

2   Knowledge management in firms (P or E):
2.1.   Identification and codification of knowledge assets in firms (P)
2.2.   Acceleration in the rate of technical change (E)
2.3.   Growing diversity of knowledge sources (E)
2.4.   Escalating R&D costs and risks (P)

3   Changes in production and distribution (P or E):
3.1.   Outsourcing and deconstruction of the value chain (P)
3.2.   The increasing strategic importance of speed (E)
3.3.   Multiplicity of end applications of technologies and customization (E)
3.4.   The growing role of information technology in alliance relationships (P).

(R) = Regulatory changes. (E) = Other changes in the business and economic environment. (P) = Policy/strategy changes internal to firms.

3 Environmental and contextual changes favoring alliances

3.1. Governmental policy changes (R):

3.1.1. Further deregulation of industries and economic liberalization (R)

Since the 1980s, old industrial structures have been dismantled in a large number of sectors from banking and insurance to utilities and airlines. *A priori*, there is no reason to believe that liberalization should necessarily lead to a growth in alliances. But as an empirical fact, such regulated industries typically had been oligopolistic and frequently exhibited strong vertical integration (Caves, 1998). Hence, upon deregulation, a greater incidence of alliances was almost inevitable (Ostry, 1998) (Safarian and Dobson, 1997).

There are many familiar tales. Competition in the international airline industry can today be said to be based on "alliance clusters" as much as on individual carriers. Since deregulation in the industry is incomplete in one vital aspect — namely landing rights — airline alliances are driven by locational or geographical complementarity. However, other synergies of cooperation also kick in, such as economies of scale or scope and the transfer of learning — such as price and revenue management algorithms.

A case in point was Enron (*Business Week*, 2001). Even though this company has gone into bankruptcy and has been at the center of much controversy, its approach to alliances remains valid. In a liberalized electricity sector, nimble market-maker firms juggle daily purchases of power on the spot market with constantly shifting customer demand. In Enron's case, via an alliance with Motorola and ABB, customers' power use was metered hourly (meters supplied by ABB) and the resulting data transmitted by wireless modem transmitters (designed by Motorola) to Enron's central IT location where they were cumulated and analyzed every few hours. Enron did not feel it worthwhile to invest in electricity meter or wireless modem technology. This was best left to partners — Motorola and ABB — who could develop specialized hardware on a lower incremental cost. Interestingly, the alliance agreement left ABB and Motorola free to sell their equipment to other competing utility companies. Enron claimed not to be concerned because of its strong proprietary expertise in data analysis and expert systems for purchasing and pricing algorithms. Incidentally, in a very loose sense, this was also an alliance involving Enron's customers who tolerated an "intrusion" of the alliance's hardware into their premises and collection of minute data on their electricity use in return for lower rates.

Skandia, an insurance and financial services company, is frequently proposed as an example of a "virtual corporation" that grew rapidly following deregulation, with a policy of alliance partners (Edvinsson, 1997). With only 1700 employees it serves 785,000 customers with insurance annuities based on mutual fund portfolios. It does this by inviting partners to co-develop its products and by using 46,000 independent investment managers and insurance agent firms as partners worldwide. At substantial cost, Skandia develops insurance products on a globally centralized basis, but then leverages this learning, at low incremental transfer cost, at the many country locations it serves. Like Enron, Skandia considers part of its core competence to be the collection, analysis and monitoring of micro-data on clients and partner agents. For a particular partner of Skandia the picture may not be so rosy, however. Skandia's network of distributors sell a portfolio of products, and a given partner may have little control over how their jointly developed product is pushed within the portfolio.

3.1.2 Harmonization of standards and reciprocal acceptance of data (R)

This is still a recent global phenomenon, but it explains some alliance formation. Two aspects of harmonization concern us in particular. First, greater and more consistent application of Intellectual property (IP) laws favors the propensity to form alliances. While intellectual property laws still vary on a national basis, and the current WTO (TRIPS) agreement is only a start, newly adopting countries have indeed mimicked US and European law. Second, continuing talks under WTO will inevitably lead to greater harmonization and reciprocal acceptance of standards (Marshall, 1997). Already, in pharmaceutical certification, some nations have agreed to accept the field test results of others. This promotes international alliances based on pooling of multi-country data. The advantages of winning the race to commercialization of a drug presumably outweigh the disadvantage of sharing territories and potential revenues with alliance partners. Another kind of "learning race" in biotechnology involves research coalitions motivated by the desire to be the first to patent and for the great payoff from doing so (Powell, 1998). Other alliance-based races are motivated by the drive to set industry technical standards.

3.1.3 Spread of intellectual property laws and effective enforcement (R)

The TRIPS-based system of patent and intellectual property laws has triumphed (Gana, 1995). Collective aboriginal cultural property, mineral and biological phenotypes treated from time immemorial as the common heritage of mankind, even local names and recipes — all of these are to be swept away in a wave of privatized ownership for the sake of a greater economic benefit. On the other hand, the greater good potentially for all of mankind includes better science, better technology, better software and books as the private rewards of intellectual property protection spur creativity. This greater good may not immediately rebound to all nations, nor will it be uniformly spread. However, studies have correlated the strength of IP protection with economic development (Gould and Gruben, 1996) and with FDI inflows into nations. Specifically, Mansfield's study links the strength of IP protection with the transfer of advanced technology to nations (Mansfield, 1994). In general, patent intensity is correlated with the market value of companies. But other studies show that patents are a crucial strategic asset, or the key to revenue appropriation, principally in the chemical, pharmaceutical, machinery, electrical and electronic sectors. For other industries and services, unregistered "know-how" or tacit knowledge can be more important.

The rate of registration of intellectual property claims in novel ways such as patents for "business methods" or in new areas such as the Internet are rising rapidly (Davies, 1999). So also is the enactment of IP legislation and its effective enforcement around the world (Ginarte and Park, 1997).

What does this mean for alliance formation? Anecdotal evidence suggests that in many cases such as the long-lived Fuji–Xerox alliance, proprietary information is shared with allies because strong patents and clearly defined territories reduce the worry of competition from partners. Greater trust, derived from strong patents or intellectual property protection, helps alliance formation. In a study of the global expansion of hotel chains, Contractor and Kundu (1998) show that alliances involving a local partner in franchising, joint ventures or management service agreements are the dominant international strategy. They posit that one reason for the ubiquity of alliance arrangements in hotels is the strategic threat of withdrawal of the global brand name wielded by the global firm over its partners. Thus, the existence of effective and valuable brands as an enforceable intellectual property right enables many alliances to occur, i.e. the Xerox brand name's value to Fuji.

This conclusion, that strong IP protection fosters alliances, is also supported in empirical studies in supply-chain alliances (Marsh and Griffiths, 1999) and in international R&D alliances in a study by Oxley (1999). In these studies, this is inferred from the fact that stronger (i.e. hierarchical) governance mechanisms are preferred when IP protection is weaker. On the other hand, more efficient markets for knowledge together has led to a preference for alliance types with stronger IP protection. This is attested by a seemingly dramatic increase in the share of non-equity alliances in total alliances in the MERIT database of technology alliances, from below 10 percent in 1970 to nearly 90 percent in 1997 (Duyesters, Kok, and Vaandrager, 2000). In general, IP protection fosters alliances of all kinds (and, within alliance types, tends to favor non-equity modes).

3.2. Knowledge management in firms (P or E)

3.2.1. Identification and codification of knowledge assets in firms (P)

In recent years there has been a conscious effort in companies to inventory technical assets and strategic capability, so-called technology-audits (Contractor and Narayanan, 2000). This reflects the recent emphasis on knowledge management (Nahapiet and Hoshal, 1998) and the growing importance of intellectual property registration and enforcement (Bordwin, 1999). By performing such an audit, and then launching an aggressive licensing program, Dow Chemicals was, for instance, able to sign licensing agreements which would yield an estimated revenue increase of over $ 100 million (Davenport, De Long and Beers, 1998). Much of high-technology or knowledge-intensive business is characterized by high fixed or sunk costs but very low variable cost. There is a creating–codifying–transferring sequence in alliance strategy.

1 The costs of creating knowledge can be very large.
2 The cost of codifying it is smaller (Nelson and Winter, 1982).
3 Once codified however, the cost of transferring the knowledge to another ally or location can be relatively small.
4 The strategy of several companies, like Skandia for instance, is predicated in part on identifying intellectual capital or "knowing what we know", then codifying this knowledge in a template, and then replicating this template in other country locations using many allies (Edvinsson, 1997).

Codification of knowledge and low-cost replication in ally firms and in other locations underlie the basic strategy of franchising, be it for fast food, hotels or servicing marine diesel engines worldwide. The sharp rise in non-equity forms of alliances, such as licensing and franchising, is partially due to advances in codification and easier replication of knowledge.

Other forms of codification involve expert systems or artificial intelligence programs (Blumentritt and Johnson, 1999). Let us, for instance, consider Precision Feeder Inc., which manufactures vibrating hoppers or feeders that precisely meter the flow of powders or liquids in packaging assembly lines. Because the materials handled are so diverse, from solid grains to liquids, and vary in particle size, density, viscosity, moisture content, etc, to name but a few variables, no single design will work. There are thousands of possible configurations, and because of the large number of design parameters, there is no deterministic design solution. When a client brings in a new material to be packaged, the traditional method in the firm was to use trial and error and the design experience residing in the minds of its engineers. However, the firm had records of over a thousand of its past jobs, covering a range of materials, over many years. With these data now computerized, an expert system software program gives design guidance that greatly reduces trial and error and saves design time for a new material. This not only confers a competitive advantage on Precision Feeder Inc. but enabled it to license its proprietary software and data to licensees around the world. With strictly defined territories, the fear of foreign allies competing with the licensor was considered low. Thus, codified design experience enabled Precision Feeder to serve, via alliance agreements, foreign markets it could never have hoped to reach on its own.

Mere data banks are little more than raw information. It is their interpretation that matters. DaimlerChrysler, for instance, is writing "books of knowledge" in several automobile design areas; for example, crash resistance. Here the focus is not just on historical crash test data, but expert engineers also include essays on how to interpret the information and use it in future designs (Davenport, De Long and Beers, 1998). Once codified, such information can be shared with allies at low transfer cost.

3.2.2. Acceleration in the rate of technical change (E)

As far back as twenty years ago, Pennings (1981) observed that the desire of companies for collective or cooperative strategies was negatively correlated with environmental or technological stability. Since then, the rate of technical development has accelerated, product cycles have shortened and the number of alliances has exploded (*Economist*, 2000). Entire industries have been shaken up by technological discontinuities. Take, for instance, the influx of biotechnology into the pharmaceutical field. Instead of new firms displacing incumbents in a classic Schumpeterian "creative destruction", we now have new firms and old ones forming alliances. As an example, Genentech licensed recombinant DNA insulin to Eli Lilly. This exemplifies a typical alliance pattern in the industry, where the industry newcomer hands over the marketing of the new drug to older, established partners that have the commercialization know-how, capital and distribution network in place. Instead of Schumpeterian creative destruction of incumbent companies, we have co-option by them towards newcomers (Greis, Dibner, and Bean, 1995) (Kogut, Walker, and Kim, 1995).

3.2.3. Growing diversity of knowledge sources (E)

In general, rapid technical change has meant that, in all sectors, but particularly in ones such as biotechnology, software, aircraft, computers, and telecommunications, knowledge and capability are fragmented. Firms increasingly consider their own internal knowledge as incomplete because the needed number of technology sources and component sources has escalated (Grandstrand, Hakanson, and Sjolander, 1993). At the same time, another recent trend, namely focusing on "core competence", has meant that companies are deliberately narrowing their focus. Hence the need for external acquisition of knowledge is inevitably greater, and alliances provide one means of acquiring capability externally. In many instances this may be the only option when dealing with advanced knowledge sources. In the above-mentioned industries, learning and capability collectively reside in a network of firms that operate in ever-shifting and re-forming coalitions reacting to each wave of technical change (Powell, Koput, and Smith-Doerr, 1996); (Mowery, Oxley, and Silverman, 1998).

3.2.4. How alliances can reduce escalating R&D costs and risks (P)

Alliances can lower the risk of escalating R&D costs in knowledge-intensive sectors in at least three ways. First, in collaborative R&D, not only can we make the obvious point that cost and risk are shared, but the technological and fixed plant synergies across the research partnership can also reduce the total project cost compared to one of the allies undertaking the task alone. The Boeing 777 model is said to have been developed at much lower cost than if Boeing alone had undertaken the development — and in half the time. This was done by using a globally connected IT network into which allies as well as future customers could plug (Kasarda and Rondinelli, 1998). For smaller products having a large model variety, designing and holding an inventory entails risks. Sharing custody of the design process with the customer virtually eliminates such risks and sunk costs, and cements ties with the client. This is illustrated by Ross Operating Valve Company whose engineers work with customers via computer to rapidly customize design parts to users' specifications, then transmit these designs instantaneously to plants in Michigan, Germany, the UK or Japan, from where the valves are quickly produced and shipped out. Joint design eliminates inventory risk and speculative sunk costs, speeds the operation and satisfies the customer. In a very loose sense, this makes the customer your "ally", and customers are thus co-creators of value (Prahalad and Ramaswamy, 2000). Dell is another example of this.

Second, in the application of the technology, alliance partners can provide increasing network returns to scale and economies of scope (Shapiro and Varian, 1998). A network of producers also reduces risk in the commercialization stage (Kotabe, Sahay, and Aulakh, 1996). The previously discussed Precision Feeder Inc. case can serve as an illustration here.

Third, R&D risk can be lowered by alliances used as a device to win "learning races" (Powell, 1998). In sectors that reward "first-to-market" or where technical standards are yet to be set, speed is perhaps particularly of the essence. If an alliance coalition's standards become the norm, that can confer enormous oligopolistic advantage and lock in market share. Particularly in situations where multiple technologies need to be applied, cross-licensing coalitions that exchange and pool their technologies can win the race to market (Grindley and Teece, 1997).

3.3. Changes in production and distribution (P or E)

Advances in Information Technology have led to new production methods, with greater emphasis on speed of execution and delivery. Moreover, customers often prefer variety and speed over lowest cost. These changes are leading to a de-construction of the value chain into greater specialization, with different pieces of the value chain occupied by different firms cooperating with each other. These cooperating allies are more agile, more flexible or more responsive to demand changes, and can make different batches to smaller efficient scale than before. In more and more sectors, flexible batch production or even mass customization is replacing the old Fordian system of mass production.

3.3.1. Trend towards outsourcing and de-construction of the value chain (P)

Cisco Systems, a company which used to have one of the world's largest capitalizations, but is still fundamentally successful, is "…quickly getting out of the business of making things…" and increasingly relies on outside procurement (Freidland and McWilliams, 2000). Interestingly, procurement in the US and

Mexico is replacing sourcing from China despite Mexican wages being four times as high and US wages over ten times as high compared to China. Why? Procurement is in fact not on an arm's-length basis, but requires close coordination of delivery, rapid turnaround, retooling and even some joint design, undertaken by Cisco with its partner suppliers — in short, a set of alliance relationships. It is typically easier to build an alliance relationship in North America than in China. Moreover, shipment from China takes two to three weeks, compared to a day or two in North America.

Agility and flexibility are needed in suppliers, and therefore there is also a greater need for close coordination with suppliers acting as allies. This would not be new to the Japanese who have long had familial relationships with suppliers in a "keiretsu" system which has been transplanted in the US to some extent by supplier firms accompanying Japanese FDI to the US (Martin, Swaminathan, and Mitchell, 1998).

Inventory is, after all, merely the physical manifestation of imperfect information and coordination. (Assuming perfect information and coordination, no inventories would be needed.) With heightened coordination and information flows across Cisco's allies, the higher manufacturing costs in Mexico and the US (compared to China) are typically more than offset by the benefits of shorter delivery, agility and flexibility. Dell's component inventories have fallen from 31 days in 1996 to just 6 days in 2000 (*Economist*, 2000).

By agility and flexibility is meant that the size of the average production run is declining. This is the counterpart to saying that the number of model changes per firm per year has escalated — witness Cisco's rate of nearly one per day. On the supply side, factories must be able to retool in hours and begin to produce a new model with minimal down time. On the demand side, customers clearly reward variety and customization. When customers "build" their own computer on Dell's web site, Dell not only delivers customized satisfaction, but also gets paid in advance, unlike traditional manufacturing where the company finances production and distribution and then waits for a sale.

Customization also occurs when a former commodity supply business turns into a service alliance relationship. Boonton Purification Inc was, for instance, ten years ago a supplier of water purification chemicals to a variety of end users, ranging from steel to plastics industries. Being almost a commodity, the company faced severe price pressure. The options seemed to be to relocate their production to a low-cost emerging nation or to go into bankruptcy. Instead, Boonton Purification turned themselves into a service firm. Today they not only supply the water purification chemicals, but also perform and manage that entire function inside the client firms. Their monitoring instrumentation is mounted inside the client's facilities from where data are fed to Boonton Purification's computers for analysis and remediation. This requires considerable trust and coordination — in short, a supply chain alliance relationship.

Many similar examples abound in marketing and distribution. Procter and Gamble have permanent staff and a whole department inside Walmart's headquarters offices (Zinn and Parasuraman, 1997). As already noted, Bose Corporation requires that a full-time representative from major supplier firms be present in their company, not only to coordinate the supply chain, but also to participate in the R&D process for new models. Elsewhere, suppliers have taken over retailer functions such as stock control and point-of-sale display in the retail establishment.

3.3.2. The increasing strategic importance of speed (P or E)

We have alluded to several aspects of the strategic importance of speed. First, there tends to be a transition from inefficient markets to speedier spot markets. This was illustrated earlier by the deregulation in the electric power sector. Oligopolistic structures in electricity supply are being replaced by agile spot market intermediaries that rely on fast and continuous demand (usage) information transmitted by wireless modem from customers to IT headquarters for aggregation. Second, supply chain alliances are becoming common, being predicated on speed, flexibility and close coordination to reduce inventories and to supply users' demand for greater variety. Third, these are learning races in innovation, where alliances are formed in order to speed R&D at a rate not possible for go–it–alone firms. Fourth, speed-to-market is more and more a critical success factor, predicated upon capturing market share (Kotabe, Sahay, and Aulakh, 1996). Fifth, speed is also driven by the awareness of a short or transient product cycle. Roy and Dugal (1999), for example, recount instances where licensing is motivated by the desire to speedily maximize returns from transitory innovations.

3.3.3. Multiplicity of end applications of technologies and customization (E)

Another trend in several industries is that the end applications of technologies have multiplied, raising uncertainty and raising the "appropriability" problem. This means that the firm considering expenditures in R&D may not feel able to capture an adequate return from "spillovers" into other areas. This dampens the incentives for R&D, unless participating in an alliance provides a means for greater appropriability. A recent study indicates that in sectors with weak appropriability there is a higher propensity to participate in R&D consortia (Sakakibara, 2000). Kotabe, Sahay and Aulakh (1996) suggested that "technology is blurring the boundaries between industries previously considered unrelated…". The chemical industry is a good example. Accounting for 2 percent of the US GDP, and recipient of 12 percent of all patents, it produces over 70,000 different products; and chemicals go into virtually every industrial segment, transportation and services. The diversity of end applications being enormous, and its totality unknown to any single firm, the chemicals industry has increased returns via alliances — and could probably do even more! Dollinger and Golden found that the more "fragmented" the industry, the greater the incidence of alliances of all types (Dollinger and Golden, 1992). Firms have set up "Technology Marketing", "Licensing" and "Alliance Management" departments to increase the returns on their corporate knowledge (Contractor and Narayanan, 2000).

When the end applications of an emerging technology are uncertain, alliances in start-up firms, involving, for instance, a small equity stake or a contractual obligation to share the fruits of R&D, can be a way of buying "real options." In 1999 Microsoft is reported to have spent a staggering $ 7 billion buying small stakes in hundreds of startups. Such stakes can be akin to buying options to potentially interesting technologies, or they could be an option to enter certain new markets.

3.3.4. The role of information technology in alliance relationships (P)

Thirty-five percent of real economic growth in the US between 1995 and 1998 was attributable to information technology (IT) according to the US Department of Commerce (1999). IT has been one of the key drivers to the formation of alliances, as we have seen in several examples earlier in the paper. We shall highlight seven aspects of IT's role in alliances.

- Joint design by spatially separated partners, as we saw in the Boeing 777 case or with Ross Operating Valve Company. Extending this further, by enabling each customer to design their own configuration, we see how IT is ushering in an era of
- Mass customization, as in the case of Dell Computers and in many other areas, ranging from course packets used in education, to garments custom cut and tailored to fit each user (*Economist*, 2000).
- Communication and coordination of allies over the value chain is illustrated by Caterpillar's on-line system that allows vendors to access not only their own deliveries and inventories, but also track sales, markets and deliveries of other vendors, in an open system.
- Codification of knowledge in Expert Systems that are then licensable or sharable with allies was illustrated by the Precision Feeder Case. This enabled a small company to have substantial additional revenues from licensees worldwide and access foreign markets that they could never have hoped to tap otherwise.
- Monitoring a large constellation of "partners." This was illustrated in the Skandia story where the insurance firm kept track of minute data on its agents and investment advisers in many nations.
- Enabling spot markets in electricity where nimble market-maker firms balance supply and demand on a continuous basis by obtaining real-time electricity usage readings from customers' meters (made by one ally) and transmitting these readings to IT headquarters by wireless modems (made by another ally firm).
- As an internalized asset for control, reservations and revenue enhancement, as in the case of airline systems such as SABRE or those used in global hotel chains.

[...]

References

Anand, B., and Khanna, T. (2000). Do firms learn to create value? The case of alliances. *Strategic Management Journal*, March 21(3), 295–315.

Blumentritt, R., and Johnson, R. (1999). Towards a strategy for knowledge management. *Technology Analysis and Strategic Management*, 11(3), 287–300.

Bordwin, M. (1999). Protecting your 21st century gold. *Management Review*, 88(9), 49–51.

Business Week (European Edition) (2001). The fall of ENRON. (17 December), 30-35

Caves, R. (1998). Research on international business: Problems and prospects. *Journal of International Business Studies*, 29(1), 5–20.

Cohen, W. M., and Levinthal, D. A. (1990). Absorptive capacity: A new perspective on learning and innovation. *Administrative Science Quarterly*, 35(1), 128–152.

Contractor, F. J. (1985). *Licensing in international strategy: A guide for planning and negotiation.* Westport, CT and London: Quorum Books.

Contractor, F. J. (1999). Licensing compared with foreign equity investment and trading for US-based multinational firms. *Journal of the Licensing Executives Society*, June, 1–10.

Contractor, F. J., and Lorange, P. (1988). Why should firms cooperate? The strategy and economics basis for cooperative ventures. In F. Contractor, and P. Lorange (Eds), *Cooperative strategies in international business* (pp. 3–28). Lexington, MA: Lexington Books.

Contractor, F. J., and Narayanan, V. (2000). Integrating strategic planning with technology management in the global firm. In M. Tayeb (Ed.), *International business: Theories, policies and practices*. Harlow, UK: Pearson.

Contractor, F. J., and Kundu, S. (1998). Modal choice in a world of alliances: Analyzing organizational forms in the international hotel sector. *Journal of International Business Studies*, 29(2), 329–358.

Davenport, T., De Long, D., and Beers, M. (1998). Successful knowledge management projects. *Sloan Management Review*, 39(2), 43–57.

Davies, L. (1999). *A model for Internet regulation?* London: Information Technology Law Unit. (Also at www.scl.org/content/ecommerce).

Dollinger, M., and Golden, P. (1992). Interorganizational and collective strategies in small firms: Environmental effects and performance. *Journal of Management*, 18(4), 695–715.

Dunning, J. (1980). Towards an eclectic theory of international production. *Journal of International Business Studies*, Spring/Summer, 9–31.

Duysters, G., Kok, G., and Vaandrager, M. (2000). Crafting successful strategic technology partnerships. *R&D Management*, 29(4), 343–351.

Economist (1999). Measuring intangible assets: A price on the priceless. (12 June), 61–62.

Economist (2000). All yours. (1 April), 57–58.

Edvinsson, L. (1997). *Intellectual Capital: Realizing Your Company's True Value by Finding Its Hidden Brainpower.* New York: Harper Business.

Freidland, J., and McWilliams, G. (2000). How a need for speed turned Guadalahara into a high-tech hub. *Wall Street Journal*, 2 March, A1.

Gana, R. (1995). Has creativity died in the Third World? Some implications of the internationalization of intellectual property. *Denver Journal of International Law and Policy*, 24(1), 109–144.

Ginarte, J., and Park, W. (1997). Determinants of patent rights: A cross-national study. *Research Policy*, 26, 283–301.

Gould, D., and Gruben, W. (1996). The role of intellectual property rights in economic growth. *Journal of Development Economics*, 48, 323–350.

Grandstrand, O., Hakanson, K., and Sjolander, S. (1993). Internationalisation of R&D – A survey of some recent research. *Research Policy*, 22(5–6), 413–430.

Greis, N., Dibner, M., and Bean, A. (1995). External partnering as a response to innovation barriers and global competition in biotechnology. *Research Policy*, 24, 609–630.

Grindley, P., and Teece, D. (1997). Managing intellectual capital: Licensing and cross-licensing in semiconductors and electronics. *California Management Review*, 39(2), 8–41.

Gulati, R., and Singh, H. (1998). The architecture of cooperation: Managing coordination costs and Appropriation Concerns in Strategic Alliances. *Administrative Science Quarterly*, 43(4), 781–814.

Harbison, J., and Pekar, P. (1997). *Smart Alliances*. New York: Booz, Allen and Hamilton.

Kasarda, J., and Rondinelli, D. (1998). Innovative infrastructure for innovative manufacturers. *Sloan Management Review*, 39(2), 73–82.

Kogut, B., Walker, G., and Kim, D.-J. (1995). Cooperation and entry induction as an extension of technological rivalry. *Research Policy*, 24, 77–95.

Kotabe, M., Sahay, A., and Aulakh, P. (1996). Emerging role of technology licensing in the development of global product strategy: Conceptual framework and research propositions. *Journal of Marketing*, 60(1), 73–88.

Lissack, M., and Roos, J. (1999). *The next common sense*. London: Nicholas Brealey Publishing.

Lorange, P., and Roos, J. (1992). *Strategic alliances: Formation. implementation and evolution*. Oxford: Blackwell.

Mansfield, E. (1994). *Intellectual property protection, foreign direct investment and technology transfer*. Washington, DC: World Bank.

Marshall, R. (1997). Patents, antitrust and the WTO/GATT: Using TRIPS as a vehicle for antitrust harmonization. *Law and Policy in International Business*, 28(4), 1165–1193.

Marsh, P., and Griffiths, F. (1999). Copyrights and wrongs. *Supply Management*, 4(19), 59.

Martin, X., Swaminathan, A., and Mitchell, W. (1998). Organizational evolution in the interorganizational environment: Incentives and constraints on international expansion strategy. *Administrative Science Quarterly*, 43, 566–601.

Mowery, D., Oxley, J., and Silverman, B. (1998). Technological overlap and interfirm cooperation: Implications for the resource based view of the firm. *Research Policy*, 27, 507–523.

Nahapiet, J., and Ghoshal, S. (1998). Social capital, intellectual capital, and the organizational advantage. *Academy of Management Review*, 23(2), 242–266.

Nelson, R., and Winter, S. (1982). *An evolutionary theory of economic change*. Cambridge, MA: Harvard University Press.

Ostry, S. (1998). Technology, productivity and the multinational enterprise. *Journal of International Business Studies*, 29(1), 85–100.

Oxley, J. (1999). Institutional environment and the mechanisms of governance: The impact of intellectual property protection on the structure of interfirm alliances. *Journal of Economic Behavior and Organization*, 38, 283–309.

Pennings, J. (1981). Strategically interdependent organizations. In P. Nystrom, and W. Starbuck (Eds.), *Handbook of organizational design* (pp. 433–455). New York: Oxford University Press.

Powell, W. (1998). Learning from collaboration: Knowledge and networks in the biotechnology and pharmaceutical industry. *California Management Review*, 40, 228–240.

Powell, W., Koput, W., and Smith-Doerr, L. (1996). Interorganizational collaboration and the locus of innovation. *Administrative Science Quarterly*, 41, 116–145.

Prahalad, C. K., and Ramaswamy, V. (2000). Co-opting customer competence. *Harvard Business Review*, January–February, 79–87.

Roy, M., and Dugal, S. (1999). The effect of technological environment and competitive strategy on licensing decisions. *American Business Review*, 17(2), 112–118.

Safarian, A. E., and Dobson, W. (1997). *The people link. Human resource linkages across the Pacific*. Toronto and London: University of Toronto Press.

Sakakibara, M. (2000). Formation of R&D consortia: Industry and company effects. Working paper 002 (UCLA CIBER).

Shapiro, C., and Varian, H. R. (1998). *Information rules: A strategic guide to the network economy*. Boston MA: Harvard Business School Press.

Survey of Current Business (1995). *The national income and product accounts of the United States*. Survey of Current Business.

Sveiby, K.-E. (1998). *Measuring intangibles and intellectual capital – An emerging first standard.* Internet Version, August: 1–10.

Tobin, J. (1969). A general equilibrium approach to monetary theory. *Journal of Money, Credit and Banking*, February, 15–29.

UNCTAD (1992 and 1995). *World Development Report*. New York: United Nations.

US Department of Commerce (1999). *The Emerging Digital Economy*. Washington, D.C.: U.S. Government Printing Office.

Von Hippel, E. (1994). 'Sticky information' and the locus of problem solving: Implications for innovation. *Management Science*, 40(4), 429–439.

Williamson, O. E. (1985). *The economic institutions of capitalism: Firms, markets and relational contracting*. New York: Free Press.

Zinn, W., and Parasuraman, A. (1997). Scope and intensity of logistics-based strategic alliances. *Industrial Marketing Management*, 26, 137–147.

15

COMPETITION FOR COMPETENCE AND INTER-PARTNER LEARNING WITHIN INTERNATIONAL STRATEGIC ALLIANCES

Gary Hamel

Source: Edited from *Strategic Management Journal*, 1991, Vol. 12, pp. 83–103.

The research question

A skills-based view of the firm

It is possible to conceive of a firm as a portfolio of core competencies on one hand, and encompassing disciplines on the other, rather than as a portfolio of product-market entities (Prahalad and Hamel, 1990). As technology bundles, core competencies make a critical contribution to the unique functionality of a range of end-products. An example is Honda's expertise in powertrains, which is applied to products as diverse as automobiles, motorcycles, generators, and lawn mowers. Encompassing disciplines includes total quality control, just-in-time manufacturing systems, value engineering, flexible manufacturing systems, accelerated product development, and total customer service. Such disciplines allow a product to be delivered to customers at the best possible price/performance trade-off. Core competencies and value-creating disciplines are precisely the kinds of firm-specific skills for which there are only imperfect external markets, and hence form the *raison d'être* for the multinational enterprise (Buckley and Casson, 1985; Caves, 1971; Teece, 1981).

Conceiving of the firm as a portfolio of core competencies and disciplines suggests that inter-firm competition, as opposed to inter-product competition, is essentially concerned with the acquisition of skills. In this view global competitiveness is largely a function of the firm's pace, efficiency, and extent of knowledge accumulation. The traditional 'competitive strategy' paradigm (e.g. Porter, 1980), with its focus on product-market positioning, focuses on only the last few hundred yards of what may be a skill-building marathon. The notion of competitive advantage (Porter, 1985) which provides the means for computing product-based advantages at a given point in time (in terms of cost and differentiation), provides little insight into the process of knowledge acquisition and skill building.

Core competencies and value-creating disciplines are not distributed equally among firms. Expansion-minded competitors, exploiting such firm-specific advantages, bring the skill deficiencies of incumbents into stark relief. The present study was unconcerned with why such discrepancies in skill endowments exist, but was very concerned with the role international strategic alliances might play in effecting a partial redistribution of skills among partners. While 'globalization' has been widely credited for provoking a shift to collaborative strategies (Ghemawat, Porter and Rawlinson, 1986; Hergert and Morris, 1988; Ohmae, 1989; Perlmutter and Heenan, 1986), the ways in which strategic alliances either enhance or diminish the skills which underlie global competitiveness have been only partially specified. The goal of the present research was to understand the extent to which and means through which the collaborative process might lead to a reapportionment of skills between the partners. While skills discrepancies have been recognized as a motivator for international collaboration (Contractor and Lorange, 1988; Root, 1988), the crucial distinction between acquiring such skills in the sense of gaining access to them – by taking out a license, utilizing a subassembly supplied by a partner, or relying on a partner's employees for some critical operation – and actually internalizing a partner's skills has seldom been clearly drawn. This distinction is crucial. As long as a partner's skills are embodied only in the specific outputs of the venture, they have no value outside the narrow terms of the agreement. Once internalized, however, they can be applied to new geographic markets, new products, and new businesses. For the partners, an alliance may be not only a means for trading access to each other's skills – what might be termed quasi-internalization – but also a mechanism for actually acquiring a partner's skills – *de facto* internalization.

A conception of strategic alliances as opportunities for *de facto* internalization was suggested during a major research project on 'competition for competence' in which the author participated (Prahalad and Hamel, 1990). In that study managers often voiced a concern that, when collaborating with a potential competitor, failure to 'out-learn' one's partner could render a firm first dependent and then redundant within the partnership, and competitively vulnerable outside it. The two premises from which this concern issued seemed to be that (1) few alliances were perfectly and perpetually collusive, and (2) the fact that a firm chose to collaborate with a present or potential competitor could not be taken as evidence that that firm no longer harbored a competitive intent *vis-à-vis* its partner. Indeed, when it came to the competitive consequences of inter-partner learning, the attitudes of some managers in the initial study had shifted from naivety to paranoia within a few short years. This seemed to be particularly true for managers in alliances with Japanese partners. What was lacking was any systematic investigation of the determinants of inter-partner learning.

[…]

The findings

The six major propositions which grew out of the data are summarized in Table 15.1. They will be discussed in turn, and the evidence which produced them briefly summarized.

Competitive collaboration

Though not always readily admitting it, several partners clearly regarded their alliances as transitional devices where the primary objective was the internalization of partner skills. As one Japanese manager put it:

> We've learned a lot from [our partner]. The [foreign] environment was very far from us – we didn't understand it well. We learned that [our partner] was very good at developing. Our engineers have learned much from the relationship.

A European manager stated that:

> [Our partner] was passionately hungry to find out the requirements of the users in the markets they wanted to serve. We were priming the market for them.

A manager in a Japanese firm that had to contend with a persistently inquisitive European partner believed that:

> The only motivation for [our European partner] is to get mass manufacturing technology. They see [the alliance] as a short circuit. As soon as they have this they'll lose interest.

This manager believed that the partner would see eventual termination of the agreement as evidence of successful learning, rather than of a failed collaborative venture.

While no manager in the study claimed a desire to 'deskill' partners, there were several cases in which managers believed this had been the outcome of the collaborative process. In these cases the competitive implications of unanticipated (and typically unsanctioned) skill transfers were clearly understood, albeit retrospectively.

The president of the Asia-Pacific division of an American industrial products company was in no doubt that his firm's Japanese partner had emerged from their 20-year alliance as a significant competitor:

> We established them in their core business. They learned the business from us, mastered our process technology, enjoyed terrific margins at home, where we did not compete in parallel, and today challenge us outside of Japan.

TABLE 15.1 A theory of inter-partner learning: Core propositions

1. Competitive collaboration

(a) Some partners may regard internalization of scarce skills as a primary benefit of international collaboration.

(b) Where learning is the goal, the termination of an agreement cannot be seen as failure, nor can its longevity and stability be seen as evidence of success.

(c) Asymmetries in learning within the alliance may result in a shift in relative competitive position and advantage between the partners outside the alliance. Thus some partners may regard each other as competitors as well as collaborators.

2. Learning and bargaining power

(a) Asymmetries in learning change relative bargaining power within the alliance: successful learning may make the original bargain obsolete and may, *in extremis*, lead to a pattern of unilateral, rather than bilateral, dependence.

(b) The legal and governance structure may exert only a minor influence over the pattern of inter-partner learning and bargaining power.

(c) A partner that understands the link between inter-partner learning, bargaining power, and competitiveness will tend to view the alliance as a race to learn.

3. Intent as a determinant of learning

(a) The objectives of alliance partners, with respect to inter-partner learning and competence acquisition, may be usefully characterized as internalization, resource concentration, or substitution.

(b) An internalization intent will be strongest in firms which conceive of competitiveness as competence-based, rather than as product-based, and which seek to close skill gaps rather than to compensate for skills failure.

(c) A substitution intent pre-ordains asymmetric learning; for systematic learning to take place, operators must possess an internalization intent.

4. Transparency as a determinant of learning

(a) Asymmetry in transparency pre-ordains asymmetric learning: some firms and some skills may be inherently more transparent than others.

(b) Transparency can be influenced through the design of organizational interfaces, the structure of joint tasks, and the 'protectiveness' of individuals.

5. Receptivity as a determinant of learning

(a) Asymmetry in receptivity pre-ordains asymmetric learning: some firms may be inherently more receptive than others.

(b) Receptivity is a function of the skills and absorptiveness of receptors, or exposure position, and of parallelism in facilities.

6. The determinants of sustainable learning

Whether learning becomes self-sustaining – that is, whether the firm eventually becomes able, without further inputs from its partner, to improve its skills at the same rate as its partner – will depend on the depth of learning that has taken place, whether the firm possesses the scale and volume to allow, in future, amortization of the investment needed to break free of dependence on the partner, and whether the firm possesses the disciplines of continuous improvement.

The divisional vice-president of a Western computer company had a similar interpretation of his firm's trans-Pacific alliance:

> A year and a half into the deal I understood what it was all about. Before that I was as naive as the next guy. It took me that long to see that [our partner] was preparing a platform to come into all our markets.

Yet another manager felt a partner had crossed the line distinguishing collaboration from competition:

> If they were really our partners, they wouldn't try to suck us dry of technology ideas they can use in their own products. Whatever they learn from us, they'll use against us worldwide.

Recognizing the potential danger of turning collaborators into competitors, a senior executive in a Japanese firm hoped his firm's European partners would be 'strong – but not too strong.'

The proposition that partners possessing parallel internalization and international expansion goals would find their relationships more contentious than partners with asymmetric intents arose, in part, from observing the markedly different relationships that existed between three partners in a triadic alliance. The British firm in the alliance, possessing neither an internalization intent nor global expansion goals, enjoyed a placid relationship with its Japanese partner. However, the French and Japanese firms in the alliance, each possessed of ambitious learning and expansion goals, were often at loggerheads. A technical manager in the Japanese firm remarked that:

> The English were easier to work with than the French. The English were gentlemen, but the French were [not]. We could reach decisions very quickly with the English, but the French wanted to debate and debate and debate.

This seemed to be a reaction to the difficulty of bargaining with a partner who possessed equally ambitious learning goals.

In general, whenever two partners sought to extract value in the same form from their partnership – whether in the form of inter-partner learning benefits or short-term economic benefits – managers were likely to find themselves frequently engaged in contentious discussions over value-sharing. The relationships where managers were least likely to be troubled by recurring arguments over value appropriation were those where one partner was pursuing, unequivocably, a learning intent and the other a short-term earnings maximization intent. In such relationships – there were three – one partner was becoming progressively more dependent on the other. That the British firm mentioned above ultimately withdrew from the business on which the alliance was based suggested a fundamental proposition: just as contentiousness does not, by itself, indicate collaborative failure (some managers recognized they had to accept a certain amount of contentiousness as the price for protecting their core skills and gaining access to their partner's), an abundance of harmony and good will does not mean both partners are benefiting equally in terms of enhanced competitiveness. Collaborative success could not be measured in terms of a 'happiness index.'

Learning and bargaining power

The link between learning and bargaining power emerged clearly in several cases, one of which is briefly summarized here. A European firm in the study had entered a sourcing agreement with a Japanese partner in the mid-1970s, and later, partly through the use of political pressure, had succeeded in enticing the Japanese partner into a European-based manufacturing joint venture to produce a sophisticated electronics product that had, heretofore, been sourced by the European firm from Japan. At the time the joint venture was entered, the European firm established a corporate-wide goal to gain an independent, 'worldclass,' capability to develop and manufacture the particular product. This was seen as part of a broader corporate-wide effort to master mass manufacturing skills that were viewed as crucial to the firm's participation in a host of electronics businesses. Over the next 7 years, the European firm worked assiduously to internalize the skills of its Japanese partner. By the late 1980s the firm had progressed through six of the seven 'steps' it had identified on the road from dependence to independence – where the journey began with a capability for assembling partner-supplied sub-assemblies using partner-specified equipment and process controls, and ended with a capability for simultaneous advance of both product design and manufacturing disciplines (i.e. design for manufacturability, component miniaturization, materials science, etc.), independent of further partner technical assistance.

In interviews with both the European firm and its Japanese partner, it became clear that the bargaining power of the Continental firm had grown as its learning had progressed. For the European firm, each stage of learning, when complete, became the gateway to the next stage of internalization. Successful learning at each stage effectively obsolesced the existing 'bargain,' and constituted a *de facto* query to the Japanese partner: 'Now what are you going to do for us?' As the firm moved nearer and nearer its goal of independence, it successively raised the 'price' for its continued participation in the alliance. The Japanese partner also learned through the alliance. Managers credited the venture with giving them insight into unique customer needs and the standards-setting environment in Europe. However, the Japanese firm could not easily obsolesce the initial bargain; this due not to any learning deficiency on its part, but to the difficulty of unwinding a politically visible relationship.

The notion of collaboration as a race to learn emerged directly from the interview data. As one Western manager put it:

If they [our partner] learn what we know before we learn what they know, we become redundant. We've got to try to learn faster than they do.

Several Western firms in the study seemed to have discovered that where bargaining power could not be maintained by winning the race to learn, it might be maintained through other means. In a narrow sense managers saw collaboration as a race to learn, but in a broader sense they saw it as a race to remain 'attractive' to their partners. A European manager stated:

You must continually add to the portfolio of things that make you desirable to your partner. Many of the things that [our partner] needed us for in the early days, it doesn't need now. It needed to establish a base of equipment in Europe and we have done this for them. You must ensure that you always have something to offer your partner – some reason for them to continue to need you.

Managers in a Japanese firm whose European partner had shown a high propensity to learn, believed that ultimate control came from being ahead in the race to create next-generation competencies. Leadership here brought partial control over standards, the benefits of controlling the evolution of technology, and the product price and performance advantages of being first down the experience curve. One senior manager put it succinctly:

Friendship is friendship, but competition is competition. Competition is about the future and that is R&D.

Here was a suggestion that partners in competitive alliances may sometimes be more likely to view collaboration as a race to get to the future first, rather than a truly cooperative effort to invent the future together. Again, this provided evidence of a subtle blending of competitive and collaborative goals.

The greater the experience of interviewees in administering or working within collaborative arrangements, the more likely were they to discount the extent to which the formal agreement actually determined patterns of learning, control, and dependence within their partnerships. The formal agreement was seen as essentially static, and the race for capability acquisition and control essentially dynamic. As the interviewing progressed it became possible to array the factors which interviewees typically associated with power and control. Power came first from the relative pace at which each partner was building new capabilities internally, then from an ability to out-learn one's partner, then from the relative contribution of 'irreplaceable' inputs by each partner to the venture, then from the relative share of value-added, then from the operating structure (which partner's employees held key functional posts), then from the governance structure (which partner was best represented on the board and key executive committees), and finally from the legal structure (share of ownership and legally specified terms for the division of equity and profits). On this basis it was possible, for several of the alliances, to construct a crude 'relative power metric.' For the triadic partnership mentioned above (British, French, and Japanese), relative power was apportioned as per Table 15.2.

While the legal and managerial power of the British partner was at least equal to that of its counterparts, it failed almost totally to exploit other potential sources of power and control. The British firm's failure to keep pace with its partners in learning and competence-building made its acquisition by one of its partners, or some other ambitious firm, almost inevitable. By way of contrast, the French firm, with no advantage in terms of ownership or executive authority, was able to substantially increase its control of the relationship through a rapid pace of learning. The French firm had substantially increased its R&D budget, hoping eventually to counterbalance its Japanese partner's faster pace of new product development and competence-building. Although the French firm's equity stake remained at 33 percent through most of the 1980s, it continued to enhance its bargaining power by internalizing the skills of its Japanese partner and gaining an

TABLE 15.2 Relative power of partners in a triadic alliance[1] (ranked by perceived importance as determinants of bargaining power)

	British	French	Japanese
1 Relative pace of competence building[2]		+++	+++++
2 Relative success at inter-partner learning		++++	++
3 Relative criticality of inputs[3]		++	+++
4 Relative share of value-added[4]	+	++	++++
5 'Possession' of key operating jobs[5]	++	++	+
6 Representation on governing bodies[6]	++	+	+
7 Legal share of ownership[7]	+	+	+

1 The number of plus signs indicates the relative power within the joint venture that each partner gained from each factor.

2 Managers in the Japanese partner believed their firm was innovating more rapidly than its European partners in the areas of miniaturization, production engineering, and advanced technologies.

3 For most of the venture's early history product designs, process equipment, and high-precision components were supplied exclusively by the Japanese partner.

4 By 1985 European content was approximately 50 percent. The French partner supplied a greater share of the European content than the British partner.

5 The Managing Directors of the two European plants were Europeans. At each plant a Japanese employee held the Deputy Managing Director's post.

6 Each partner was responsible for appointing two representatives to the Supervisory Board and one representative to the Management Board. The agreement stipulated that a European was to be the President of the Supervisory Board. An executive seconded from the British partner occupied this position.

7 Each of the three partners held 33.33 percent of the joint venture's equity.

ever-increasing share of value-added. From the very different experiences of the British and French firms in this alliance came the proposition that power vested in a particular firm through the formal agreement will almost certainly erode if its partners are more adept at internalization or quicker to build valuable new competencies.

The perspectives on bargaining power and learning which emerged from the case analysis also gave rise to propositions regarding the longevity of rivalrous alliances. In general, it appeared that competitively oriented partners would continue to collaborate together so long as they were: (1) equally capable of inter-partner learning or independent skills development, and/or (2) both substantially smaller, and mutually vulnerable, to industry leaders.

Three broad determinants of learning outcomes emerged during the study and constitute the core of the internalization model. Intent refers to a firm's initial propensity to view collaboration as an opportunity to learn; transparency to the 'knowability' or openness of each partner, and thus the potential for learning; and receptivity to a partner's capacity for learning, or 'absorptiveness.' While there was much a firm could do to implant a learning intent, limit its own transparency, and enhance its receptivity, there seemed to be some inherent determinants of inter-partner learning, more or less exogenous to the partnership itself, that either predisposed a firm to positive learning outcomes, or rendered it unlikely to successfully exploit opportunities to learn. [...]

[...]

Discussion

Though this research grew out of an interest in skills-based competition (Nelson and Winter, 1982; Dierickx and Cool, 1989; Quinn, Doorley and Paquette, 1990; Prahalad and Hamel, 1990; Barney, 1990; Teece, Pisano and Shuen, 1990), it is also important to set it within the context of existing research on the management of strategic alliances. The way in which the present study both complements and challenges prior research on collaboration is now discussed.

Joint ventures and other non-market inter-firm agreements have typically been pictured as an intermediate level of integration between arm's-length contracts in open markets and full ownership (Nielsen, 1988; Thorelli, 1986). But where the goal of the alliance is skills acquisition, an alliance may be seen, by one or both partners, not as an optimal compromise between market and hierarchy, to use Williamson's (1975) nomenclature, but as a half-way house on the road from market to hierarchy. In this sense the alliance is viewed not as an alternative to market-based transactions or full ownership, but as an alternative to other modes of skill acquisition. These might include acquiring the partner, licensing from the partner, or developing the needed skills through internal efforts. There are several reasons collaboration may in some cases be the preferred mode of skills acquisition.

For some skills, what Itami (1987) terms 'invisible assets,' the cost of internal development may be almost infinite. Complex skills, based on tacit knowledge, and arising out of a unique cultural context may be acquirable only by up-close observation and emulation of 'best in class.' Alliances may offer advantages of timeliness as well as efficiency. Where global competitors are rapidly building new sources of competitive advantage, as well as enhancing existing skills, a go-it-alone strategy could confine a firm to permanent also-ran status. Alliances may be seen as a way of short-circuiting the process of skills acquisition and thus avoiding the opportunity cost of being a perpetual follower. Motorola's reliance on Toshiba for re-entry to the DRAM semiconductor business seems to reflect such a concern. Internalization via collaboration may be more attractive than acquiring a firm in total. In buying a company the acquirer must pay for non-distinctive assets, and is confronted with a substantially larger organizational integration problem.

Capturing value vs. creating value

There are two basic processes in any alliance: value creation and value appropriation. The extent of value creation depends first on whether the market and competitive logic of the venture is sound, and then on the efficacy with which the two partners combine their complementary skills and resources; that is, how well they perform joint tasks. Each partner then appropriates value in the form of monetary or other benefits. In general, researchers have given more attention to the process of value creation than the process of value appropriation. The primary concern of both the transactions' cost (Hennart, 1988) and strategic position (e.g. Harrigan, 1985) perspectives is the creation of joint value. Transactional efficiency gained through quasi-internalization is one form of value creation; improvement in competitive position is another. Both perspectives provide insights into why firms collaborate; neither captures the dynamics which determine collaborative outcomes, and the individual monetary and long-term competitive gains taken by each partner. Making a collaborative agreement 'work' has generally been seen as creating the preconditions for value creation (Doz, 1988; Killing, 1982, 1983). There is much advice on how to be a 'good' partner (Goldenberg, 1988; Perlmutter and Heenan, 1986) – firms are typically urged to build 'trust' (Harrigan, 1986; Peterson and Shimada, 1978) – but little advice on how to reap the benefits of being a good partner.

There appear to be two mechanisms for extracting value from an alliance: bargaining over the stream of economic benefits that issues directly from the successful execution of joint tasks, and internalizing the skills of partners. These 'value pools' may be conceptually distinct, but they were shown to be related in an important way. Bargaining power at any point in time within an alliance is, *ceteris paribus*, a function of who needs whom the most. This, in turn, is a function of the perceived strategic importance of the alliance to each partner and the attractiveness to each partner of alternatives to collaboration. Depending on its bargaining power a partner will gain a greater or lesser share of the fruits of joint effort. An important issue then is what factors prompt changes in bargaining power. Some factors will be exogenous to the partnership. A change in strategic priorities may suddenly make a partnership much more or much less vital for one of the partners (Franko, 1971). Likewise, a shift in the market or competitive environment could devalue the contribution of one partner and revalue the contribution of the other. Rapid change in technology might produce a similar effect (Harrigan, 1985). However, there is one determinant of relative bargaining power that is very much within the firm's control: its capacity to learn.

While Westney (1988) and Kogut (1988) recognize that learning may be an explicit goal in an alliance, they do not specify the critical linkages between learning, dependency, and bargaining power. Conversely, while Pfeffer and Nowak (1976) and Blois (1980) correctly view alliances as mechanisms for managing interorganizational dependence, they do not take a dynamic view of interdependence, and hence miss the linkage between learning and changes in relative dependency. If bargaining power is a function of relative dependence it should be possible to lessen dependency and improve bargaining power by out-learning one's partner. Most bargains obsolesce with time (Kobrin, 1986); by actively working to internalize a partner's skills it should be possible to accelerate the rate at which the bargain obsolesces. This seems to have been the motivation for Boeing's Japanese partners in recent years (Moxon, 1988). It was clearly the motivation of two of the Japanese partners in the study.

The process of collaborative exchange

Researchers have tended to look at venture and task structure when attempting to account for partnership performance. An equally useful perspective might be that of a collaborative membrane, through which flow skills and capabilities between the partners. The extent to which the membrane is permeable, and in which direction(s) it is permeable determines relative learning. Though researchers and practitioners often seem to be preoccupied with issues of structure – legal, governance and task (Harrigan, 1988; Killing, 1983; Schillaci, 1987; Tybejee, 1988) – the study suggests that these may be only partial determinants of permeability. Conceiving of an alliance as a membrane suggests that access to people, facilities, documents, and other forms of knowledge is traded between partners in an on-going process of collaborative exchange. As operating employees interact day-by-day, and continually process partner requests for access, a series of micro-bargains are reached on the basis of considerations of operational effectiveness, fairness, and bargaining power. Though these bargains may be more implicit than explicit, outlearning a partner means 'winning' a series of micro-bargains. The simple hypothesis is that the terms of trade in any particular micro-bargain may be only partially determined by the terms of trade which prevailed at the time the macro-bargain was struck by corporate officers. A firm may be in a weak bargaining position at the macro level, as NEC undoubtedly was when it entered its alliance with Honeywell in the computer business in the early 1960s, but may be able to strike a series of advantageous micro-bargains if, at the operational level, it

TABLE 15.3 Distinctive attributes of a theory of competitive collaboration

	Traditional perspective	*Alternative perspective*
Collaborative logic	Quasi-internalization	*De facto* internalization
Unit of analysis	Joint outcomes	Individual outcomes
Underlying process	Value creation	Value appropriation
Success determinants	Form and structure (macro-bargain)	Collaborative exchange (micro-bargains)
Success metrics	Satisfaction and longevity	Bargaining power and competitiveness

uniquely possesses the capacity to learn. Restating the bargaining power argument advanced earlier, the cumulative impact of micro-bargains will, to a large extent, determine in whose favor future macro-bargains are resolved.

Success metrics

Where internalization is the goal, the longevity and 'stability' of partnerships may not be useful proxies for collaborative success. Nevertheless, they have often been used as such (Beamish, 1984; Franko, 1971; Gomes-Casseres, 1987; Killing, 1983; Reynolds, 1979). A long-lived alliance may evince the failure of one or both partners to learn. It was interesting to note in the study that, despite collaborative agreements in Japan with Japanese firms spanning several decades, several Western partners were still unable to 'go it alone' in the Japanese market. By way of contrast, there were few cases in which Japanese firms had remained dependent on Western partners for continued access to Western markets (though in one case the Japanese partner ultimately acquired its European partner). Likewise, an absence of contention in the relationship is not, by itself, an adequate success metric. A firm with no ambition beyond investment avoidance and substitution of its partner's competitiveness for its own lack of competitiveness may be perfectly content not to learn from its partner. But where a failure to learn is likely to ultimately undermine the competitiveness and independence of the firm, such contentedness should not be taken as a sign of collaborative success. The theoretical perspective on collaboration developed in this paper is summarized in Table 15.3.

References

Argyris, C. and D. A. Schön. *Organizational Learning*, Addison-Wesley, Reading, MA, 1978.

Baba, Y. 'The dynamics of continuous innovation in scale-intensive industries,' *Strategic Management Journal*, 10, 1989, pp. 89–100.

Ballon, R. J. 'A lesson from Japan: Contract, control, and authority,' *Journal of Contemporary Business*, 8(2), 1979, pp. 27–35.

Barney, J. B. 'Firm resources and sustained competitive advantage.' Unpublished manuscript, Department of Management, Texas A&M University, 1990.

Beamish, P. W. 'Joint venture performance in developing countries.' Unpublished doctoral dissertation, University of Western Ontario, 1984.

Benedict, R. *The Chrysanthemum and the Sword*, reprint (1974), New American Library, New York, 1946.

Block, A. and H. Matsumoto. 'Joint venturing in Japan.' *Conference Board Record*, April 1972, pp. 32–36.

Blois, K. J. 'Quasi-integration as a mechanism for controlling external dependencies,' *Management Decision*, 18(1), 1980, pp. 55–63.

Buckley, P. J. and M. Casson. *Economic Theory of the Multinational Enterprise. Selected Papers*, Macmillan, London, 1985.

Buckley, P. J. and M. Casson. 'A theory of cooperation in international business.' In F. J. Contractor and P. Lorange (eds), *Cooperative Strategies in International Business*, D.C. Heath, Lexington, MA, 1988, pp. 31–53.

Burgelman, R. A. 'A model of the interaction of strategic behavior, corporate context and the concept of strategy,' *Academy of Management Review*, 8(1), 1983a, pp. 61–70.

Burgelman, R. A. 'A process model of internal corporate venturing in the diversified major firm,' *Administrative Science Quarterly*, 28(2), 1983b, pp. 223–244.

Business Week. 'When U.S. joint ventures with Japan go sour,' 24 July 1989, pp. 14–16.

Caves, R. E. 'International corporations: The industrial economics of foreign investment', *Economica*, February 1971, pp. 1-27.

Contractor, F. J. and P. Lorange. 'Why should firms cooperate: The strategy and economic basis for cooperative ventures.' In F. J. Contractor and P. Lorange (eds), *Cooperative Strategies in International Business*, D.C. Heath, Lexington, MA, 1988, pp. 3–28.

Cyert, R. M. and J. G. March. *A Behavioral Theory of the Firm*, Prentice-Hall, Englewood Cliffs, NJ, 1963.

Dierickx, I. and K. Cool. 'Asset stock accumulation and sustainability of competitive advantage,' *Management Science*, December 1989, pp. 1504–1514.

Doz, Y. 'Technology partnerships between larger and smaller firms: Some critical issues.' In F. J. Contractor and P. Lorange (eds), *Cooperative Strategies in International Business*, D.C. Heath, Lexington, MA, 1988, pp. 317–328.

Franko, L. G. *Joint Venture Survival in Multinational Corporations*, Praeger, New York, 1971.

Ghemawat, P., M. E. Porter and R. A. Rawlinson. 'Patterns of international coalition activity.' In M. E. Porter (ed.), *Competition in Global Industries*, Harvard University Press, Boston, MA, 1986, pp. 345–365.

Glaser, B. G. and A. L. Strauss. *The Discovery of Grounded Theory: Strategies for Qualitative Research*, Aldine, New York, 1967.

Goldenberg, S. *International Joint Ventures in Action: How to Establish, Manage and Profit from International Strategic Alliances*, Hutchinson Business Books, London, 1988.

Gomes-Casseres, B. 'Joint venture instability: Is it a problem?' *Columbia Journal of World Business*, Summer 1987, pp. 97–102.

Hamel, G. 'Competitive collaboration: Learning, power and dependence in international strategic alliances.' Unpublished doctoral dissertation, Graduate School of Business Administration, University of Michigan, 1990.

Harrigan, K. R. *Strategies for Joint Ventures*. Lexington Books, Lexington, MA, 1985.

Harrigan, K. R. *Managing for Joint Venture Success*. Lexington Books, Lexington, MA, 1986.

Harrigan, K. R. 'Joint ventures and competitive strategy,' *Strategic Management Journal*, 9, 1988, pp. 141–158.

Hedberg, B. L. T. 'How organizations learn and unlearn.' In P. C. Nystrom and W. H. Starbuck (eds), *Handbook of Organizational Design*, Oxford University Press, Oxford, 1981.

Hennart, J. 'A transaction cost theory of equity joint ventures,' *Strategic Management Journal*, July–August, 9, 1988, pp. 36–74.

Hergert, M. and D. Morris. 'Trends in international collaborative agreements.' In F. J. Contractor and P. Lorange (eds), *Cooperative Strategies in International Business*, D.C. Heath, Lexington, MA, 1988, pp. 99–109.

Imai, M. *Kaizen: The Key to Japan's Competitive Success*, Random House, New York, 1986.

Itami, H. with T. W. Roehl. *Mobilizing Invisible Assets*. Harvard University Press, Cambridge, MA, 1987.

Killing, J. P. 'How to make a global joint venture work,' *Harvard Business Review*, May–June 1982, pp. 120–127.

Killing, J. P. *Strategies for Joint Venture Success*. Praeger, New York, 1983.

Kobrin, S. J. 'Testing the bargaining hypothesis in the manufacturing sector in developing countries,' Unpublished manuscript, 1986.

Kogut, B. 'Joint ventures: Theoretical and empirical perspectives,' *Strategic Management Journal*, 9(4), 1988, pp. 319–322.

Mintzberg, H. 'Patterns in strategy formulation,' *Management Science*, 24(9), 1978, pp. 934–948.

Moxon, R. W., T. W. Roehl and J. F. Truitt. 'International cooperative ventures in the commercial aircraft industry: Gains, sure, but what's my share?' In F. J. Contractor and P. Lorange (eds), *Cooperative Strategies in International Business*, D.C. Heath, Lexington, MA, 1988, pp. 255–278.

Nakane, C. *Japanese Society*. University of California Press, Berkeley, CA, 1970.

Nelson, R. R. and S. G. Winter. *An Evolutionary Theory of Economic Change*, Belknap Press, Cambridge, MA, 1982.

Nielsen, R. P. 'Cooperative strategy,' *Strategic Management Journal*, 9, 1988, pp. 475–492.

Nystrom, P. C. and W. H. Starbuck. 'To avoid organizational crises, unlearn,' *Organizational Dynamics*, 12(4), 1984, pp. 53–65.

Ohmae, K. 'The global logic of strategic alliances,' *Harvard Business Review*, March–April 1989, pp. 143–155.

Ouchi, W. G. 'Markets, bureaucracies, and clans,' *Administrative Science Quarterly*, 25, 1980, pp. 129–141.

Ouchi, W. G. and R. T. Johnson. 'Made in America (under Japanese management),' *Harvard Business Review*, September–October 1974, pp. 61–69.

Perlmutter, H. V. and D. H. Heenan. 'Cooperate to compete globally,' *Harvard Business Review*, March–April 1986, pp. 136–152.

Peterson, R. B. and H. F. Schwind. 'A comparative study of personnel problems in international companies and joint ventures in Japan,' *Journal of International Business Studies*, 8(1), 1977, pp. 45–55.

Peterson, R. B. and J. Y. Shimada. 'Sources of management problems in Japanese–American joint ventures,' *Academy of Management Review*, 3, 1978, pp. 796–804.

Pettigrew, A. M. 'On studying organizational cultures,' *Administrative Science Quarterly*, 24(4), 1979, pp. 570–581.

Pfeffer, J. and P. Nowak. 'Joint ventures and interorganizational interdependence,' *Administrative Science Quarterly*, 21, 1976, pp. 398–418.

Porter, M. E. *Competitive Strategy: Techniques for Analyzing Industries and Competitors*, Free Press, New York, 1980.

Porter, M. E. *Competitive Advantage*, Free Press, New York, 1985.

Postman, L. and B. J. Underwood. 'Critical issues in interference theory,' *Memory and Cognition*, 1, 1973, pp. 19–40.

Prahalad, C. K. and Y. Doz. *Multinational Mission*, Free Press, New York, 1987.

Prahalad, C. K. and G. Hamel. 'The core competence and the corporation,' *Harvard Business Review*, May–June 1990, pp. 71–91.

Quinn, J. B., T. L. Doorley and P. C. Paquette. 'Building leadership in high technology industries: Focus technology strategies on services innovation.' Unpublished paper presented at the Second International Conference on Managing the High Technology Firm, University of Colorado, Boulder, CO, 10 January 1990.

Reich, R. B. and E. D. Mankin. 'Joint ventures with Japan give away our future,' *Harvard Business Review*, March–April 1986, pp. 78–86.

Reynolds, J. I. *Indian–America Joint Ventures. Business Policy Relationships*. University Press of America, Washington, DC, 1979.

Root, F. R. 'Some taxonomies of cooperative arrangements.' In F. J. Contractor and P. Lorange (eds), *Cooperative Strategies in International Business*, D.C. Heath, Lexington, MA, 1988, pp. 69–80.

Schillaci, C. E. 'Designing successful joint ventures,' *Journal of Business Strategy*, 8(2), 1987, pp. 59–63.

Seyle, H. *From Dream to Discovery: On Being a Scientist*, McGraw-Hill, New York, 1964.

Sullivan, J. and R. B. Peterson. 'Factors associated with trust in Japanese–American joint ventures,' *Management International Review*, 22(2), 1982, pp. 30–40.

Teece, D. J. 'The multinational enterprise: Market failure and market power considerations,' *Sloan Management Review*, 22(3), 1981, pp. 3–17.

Teece, D. J., G. P. Pisano and A. Shuen. 'Firm capabilities, resources, and the concept of strategy,' CCC Working Paper No. 90–8, Center for Research in Management, University of California at Berkeley, 1990.

Terpstra, V. and K. David. *The Cultural Environment of International Business*. South-eastern, Cincinnati, OH, 1985.

Thorelli, H. B. 'Networks: Between markets and hierarchies,' *Strategic Management Journal*, 7, 1986, pp. 37–51.

Tybejee, T. T. 'Japan's joint ventures in the United States.' In F. J. Contractor and P. Lorange (eds), *Cooperative Strategies in International Business*, D.C. Heath, Lexington, MA, 1988, pp. 457–472.

Watzlawick, P., J. H. Weakland and R. Fisch. *Change*. Norton, New York, 1974.

Westney, D. E. 'Domestic and foreign learning curves in managing international cooperative strategies.' In F. J. Contractor and P. Lorange (eds), *Cooperative Strategies in International Business*, D.C. Heath, Lexington, MA, 1988, pp. 339–346.

Williamson, O. E. *Markets and Hierarchies: An Analysis and Antitrust Implications*. Free Press, New York, 1975.

16

THE IMPORTANCE OF SOCIAL CAPITAL TO THE MANAGEMENT OF MULTINATIONAL ENTERPRISES
Relational networks among Asian and Western firms

Michael Hitt, Ho-Uk Lee and Emre Yucel

Source: *Asia Pacific Journal of Management*, 2002, Vol. 19.

1 Introduction

> The image of atomistic actors competing for profits against each other in an impersonal marketplace is increasingly inadequate in a world in which firms are imbedded in networks of social, professional and exchange relationships with other organizational actors. ... Such networks encompass a firm's set of relationships, both horizontal and vertical, with other organizations — be they suppliers, customers, competitors, or other entities — including relationships across industries and countries.
>
> (Gulati, Nohria and Zaheer, 2000: 203).

The above quote explains the increasing importance of relationships between firms. Firms navigate in the competitive landscape competing against networks of firms as opposed to individual competitors (Hitt, Keats and DeMarie, 1998b). Firms operating in a network have many more resources they can access to increase their ability to compete than do single firms operating independently. To be competitive, most firms need additional resources and thus attempt to develop their own networks to gain competitive parity or, more importantly, a competitive advantage. In this competitive environment, firms with social capital have an advantage. While the concept of social capital has been embraced by several disciplines with partially varying definitions, relationships, or relational capital, represent a major component of all of them. Thus, for our purposes, we define social capital as the relationships between individuals and organizations that facilitate action and thereby create value (Adler and Kwon, 2002; Seifert, Kraimer and Liden, 2001). The web of social relationships that develops entails norms, values and obligations and yields potential opportunities for the members (Haley and Haley, 1999; Yli-Renko, Autio and Sapienza, 2001).

Social capital has become an important asset to multinational firms because of the need for appropriate resources (e.g. information, technology, knowledge, access to distribution networks, etc.) to compete effectively in global markets. Therefore, multinational firms may be able to gain a competitive advantage because of their social capital. The focus of this work is on social capital, its importance and effects in multinational firms. Importantly, we focus on the differences in the social capital held traditionally by Asian and Western firms.

In the West (i.e. North America, Western Europe), business dealings have been largely based on the concept of transactions. However, in most Asian societies, they are based on relationships. For example, when an executive is regarded as successful in Western societies, s/he is often described as wealthy. However, an executive of similar success in China is referred to as well connected (Chen, 2001). While social capital has become an important concept in recent management literature (e.g. Adler and Kwon, 2002; Tsai and Ghoshal, 1998), the relationships, or relational capital, have been important in the culture, business dealings and academic writings in Asian countries for many centuries (e.g. Wee and Lan, 1998).

Asia encompasses many countries within its geographic borders, however, the three leading countries with the strongest economic impact in world markets are China, Japan, and Korea (Dafter, 2001); thus we focus on these three countries in this chapter. In all three, relationships provide a basis for the culture, business transactions and business operations. For example, the concepts of guanxi in China, kankei in Japan, and *inmak* in Korea all emphasize the importance of relationships or connections in these societies. However, while all three concepts share many similarities, they also have some subtle differences. We elaborate on these concepts in a later section.

The comments above suggest that cultures and institutionalized practices within countries can affect the general managerial practices within firms (Sullivan and Weaver, 2000). For example, research has shown that managers from Asia and from the U.S. develop and apply different strategic orientations (Hitt *et al.*, 1997). These differences may be related to the Asian economic prosperity as well as to the moral hazard that led to the so-called Asian crisis.

Asia experienced a major financial crisis in the late 1990s carrying into the 21st century. However, Asia is composed of multiple markets, not all of which were equally affected by the problems. For example, China continued to experience significant economic growth during the financial crisis. Korea suffered but has rebounded and Japan continues to suffer in 2002. Still, these countries, their cultures and management practices have much to offer that can enhance our knowledge of effective management of multinational firms. Additionally, Asia will continue to grow in economic importance in global markets. For example, it is predicted that 360 million Asians will be accessing the Internet by 2005 (Powell, 2000). This number exceeds the combined total population base of the U.S. and Canada. Also, privately owned Chinese companies, mostly located outside of

China, represent an economic power only behind the U.S., Europe, and Japan (Tsang, 2002).

Chinese, Japanese and Korean management approaches represent significant forces in global markets. As such, managers throughout the world should try to understand and learn from Asian management practices because these perspectives offer alternative applications of successful and effective management in dynamic and uncertain environments (Fruin, 1998). We focus on their contribution to and the importance of the development and management of social capital in multinational organizations. First, we examine the concept of social capital in more depth.

2 Social capital

Social capital has been defined in different ways especially across disciplines. For example, Coleman (1990) states that social capital is created when the relations among individuals change in a manner that facilitates action; whereas Burt (1992), defines social capital as opportunities a player receives through relationships with other players such as colleagues. But both Coleman (1990) and Burt (1992), suggest that social capital springs from the relationships among people. Tsai and Ghoshal (1998) suggest that the norms and values associated with relationships contribute to social capital as well. Thus, most conceptions of social capital include relations or networks of relationships among individuals and organizations. And these relationships facilitate action and thereby create value (Adler and Kwon, 2002; Seifert, Kraimer and Liden, 2001). Therefore, relationships are the most critical dimension of social capital.

Adler and Kwon (2002) noted that the importance of the social capital concept has been increasingly recognized by a number of social science disciplines. They suggested that in recent years social capital has been acknowledged in the field of organization studies as contributing to success in a number of important organizational activities. Among them are inter-unit and inter-firm resource exchange, the creation of intellectual capital, inter-firm learning, supplier relationships, product innovation and entrepreneurship (Adler and Kwon, 2002). Social capital effects range from substantive (e.g. supplier relationships) to facilitative (e.g. innovation and entrepreneurship) (Ahuja, 2000a).

Effective management of businesses requires dissemination, absorption, and utilization of knowledge (Lane and Lubatkin, 1998), especially in the current competitive landscape (Davenport and Prusak, 1997). Firms may acquire knowledge from external sources or develop knowledge internally. Regardless of the source, knowledge must be disseminated throughout the organization for maximum effect. Such dissemination occurs through knowledge networks based on the frequent, repeated, and significant interactions among different members of the organization (Ghoshal and Bartlett, 1990). Knowledge networks extend externally as well to include market relations, hierarchical relations, and social relations (Adler and Kwon, 2002). Knowledge resides in different nodes of the network in the forms of 'conscious knowledge' (articulate knowledge that can be retrieved and stored from records), 'automatic knowledge' (tacit knowledge of individuals), 'objectified knowledge' (the highest form of socially explicit and shared knowledge available) and 'collective knowledge' (tacit experiences and enactment of the collective, routines, etc.) (Brown and Duguid, 1991; Nahapiet and Ghoshal, 1998; Spender, 1996). The most valuable technical and commercial knowledge in organizations is embedded in tacit collective knowledge because of its inimitability and difficulty to transfer.

Social capital can be used to access knowledge but it also is helpful in leveraging and exploiting collective knowledge (Nahapiet and Ghoshal, 1998). Ahuja (2000b) demonstrated how social capital facilitates the creation of inter-firm linkages useful for leveraging and exploiting a firm's knowledge. For example, exchanges based on these linkages can facilitate product innovation, expedite resource exchange (Gabbay and Zuckerman, 1998; Hansen, 1998), and create intellectual capital (Hargadon and Sutton, 1997; Nahapiet and Ghoshal, 1998). While these are positive outcomes, most firms experience information asymmetries that create knowledge gaps because of inadequate knowledge dissemination (Hoopes and Postrel, 1999). However, effective social capital helps to overcome this problem. Social relations impose symmetry through exchanges (Adler and Kwon, 2002) due to 'norms of general reciprocity' (Putnam, 1993), thereby producing information symmetries between members of the organization. Information symmetry, then, contributes to a shared vision through continuous interaction of managers and employees (Lovas and Ghoshal 2000). Multinational firms use internal social capital to integrate units operating in disparate locations and cultures. The internal units operating in multiple and diverse country markets must be bound together by shared values, goals and global vision. Orton and Weick (1990) refer to this as 'loose coupling.' Internal social capital can also contribute to more effective integration in merging acquired firms into the acquiring firm's assets (Harrison et al., 2001). Thus, while social capital partially results from actions to produce harmony, harmony also results from the exercise of social capital, producing a reciprocally interdependent relationship.

Burt (1997) suggests that social capital is a quality of individuals; it contributes to an individual's human capital. For example, a partner's knowledge of and relationship with important clients of a law firm adds value to the partner's human capital and also adds value to the firm (Hitt et al., 2001b). As such, the firm's social capital becomes a partial extension of the partner's social capital. Therefore, it is difficult to separate the firm's social capital from its managers' and employees' relationships with internal and external parties. The firm's strategy is based on its resources, human capital critical among them (Hitt et al., 2001b). The resources such as human capital and social capital are leveraged to implement the firm's strategy and create a competitive advantage. Thus, the firm's relationships with all of its stakeholders produce social capital that serves as input to both strategy formulation and implementation (Lovas and Ghoshal, 2000).

The arguments above suggest that all forms of social capital are critical to the firm's success. For example, social capital is vitally important to multinational firms because they need to effectively integrate internal business units across geographic (e.g. country) boundaries, as well as manage relationships within a large external network of firms (Bartlett and Ghoshal, 1998). Similarly, continuing exchange relations with other organizations often transform into inter-organizational networks. These inter-corporate relationships extend vital advantages. For example, this form of social capital can be used to facilitate market expansion and competitive positioning (Park and Luo, 2001). These actions, in turn, may lead to competitive advantage.

Three dimensions of social capital help to produce competitive advantages. Yli-Renko, Autio and Sapienza (2001) examined social interaction, relationship quality and network ties as dimensions of social capital. Social interaction is necessary to establish the network ties and relationship quality defines the strength of those ties. The quality and strength of a firm's inter-organizational linkages affect its overall success and the value created (Ghoshal and Bartlett, 1990). For example, a firm's relationships with its customers and suppliers have a major effect on its performance and therefore the value it creates for the shareholders.

While most results of social capital are positive, there are some negative consequences as well. For example, firms draw resources from networks and leverage their network ties to take advantage of opportunities. However, they are limited by the boundaries of their network. Firms may be unable to take advantage of some opportunities because the network does not provide access to the appropriate resources to do so. In fact, because of the network's boundaries, the firm may be unable to identify some opportunities. Thus, the boundaries of social capital create opportunity costs. The ties within one network may forestall ties in other networks. Network relationships built over time become self-reinforcing. As such, they lead to a form of path dependency. Firms can only access and/or develop resources allowed by the network ties. Constraints on resources sometimes lead to political behavior.

Locke (1999) noted that interrelationships within networks could become enmeshed in 'politics'. When this occurs, firms begin competing for resources and network ties that produce dysfunctional behaviors by firms within the network. Therefore, social capital can become an organizational liability if it leads to dysfunctional competition over scarce resources due to political fragmentation within an organization or network and/or institutional factors (i.e. legal regulations) in the region (Talmud, 1999). Legal infrastructure and ideologies can produce conscientious exploitation of eminent relationships with political, regulatory, and governmental posts. Firms with such linkages to political offices may have access to resources and information not available to those without such relationships (Talmud, 1992; Talmud and Mesch, 1997). Additionally, internal political fragmentation can serve as a barrier to knowledge and resource transfer, impede procedural and distributional justice, and inhibit strategic flexibility. The negative effects may be greater when resources are constrained. When resources are controlled by political centers, the threat of moral hazard and bribery is greater, and can lead to a rapid deterioration of firm resources (Adler and Kwon, 2000). Finally, social, or relational capital could lead to business actions that are difficult to justify such as loans to money-losing companies by banking officials yielding to pressure from network members (Kakinuma and Fukunaga, 1995).

3 Asian relationships, networks and management practices

3.1 Building relationships

East Asian countries in general and China, Japan, and Korea in particular have been greatly influenced by Confucianism. The philosophy of Confucius stresses that individuals are not isolated entities but a part of a larger system of interdependent relationships. As such, building and managing effective relationships have been innate in the cultures of China, Japan, and Korea as observed in their concepts of guanxi, kankei, and inmak, respectively. However, because all three countries interpreted and practiced Confucianism in different ways, the concepts of guanxi, kankei, and inmak share many similarities but also have subtle differences.

Guanxi in China has become a popular topic in both the academic and popular press. Guanxi refers to connections, often individual, that provide or imply the exchange of favors (Luo, 2000). These interpersonal relationships often form a vast relational network that is ubiquitous in all business dealings in China (Luo, 2000). Several empirical studies highlight the importance of guanxi. For example, Xin and Pearce (1996) found that executives of private companies developed and utilized guanxi more than executives of state-owned companies to compensate for the lack of formal institutional mechanisms. In a more recent study, Park and Luo (2001) found that institutional, strategic, and organizational factors were important antecedents to the use of guanxi in China. Moreover, Park and Luo (2001) found guanxi to be positively related to firm performance (i.e. sales growth). Thus relationship building in China has been and continues to be an important topic for research.

Relationships or connections are also important in Japan as can be seen in the concept of kankei. Kankei is a combination of two Japanese words, 'kan', meaning a barrier-gate and 'kei' connoting obligation and allegiance to fixed order. When combined, kankei reflects the subconscious notion of granting access through relationship, controlled by the 'barrier-gate' and letting go those who proved their loyalty and obligations to the larger social arrangement. Using this premise access to transactions is granted to insiders (uchi) and denied to outsiders (soto). Through kankei, Japanese business people distinguish those who are trustworthy, committed, and loyal from those who may be less so using an elaborate scheme of relationships. The aim in kankei relationships is to identify the outsiders and insiders with respect to the network (Scher, 1997).

Finally, the concept of inmak in Korea literally refers to people connections. Inmak includes whom and how many one knows and relates to family, educational and/or regional ties. All three ties are important and form the basis for doing business in Korea. For example, educational credentials (e.g. attending a prestigious college) are critical for career advancement in major Korean companies. Steers, Shin and Ungson (1989) state that, "When Korean managers are introduced, one of the first questions they ask each other concerns where they went to school. Discovering that both attended the same high school or university (even at different times) often brings an instant feeling of closeness" (p. 45).

Thus, all three countries having been influenced by Confucianism emphasizing the importance of relationship building (i.e. guanxi, kankei, inmak) for success. However, there are subtle yet important differences among these concepts. These differences stem from the way in which each country interpreted and adapted Confucianism. Confucianism originated in China around 500 B.C. and spread to both Japan and Korea. Confucius promulgated a code of ethical behavior that was to guide interpersonal relationships in everyday life. This code can be summarized by the so-called "five relationships": ruler/subject, father/son, husband/wife, elder brother/younger brother, and friend/friend (Chen, 2001).

Korea and Japan differed in the way they adopted Confucianism. For example, the Korean form of Confucianism placed more emphasis on interpersonal relationships and interactions among "unequals" (e.g. the son had to always defer to the father; the wife had to always obey the husband) (Steers, Shin and Ungson, 1989). More specifically, the various relationships formed in Korean society could be characterized as "blind" or "reckless". As a result, authoritarianism has been a major characteristic of Korean society. This has led to many factions and partisan behavior throughout Korean history. In particular, the 500 years of the Yi dynasty have been marred by partisan battles. The major goal for these various factions was to engage in relationships with whomever they could so that they could have many people join their factions. Japan, on the other hand, modified the doctrines of Confucianism to suit their own culture and needs while keeping Buddhism as their main philosophy (or religion). Thus, the Japanese emphasized relationships that were rational, logical, and even flexible.

Thus, one difference among guanxi, kankei, and inmak is that ascriptive ties (e.g. common birthplace, same school, and family) are much more important in establishing relationships in China and Korea than Japan. That is, guanxi networks and inmak networks of reciprocal obligations in China and Korea are formed among people who have shared a common and meaningful experience (e.g. common background characteristics). However, the network of reciprocal obligations is more pronounced in Korea than in China due to the authoritarian nature of Korean society and fractional battles that necessitated forming relationships for power.

While relationships in China and Korea are often based on visible and common background characteristics, in Japan, kankei relationships tend to be more idiosyncratic and situation specific (Whitley, 1991). That is, Japanese kankei networks can be formed with people who have different backgrounds. The Japanese place more emphasis on forming rational and logical relationships based on social factors rather than similar backgrounds.

A second difference among guanxi, kankei, and inmak relates to trust. While trust is important in forming guanxi, kankei, and inmak, it may be more important in forming kankei networks. The Japanese do not blindly engage in relationships because people share some background commonality(ies). The concept of kankei is based strongly on trust. Without trust, it is unlikely that a kankei can be formed. However, in Korea inmak can be formed even without first establishing trust.

Finally, although both the guanxi and inmak networks emphasize common background characteristics, the Chinese guanxi is much more family-tie orientated than the Korean inmak or Japanese kankei. In Chinese society, family life is central. Many businesses in China are family owned and operated and thus family-oriented behavior is natural to the Chinese (Chen, 2001). Commitment to one's family takes precedence over everything else in China. While family ties are important in Korea and to a lesser extent in Japan as well, the Korean concept of inmak places most emphasis on geographic ties. For example, there are eight provinces in Korea. The current President, Kim Dae Jung, is from the "Chulla Province". Since he became President, the Chulla Province has enjoyed substantially more investments than the other seven provinces. In addition, compared to previous administrations, many of Kim Dae Jung's cabinet members as well as lower level government officials are from the Chulla Province. Thus, the people of the Chulla Province with their inmak (i.e. relationships) to the President have enjoyed prosperity.

Regardless of the subtle differences among guanxi, kankei, and inmak, they all imply effective relationships in each country's context. Asian firms are able to reduce transaction costs through the use of guanxi, kankei, and inmak because of the low need for monitoring of the other party's actions. In addition, relationships based on guanxi, kankei, and inmak are particularly effective in acquiring resources needed for gaining a competitive advantage (Standifird and Marshall, 2000). For example, research has shown that relationships based on guanxi help firms build legitimacy and enhance a firm's competitive position. Firms with strong external relationships are better able to obtain resources necessary to gain a competitive advantage. In so doing, these relationships contribute to firm growth in the market and increases in market share (Park and Luo, 2001). Alternatively, firms investing in guanxi, kankei or inmak cannot easily transform internally because of the potential path dependence created by the relationships and resources required to maintain them (Park and Luo, 2001).

Relationships can be informal or formal. The formal relationships exist through interlocking directorates or other interactions and purposeful interdependencies among firms such as strategic alliances (Heracleous and Murray, 2001; Li, 2001). In China, interlocking directorates represent a formal type of guanxi (Peng, Au and Wang, 2001). Whether formal or informal, the resulting networks represent a cluster of interdependent firms that cooperate to achieve and maintain a competitive advantage (Li, 2001).

We may conclude that guanxi, kankei, and inmak represent a form of social capital for Asian firms. This social capital provides the basis for business dealings in each of the respective countries. Additionally, it contributes to the development of business networks in each of the countries.

Family-based decision structures, extended business networks and interdependent conglomerate organizations (formal and informal interrelationships) predominate in Asian organizations (Peng et al., 2001). The conglomerate organizations referred to as business groups include the Chaebol in Korea, Keiretsu in Japan and Jituanqiye in Taiwan. While we recognize that the formation and development of these business groups have been influenced by a variety of institutional (e.g. political and financial structures) and industry factors, we focus on relational capital and its importance to the functioning of business groups; the interdependent nature of these business groups suggests that cooperation and relational capital are important for their success. Our discussion focuses on the Japanese keiretsus because of the criticality of relationships to their success and perhaps failure (Whitley, 1991).

Keiretsus were derived from the earlier zaibatsu which were large industrial organizations evolving from large groups of family businesses involved in multiple industries (zaibatsu translated literally means financial clique) (Richter, 1999: xiii), with origins as early family enterprises (dozuku) (Bhappu, 2000). Keiretsus seemed to have provided Japanese firms with an advantage over Western competitors for many years. The access to financial capital from the main bank and special deals made by suppliers in the keiretsu contributed to a competitive advantage. But the competitive advantage may have been due in large part to the 'relational access to resources, contracts, and people' (Scher, 1997, 1999), a characteristic of social or relational capital that produces an extensive network that diffuses tacit knowledge.

The competitive advantage created by a keiretsu is the informal yet powerful and effective system of relational access to those proven to be trustworthy and committed (Dyer, 1998). The benefactors of the keiretsu relationships are rewarded by repeated transactions due to commitment, obligation, and reciprocity, a characteristic especially valuable in uncertain environments.

Membership in the keiretsu provides firms with a form of strategic flexibility. In support of this conclusion, research has shown that firms in keiretsus have a different strategic profile from non-keiretsu firms (Geringer, Tallman and Olsen, 2000). Toyota, a keiretsu firm, has strong network ties that have contributed to its high positive performance over time. For example, the network has developed institutionalized routines that have facilitated knowledge transfer between Toyota and its suppliers. According to Dyer and Nobeoka (2000), the network has helped Toyota develop a dynamic learning capability that contributes strongly to its competitive advantage.

Dyer (1998) also found that suppliers in the Japanese automobile keiretsus (kankei kaisha) interacted face-to-face with their parent company 7,270 person-days in comparison to 3,181 person-days for their independent supplier counterparts. Dyer (1998) argued that this interaction produced rich and committed relationships (e.g. 31% of highly specialized capital investments of a kankei kaisha in comparison to 15% in independent suppliers on average).

While there are many benefits to keiretsu membership, the interdependencies among the firms also have some disadvantages similar to some of the negative outcomes of social capital explained earlier. The interdependencies within keiretsus, for example, place an implied obligation on firms to help others in the network that experience problems. If those problems are severe, all firms in the network can be harmed, as shown in the current-day problems experienced by many keiretsus in Japan. These problems are highly evident in the Japanese high technology industries (e.g. semiconductors), for example (Langlois and Steinmueller, 2000). In addition, members in a keiretsu may have become too complacent with their current relationships and do not seek opportunities beyond the network.

In conclusion, control in many Asian firms is maintained through interdependencies, informal relationships and even cross holdings (ownership rights) among firms in the networks (Claessens, Djankov and Lang, 2000). In all cases, managers of the firms in the networks must develop and maintain effective working relationships in order to operate their firm successfully and achieve performance goals. Thus, relationship building and maintenance has been a special managerial skill of importance in Asian firms. Long before it was "popular" in Western firms, Asian companies developed and carefully managed their "social capital."

4 Alliances and trust

As implied in the opening quote, alliances and networks of firms have become a common means of doing business in the 21st century. Networks play a central role in the formation of new firms and the growth of existing firms, primarily because they provide access to resources needed to survive and compete in local, national and global markets (Hite and Hesterly, 2001). This fact has greatly increased the effects of social capital on the competitive capabilities of firms. Social capital facilitates the formation of alliances and contributes to the management of relationships in networks. Firms without adequate social capital may experience challenges in gaining access to resources necessary to compete, especially in global markets.

References

Adler, P.S. (2001). "Market, Hierarchy, and Trust: The Knowledge Economy and the Future of Capitalism." *Organization Science* 12, 215–234.

Adler, P.S. and S.-W. Kwon. (2000). "Social Capital: The Good, the Bad, and the Ugly." In E.L. Lesser (ed.), *Knowledge and Social Capital: Foundations and Applications*. Boston, MA: Butterworth Heinemann.

Adler, P.S. and S.-W. Kwon. (2002). "Social Capital: Prospects for a New Concept." *Academy of Management Review* 27, 17–40.

Ahuja, G. (2000a). "The Duality of Collaboration: Inducements and Opportunities in the Formation of Interfirm Linkages." *Strategic Management Journal* 21, 317–343.

Ahuja, G. (2000b). "Collaboration Networks, Structural Holes, and Innovation: A Longitudinal Study." *Administrative Science Quarterly* 45, 425–455.

Barney, J.B. and M. Hansen. (1994). "Trustworthiness as a Source of Competitive Advantage." *Strategic Management Journal* 25, 175–190.

Bartlett, C.A. and S. Ghoshal. (1998). *Managing Across Borders*. Boston, MA: Harvard Business Press.

Bhappu, A.D. (2000). "The Japanese Family: An Institutional Logic for Japanese Corporate Networks and Japanese Management." *Academy of Management Review* 25, 409–415.

Blois, K.J. (1999). "Trust in Business to Business Relationships: An Evaluation of its Status." *Journal of Management Studies* 36, 197–215.

Boisot, M. and J. Child. (1996). "From Fiefs to Clans and Network Capitalism: Explaining China's Emerging Economic Order." *Administrative Science Quarterly* 41, 600–628.

Brown, J.S. and P. Duguid. (1991). "Organizational Learning and Communities-of-Practice: Toward a Unified View of Working, Learning and Innovation." *Organization Science* 2, 40–57.

Burt, R.S. (1992). *Structural Holes: The Social Structure of Competition*. Cambridge, MA: Harvard University Press.

Burt, R.S. (1997). "The Contingent Value of Social Capital." *Administrative Science Quarterly* 42, 339–365.

Chen, M.-J. (2001). *Inside Chinese business: A Guide for Managers Worldwide*. Boston, MA: Harvard Business School Press.

Child, J. and Y. Yan. (2001). "National and Transnational Effects in International Business: Indications from Sino-Foreign Joint Ventures." *Management International Review* 41, 53–75.

Claessens, S., S. Djankov, and L.H.P. Lang. (2000). "The Separation of Ownership and Control in East Asian Corporations." *Journal of Financial Economics* 58, 81–112.

Cohen, W.M. and D.A. Levinthal. (1990). "Absorptive Capacity: A New Perspective on Learning and Innovation." *Administrative Science Quarterly* 35, 128–152.

Coleman, J.S. (1990). *Foundations of Social Theory*. Cambridge, MA: Harvard University Press.

Dafter, R. (2001). "Oil Pricing Paradox Costs: Asia." *Far Eastern Economic Review* April 26, www.feer.com.

Das, T.K. and B.-S. Teng. (1998). "Resource and Risk Management in the Strategic Alliance Making Process." *Journal of Management* 24, 21–42.

Das, T.K. and B.-S. Teng. (2000). "A Resource-Based Theory of Strategic Alliances." *Journal of Management* 26, 31–61.

Davenport, T. and L. Prusak. (1997). *Working Knowledge: How Organizations Manage What They Know*. Cambridge, MA: Harvard Business School Press.

Dussauge, P., B. Garrette, and W. Mitchell. (2000). "Learning from Competing Partners: Outcomes and Durations of Scale and Link Alliances in Europe, North America and Asia." *Strategic Management Journal* 21, 99–126.

Dyer, J.H. (1998). "To Sue or Keiretsu: A Comparison of Partnering in the United States and Japan." In W.M. Fruin (ed.), *Networks, Markets, and the Pacific Rim*. New York: Oxford University Press.

Dyer, J.H. and K. Nobeoka. (2000). "Creating and Managing a High-Performance Knowledge-Sharing Network: The Toyota Case." *Strategic Management Journal* 21, 345–367.

Dyer, J.H. and H. Singh. (1998). "The Relational View: Cooperative Strategy and Sources of Interorganizational Competitive Advantage." *Academy of Management Review* 23, 660–679.

Fruin, W.M. (1998). "Analyzing Pacific Rim Networks and Markets: An Introduction." In W.M. Fruin (ed.), *Networks, Markets, and the Pacific Rim: Studies in Strategy*. New York: Oxford University Press.

Gabbay, S.M. and E.W. Zuckerman. (1998). "Social Capital and Opportunity in Corporate R&D: The Contingent Effect of Contact Density on Mobility Expectations." *Social Science Research* 27, 189–217.

Geringer, J.M., S. Tallman, and D.M. Olsen. (2000). "Product and International Diversification Among Japanese Multinational Firms." *Strategic Management Journal* 21, 51–80.

Ghoshal, S. and C.A. Bartlett. (1990). "The Multinational Corporation as an Interorganizational Network." *Academy of Management Review* 15, 603–625.

Granovetter, M.S. (1985). "Economic Action and Social Structure." *American Journal of Sociology* 91, 481–510.

Gulati, R. (1999). "Network Location and Learning: The Influence of Network Resources and Firm Capabilities on Alliance Formation." *Strategic Management Journal* 20, 397–420.

Gulati, R., N. Nohria, and A. Zaheer. (2000). "Strategic Networks." *Strategic Management Journal* 21, 203–215.

Haley, G.T. and U.C.V. Haley. (1999). "Weaving Opportunities: The Influence of Overseas Chinese and Overseas Indian Business Networks on Asian Business Operations." In F.J. Richter (ed.), *Business Networks in Asia: Promises, Doubts, and Perspectives*. Westport, CT and London: Quorum Books.

Hamel, G. (1991). "Competition for Competence and Inter-Partner Learning Within International Strategic Alliances." *Strategic Management Journal* 12, 83–103.

Hansen, M.T. (1998). "Combining Network Centrality and Related Knowledge: Explaining Effective Knowledge Sharing in Multiunit Firms." Working paper, Harvard Business School, Boston.

Hargadon, A. and R.I. Sutton. (1997). "Technology Brokering and Innovation in a Product Development Firm." *Administrative Science Quarterly* 42, 716–749.

Harrison, J.S., M.A. Hitt, R.E. Hoskisson, and R.D. Ireland. (2001). "Resource Complementarity in Business Combinations: Extending the Logic to Organizational Alliances." *Journal of Management* 27, 679–690.

Heide, J. and G. John. (1990). "Alliances in Industrial Purchasing: The Determinants of Joint Action in Buyer–Supplier Relationships." *Journal of Marketing Research* 28, 24–36.

Heracleous, L. and J. Murray. (2001). "Networks, Interlocking Directors and Strategy: Toward a Theoretical Framework." *Asia Pacific Journal of Management* 18, 137–160.

Hite, J.M. and W.S. Hesterly. (2001). "The Evolution of Firm Networks: From Emergence to Early Growth of the Firm." *Strategic Management Journal* 22, 275–286.

Hitt, M.A., D. Ahlstrom, M.T. Dacin, and E. Levitas. (2001a). "The Economic and Institutional Context of International Strategic Alliance Partner Selection: China vs. Russia." Paper Presented at the Academy of Management Meetings, Washington D.C.

Hitt, M.A., L. Bierman, K. Shimizu, and R. Kochhar. (2001b). "Direct and Moderating Effects of Human Capital on Strategy and Performance in Professional Service Firms: A Resource-Based Perspective." *Academy of Management Journal* 44, 13–28.

Hitt, M.A., M.T. Dacin, E. Levitas, J.-L. Arregle, and A. Borza. (2000). "Partner Selection in Emerging and Developed Market Contexts: Resource-Based and Organizational Learning Perspectives." *Academy of Management Journal* 43, 449–467.

Hitt, M.A., M.T. Dacin, B.B. Tyler, and D. Park. (1997). "Understanding the Differences in Korean and U.S. Executives' Strategic Orientations." *Strategic Management Journal* 18, 159–167.

Hitt, M.A., R.D. Ireland, S.M. Camp, and D.L. Sexton. (2001c). "Strategic Entrepreneurship: Entrepreneurial Strategies for Wealth Creation. *Strategic Management Journal* 22, 479–491 (special issue).

Hitt, M.A., B.W. Keats, and S.M. DeMarie. (1998b). "Navigating in the New Competitive Landscape: Building Strategic Flexibility and Competitive Advantage in the 21st Century." *Academy of Management Executive* 12, 22–42.

Hitt, M.A., R.D. Nixon, P.G. Clifford, and K.P. Coyne. (1998a). "The Development and use of Strategic Resources." In M.A. Hitt, P.G. Clifford, R.D. Nixon, and K.P. Coyne (eds), *Dynamic Strategic Resources: Development, Diffusion and Integration*. Chichester, UK: John Wiley & Sons, pp. 1–14.

Hoopes, D.G. and S. Postrel. (1999). "Shared Knowledge, 'Glitches', and Product Development Performance." *Strategic Management Journal* 20, 837–865.

Inkpen, A.C. (2001). "Strategic Alliances." In M.A. Hitt, R.E. Freeman, and J.S. Harrison (eds.), *Handbook of Strategic Management*. Oxford: Blackwell Publishers, pp. 409–432.

Ireland, R.D., M.A. Hitt, and D. Vaidyanath. (2002). "Managing Strategic Alliances to Achieve a Competitive Advantage." *Journal of Management* 28, in press.

Jennings, D.F., K. Artz, L.M. Gillin, and C. Christodouloy. (2000). "Determinants of Trust in Global Strategic Alliances: Amrad and the Australian Biomedical Industry." *Competitiveness Review* 10, 25–44.

Jones, G.R. (2001). "Towards a Positive Interpretation of Transaction Cost Theory: The Central Roles of Entrepreneurship and Trust." In M.A. Hitt, R.E. Freeman, and J.S. Harrison (eds), *Handbook of Strategic Management*. Oxford: Blackwell Publishers, pp. 208–228.

Kakinuma, S. and H.i. Fukunaga. (1995). "The $4 Trillion Question." *Tokyo Business Today* 63(11), 28–32.

Koh, A.-T. (1998). "Organizational Learning in Successful East Asian Firms: Principles, Practices and Prospects." *Technological Forecasting and Social Change* 58, 285–295.

Lane, P.J. and M. Lubatkin. (1998). "Relative Absorptive Capacity and Interorganizational Learning." *Strategic Management Journal* 19, 461–478.

Langlois, R.N. and W.E. Steinmueller. (2000). "Strategy and Circumstance: The Response of American Firms to Japanese Competition in Semiconductors 1980–1995." *Strategic Management Journal* 21, 1163–1173.

Larsson, R., L. Bengtsson, K. Henriksson, and J. Sparks. (1998). "The Interorganizational Learning Dilemma: Collective Knowledge Development in Strategic Alliances." *Organization Science* 9, 285–305.

Lee, H., M.A. Hitt, and E.K. Jeong. (2002). "The Impact of CEO and TMT Characteristics on Strategic Flexibility and Firm Performance." University of Connecticut, working paper.

Li, J., G. Qian, K. Lam, and D. Wang. (2000). "Breaking into China: Strategic Considerations for Multinational Corporations." *Long Range Planning* 33, 673–687.

Li, L. (2001). "Networks, Transactions, and Resources: Hong Kong Trading Companies' Strategic Position in the China Markets." *Asia Pacific Journal of Management* 18, 279–293.

Locke, E.A. (1999). "Some Reservations About Social Capital." *Academy of Management Review* 24, 8–11.

Lovas, B. and S. Ghoshal. (2000). "Strategy as Guided Evolution." *Strategic Management Journal* 21, 875–896.

Luo, Y. (2000). *Guanxi and Business*. Singapore: World Scientific.

Luo, Y. (2001). "Determinants of Entry in an Emerging Economy: A Multilevel Approach." *Journal of Management Studies* 38, 443–472.

Luo, Y. (2002). "Building Trust in Cross-Cultural Collaborations: Toward a Contingency Perspective." *Journal of Management* 28, in press.

Nahapiet, J. and S. Ghoshal. (1998). "Social Capital, Intellectual Capital, and the Organizational Advantage." *Academy of Management Review* 23, 242–266.

Orton, D. and K.E. Weick. (1990). "Loosely Coupled Systems: A Reconsideration." *Academy of Management Review* 15, 203–223.

Pant, P.N. and V.G. Rajadhyaksha. (1996). "Partnership with an Asian Family Business— What Every Multinational Corporation Should Know." *Long Range Planning* 29, 812–820.

Park, S.H. and Y. Luo. (2001). "Guanxi and Organizational Dynamics: Organizational Networking in Chinese Firms." *Strategic Management Journal* 22, 455–477.

Parkhe, A. (1993). "Strategic Alliance Structuring: A Game Theoretic and Transaction Cost Examination of Interfirm Cooperation." *Academy of Management Journal* 36, 794–829.

Peng, M.W., K.Y. Au, and D.Y.L. Wang. (2001). "Interlocking Directorates as Corporate Governance in Third World Multinational: Theory and Evidence from Thailand." *Asia Pacific Journal Of Management* 18, 161–181.

Peng, M.W., S.-H. Lee, and J.J. Tan. (2001). "The *Keiretsu* in Asia: Implications for Multilevel Theories of Competitive Advantage." *Journal of International Management* 7, 253–276.

Peng, M.W., Y. Lu, O. Shenkar, and D.Y.L. Wang. (2001). "Treasures in the China House: A Review of Management and Organizational Research on Greater China." *Journal of Business Research* 52, 95–110.

Powell, B.A. (2001). "More Than One Market." *Red Herring Magazine* Oct. 1, www.redherring.com.

Putnam, R.D. (1993). "The Prosperous Community: Social Capital and Public Life." *The American Prospect* 13, 37.

Richter, F.-J. (1999). *Business Networks in Asia.* Westport, CT and London: Quorum Books.

Ross, W. and J. LaCroix. (1996). "Multiple Meanings of Trust in Negotiation Theory and Research: A Literature Review and Integrative Model." *The International Journal of Conflict Management* 7, 314–360.

Scher, M. (1997). *Japanese Interfirm Networks and Their Main Banks.* New York, NY: St. Martin's Press, Inc.

Scher, M. (1999). "Japanese Interfirm Networks: High Trust or Relational Access." In A. Grandori (ed.), *Interfirm Networks: Organization and Industrial Competitiveness.* Abingdon and New York, NY: Routledge.

Schifrin, M. (2001). "Partner or Perish." *Forbes* 26–28.

Seifert, S.E., M.L. Kraimer, and S.C. Liden. (2001). "A Social Capital Theory of Career Success." *Academy of Management Journal* 44, 219–237.

Singh, K. and G.S. Yip. (2000). "Strategic Lessons From the Asian Crisis." *Long Range Planning* 33, 706–729.

Spender, J.C. (1996). "Making Knowledge the Basis of a Dynamic Theory of the Firm." *Strategic Management Journal* 17, 45–62 (Special Issue).

Standifird, S.S. and R.S. Marshall. (2000). "The Transaction Cost Advantage of Guanxi-Based Business Practices." *Journal of World Business* 35, 21–42.

Steers, R.M., Y.K. Shin, and G.R. Ungson. (1989). *The Chaebol: Korea's New Industrial Might.* New York: Harper and Row.

Sullivan, D.P. and G.R. Weaver. (2000). "Cultural Cognition in International Business Research." *Management International Research* 40, 269–297.

Talmud, I. (1992). "Industry Market Power, Industry Political Power, and State Support: The Case of Israeli Industry." In G. Moore and J.A. Whitt (eds.), *Research in Politics and Society.* Vol. 4, Greenwich: JAI Press, pp. 35–62.

Talmud, I. (1999). "Corporate Social Capital and Liability: A Conditional Approach to Three Consequences of Corporate Social Structure." In R. Leenders and S.M. Gabbay (eds), *Corporate Social Capital and Liability.* Norwell, MA: Kluwer Academic Publishers, pp. 106–117.

Talmud, I. and G.S. Mesch. (1997). "Market Embeddedness and Corporate Instability: The Ecology of Inter-Industrial Networks." *Social Science Research* 26, 419–441.

Tan, E.K.-B. (2000). "Success Amidst Prejudice: Guanxi Networks in Chinese Business in Indonesia and Malaysia." *Journal of Asian Business* 16(1), 65–83.

Tsai, W. and S. Ghoshal. (1998). "Social Capital and Value Creation: The Role of Intrafirm Networks." *Academy of Management Journal* 41, 464–476.

Tsang, E.W.K. (2001). "Managerial Learning in Foreign-Invested Enterprises in China." *Management International Review* 41, 29–51.

Tsang, E.W.K. (2002). "Learning from Overseas Venturing Experience: The Case of Chinese Family Business." *Journal of Business Venturing* 17, 21–40.

Wee, C.H. and L.L. Lan. (1998). *The 36 Strategies of the Chinese.* Singapore: Addison-Wesley.

Whitley, R.D. (1991). "The Social Construction of Business Systems in East Asia." *Organiation Studies* 12, 1–28.

Wicks, A.C., S.L. Berman, and T.M. Jones. (1999). "The Structure of Optimal Trust: Moral and Strategic Implications." *Academy of Management Review* 24, 99–116.

Woolcock, M. and D. Narayan. (2000). "Social Capital: Implications for Development Theory, Research and Policy. *World Bank Research Observer* 15, 225–250.

Xin, K.R. and J.L. Pearce. (1996). "Guanxi: Connections as Substitutes for Formal Institutional Support." *Academy of Management Journal* 39, 1641–1658.

Yamagishi, T. and M. Yamagishi. (1998). "Trust and Commitment as Alternative Responses to Social Uncertainty." In W.M. Fruin (ed.), *Networks, Markets, and the Pacific Rim: Strategies in Strategy*. New York: Oxford University Press.

Yli-Renko, H., E. Autio, and H.J. Sapienza. (2001). "Social Capital, Knowledge Acquisition, and Knowledge Exploitation in Young Technology-Based Firms." *Strategic Management Journal* 22, 587–613.

Zimmerman, M. (1985). "Getting on the Japanese Wavelength." *Across the Board* 22(4), 30–37.

17

VIRTUAL TEAM COLLABORATION
Building shared meaning, resolving breakdowns and creating translucence

Pernille Bjørn and Ojelanki Ngwenyama

Source: Edited from *Information Systems Journal*, 2009, 19 (3), May.

1 Introduction

Globally distributed organizations often bring people of different cultures and languages across heterogeneous locations together to collaborate on specific projects. Virtual teams are groups of geographically and/or organizationally distributed participants who collaborate towards a shared goal using a combination of information and communication technologies (ICT) to accomplish a task (Townsend *et al.*, 1998; Lipnack and Stamps, 2000; Majchrzak *et al.*, 2000; Kirkman *et al.*, 2004). Virtual teams can refer to teams comprising of participants who never meet physically (Jarvenpaa *et al.*, 1998), or to situations in which team members rarely meet face-to-face (Chudoba *et al.*, 2005); thus, use ICT as the primary medium of interaction. Other concepts such as 'hybrid teams' or 'far-flung teams' are also used to describe teams with geographically distributed participants performing highly interdependent tasks that meet face-to-face occasionally (Bell and Kozlowski, 2002; Griffith *et al.*, 2003; Malhotra and Majchrzak, 2004; Fiol and O'Connor, 2005). In this paper we investigate the communication practices of international virtual teams organized within a hybrid work arrangement.

Virtual teams must place the ongoing challenge of managing the collaboration at the very centre of teamwork. Some researchers view the management of virtual collaboration as articulation work (Gerson and Star, 1986; Schmidt and Bannon, 1992), that comprises all tasks involved in assembling, scheduling, monitoring and coordinating individual yet interdependent activities between the geographical distributed participants. Articulation work requires shared meaning in order to engage in fruitful negotiations and to avoid or quickly recover from communication breakdowns. The team members need to develop a shared meaning context and common language for making sense of each other's actions. Creating shared meaning normally develops over time and by means of face-to-face interaction (Chudoba *et al.*, 2005). Therefore, geographically distributed participants have a significantly more difficult task when developing shared meaning, because access to each other is only mediated via the traces left in the technology. However, there is a risk that participants ascribe individual interpretations to the traces that are quite different from the intended meanings of the traces. The lack of regular co-located encounters for social or work related activities inhibits the development of a shared meaning context and increases the risk of communication breakdowns. So the questions that remain are: How can we conceptualize the organizational context which is the foundation for building shared meaning in virtual teams and how can we improve the conditions for building shared meaning without co-location?

In this paper we propose the concepts shared meaning and translucence, and demonstrate their usefulness for analysing and theorizing about collaboration within virtual teams. Briefly, translucence can be defined as the triangulation of visibility, awareness and accountability. Likewise, we define the shared meaning context as the background knowledge that guides actors in organizing and shaping their interpretations of events. Our primary interest is to explicate how these two concepts are important when investigating the collaborative practice and for designing collaborative technologies to be used in virtual teams. The empirical work presented in this paper is the case study of two virtual teams engaged in hybrid work arrangements.

2 Theoretical framework

2.1 Shared meaning in virtual teams

Teamwork is highly dependent on how well participants are socialized into the organizational context and their ability to make sense of and respond to each other's actions (Suchman, 1987; Weick, 1993). An essential feature of virtual teamwork is communicative action or the ability to successfully negotiate and communicate with each other (Clark and Brennan, 1991). Many studies note that communicative action in virtual collaboration is dependent upon the emergent and time-consuming process of establishing common ground (Olson and Olson, 2000; Cramton, 2001; Malhotra and Majchrzak, 2004; Bjørn and Hertzum, 2006). Establishing common ground is a process of creating a shared meaning context; failure to establish and maintain such a context can result in serious breakdowns in collaboration (Cramton, 2001). Knowledge sharing is another fundamental feature of collaboration that is closely related to the process of building a shared meaning context. It is in 'the process of consensus building that knowledge is shared and vice versa' (Malhotra and Majchrzak, 2004). However, a key problem is how to conceptualize and articulate the shared meaning context as a fundamental aspect of virtual teamwork.

Some information systems researchers have pointed out that all actions within an organization are socially oriented and take place within a predefined organizational context (Lyytinen and Ngwenyama, 1992; Ngwenyama and

Lee, 1997; Ngwenyama, 1998). The organizational context is the foundation for building shared meaning (Daft and Weick, 1984). For the sake of analytical clarity, we will delineate three conceptual structures of the organizational context: (1) the lifeworld; (2) organizational structures; and (3) work practice. The lifeworld is the intersubjective reality that is built on the interpretations of all personal work experiences as well as the collective experiences of the members of an organization (Ngwenyama and Klein, 1994). Habermas (1981) defines lifeworld as formed by the lived experiences and beliefs that guide people's attitudes, behaviours and actions in their interaction. It consists of the unarticulated and taken-for-granted assumptions, knowledge, culture, beliefs and values. According to Schütz (1982), the lifeworld is the frame of reference that provides individuals with implicit guidelines for organizing, shaping their interpretations and enacting meaning to events and situations. The lifeworld schemes serve as filters of the collective reality like a veil through which people observe and interpret the actions of others (Ngwenyama and Klein, 1994, p. 133). Fractures in lifeworld schemes surface only during breakdowns of understanding or when seemingly contradictory organizational actions are closely investigated (Schein, 1992).

Organizational structures comprise explicit, articulated and visible structures, such as policies, norms, symbolic artefacts, ritual activity and patterned behaviour (Gioia, 1986; Lundberg, 1989). Examples of organizational structures related to virtual teams can be travel and email policies. The initiation of a virtual team comprising people from different sub-groups of the wider organization can be viewed as the emerging of a new organizational context in which a shared meaning context, new organizational structures and work practices need to be negotiated and enacted. The initiation of the virtual team must also include articulation work, setting boundaries, negotiating commitment to common goals, resources and so on (Strauss, 1988; Mark and Poltrock, 2003). While such initiation processes are essential for articulating organization structures (norms and policies), work practices – it must be understood that these structures are emergent – are continually being reshaped due to ongoing social interactions and negotiations among the participants (Klein and Truex, 1996).

The work practice level comprises the profession-specific norms, collaborative practices and languages. In organizations, various groups develop different vocabularies (i.e. lexicons) and everyday speech usage (i.e. parole) based on their professional background, the nature and the organization of their work. Different groups develop different lexicons and parole based on their traditional workplace experiences. Developing a common work language is a process in which various uses of language influence each other and create new language forms and meanings (Holmqvist, 1989). For international teams, the complexity increases since participants do not necessarily share a common language. Further, geographic dispersion restricts the mediation of lexical differences and adoption of new vocabularies among the participants. Consequently, the potential for creating a new language form and building shared meaning is limited. Moreover, the interplay between formal and informal language can lead to problems of understanding when the participants don't share the same meaning context (Robinson, 1991). For example, ordinary artefacts such as text documents (emails, memos, etc.) have a formal language as well as a context of meaning. The context of meaning enables the actor to enact meanings not explicit in the document but relevant to reading the text (Ngwenyama and Lee, 1997). In virtual teams, participants have limited access to developing a shared meaning context because they do not have regular face-to-face encounters, which support the development and alignment of common frames of reference. Thus, the risk of communication breakdowns increases.

The organizational context is a foundational element for the development of shared meaning for all organizational actors (Ngwenyama and Lee, 1997). The lifeworld and organizational structures define the possibilities and potential for action, providing stocks of knowledge, rules and resources upon which actors can draw to interpret each other's actions. In everyday action situations (work practices), the organization's policies, norms and resources serve to enable, constrain and sometimes prescribe what is proper or improper, and to lend meaning to an individual's actions. The organizational structures also define authority and status of the individuals within the organization. As actors mediate action situations employing technology, they draw upon these stocks of knowledge, as well as material and non-material resources of the organization (Giddens, 1984; Lyytinen and Ngwenyama, 1992). While executing their work activities, actors rely upon the fact that they share aspects of the organizational context on key elements and categories. Thus, the organizational context can be viewed as a fundamental element of the shared meaning context having practical consequences for the construction and negotiation of teamwork (see Figure 17.1).

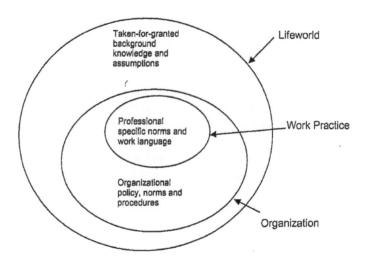

FIGURE 17.1 Three analytical levels of the organizational context providing the basis for shared meaning

2.2 Technology mediation and translucence in virtual teams

Employing technology to mediate communication and actions is essential to virtual teamwork. However, the communicative activities of virtual teams can be highly influenced by the collaboration technology and the organizational context (Ngwenyama and Lyytinen, 1997). Groupware technologies are open-ended applications (collections of rules and resources), but while their use is determined by how the participants adapt the application to their organizational context and work requirements, the functionality of the specific technology can constrain its users (Ngwenyama and Klein, 1994; Orlikowski and Hofman, 1997). A necessary requirement for virtual collaboration in a groupware technology is a common information space that comprises a common repository and functionality to create and share objects-of-work amongst the participants (Carstensen and Schmidt, 1999). To effectively use the information space requires 'articulation work', that is participants must construct meanings related to the shared objects and negotiate agreements on how to enact meaning in the shared information items (Strauss, 1988; Hertzum, 1999; Weick *et al.*, 2005). The common information space also provides visibility so that each participant can monitor and remain aware of the collaboration. In this regard the common information space serves as a kind of social 'sphere' within which social actions are propagated, 'objects-of-work' are operated upon and articulation work (see page 224) is achieved (Ngwenyama and Lyytinen, 1997).

New virtual teams have an increased risk of communication breakdowns (Hinds and Mortensen, 2005). This results from an underdeveloped shared context of meaning, and articulation work upon which smooth communication depends, leaves no digital traces in the groupware (Cramton, 2001). Further, geographic and mental distance among participants often lead to simplified views of the work situation (Suchman, 1995). Important aspects of collaborative practice become invisible at a distance and the boundaries shadowing the work increase. Hence, achieving and maintaining visibility is essential to collaborative practices within virtual teams (see Table 17.1).

TABLE 17.1 Types of communication breakdowns at the three levels of shared meaning

Level of shared meaning	Communication breakdown	Resolving breakdown
Lifeworld	Challenging the taken-for-granted constitutive knowledge	Re-assessment of both their mental models and work routines
Organization	Challenging existing organizational policies, procedures, technologies and norms	Re-assessment of policies, procedures, technology and norms
Work practice	Questioning the efficacy of teamwork practices and routines	Re-assessment and re-design of teamwork practices

Translucence refers to groupware design features that permit important but invisible social clues to be visible, thus enabling distributed collaborators to monitor and interpret each other's actions during collaboration. Translucence is an important feature of collaborative technologies, and should be provided in a low-effort, seamless way that does not interfere with the user's primary task (Ebling *et al.*, 2002). The main purpose of translucence within collaborative technologies is to avoid or recover from communication breakdowns. A communication breakdown is a disruption that occurs when previously successful work practices fail, or changes in the work situation (new workgroup, new technology, policy, etc.) nullify specific work practices or routines of the organizational actors and there are no ready-at-hand recovery strategies (Ngwenyama, 1998). Rennecker and Godwin (2005) identify two types of communication breakdowns that result from lack of translucence: (1) delays from blocked access to a needed resource and (2) interruptions due to unscheduled synchronous interactions that cause discontinuity in a current activity. While breakdowns manifest at the level of work practice, they can involve any of the three levels. On the lifeworld level, breakdowns can challenge the taken-for-granted constitutive knowledge of actors forcing them to reassess mental models of the work situation. On the work process level, breakdowns call into question the efficacy of teamwork practices and routines and force their reassessment and redesign. Furthermore, at the organizational level they may force changes in policy, procedures and technologies.

[...]

3 The organizational context of the case study

The case study reported upon took place in a global transportation company with 100,000 employees located in Europe, Canada, the US and Asia. The company develops and builds a variety of transport vehicles as well as programmable transport-related electronic devices (e.g. doors and train signalling systems). As a result of mergers, the company develops software at different locations including Scandinavia and Asia. In 2002, they launched a capability maturity model based software process improvement (SPI) program. The initial mandate of the project was the development of common software processes. The two teams we studied were involved with different initiatives related to the SPI program.

3.1 Team 1

Team 1 consisted of ten participants located in Denmark, Germany, Thailand, Finland and Sweden. The team project manager was located in Germany, and the participants were chosen by their local managers. The main objective of the project was to develop one set of common software development processes. This task was overwhelming and difficult, since neither top management nor the team members had a common understanding of the project goals or activities. Team 1 met initially in April 2002 at a 3-day co-located kick-off workshop.

At this meeting, the project manager presented rules for communication (e.g.

when to use email or telephone), and fixed dates and times were established for telephone meetings. Lotus Notes was selected as the groupware and a Notes Database was configured to serve as a common repository for the project. Each team member was expected to fill in a weekly flash report describing their progress. Each member of the team was also given a toy figure of a knight as a symbolic representation of their membership in the virtual team. Team members placed these figurines on their computer monitors. The project of Team 1 failed; after one year, top management disbanded the team and the project was terminated. It is ironic that the symbol of choice of this team was the Templar Knights of the crusades who failed due to their inability to 'share meaning' (or ideology) across distances.

3.2 Team 2

Team 2 consisted of five participants located in the US, Canada, UK and two different locations in Sweden. The goals of the project were the development of a high-level software configuration management (SCM) process grounded in existing software practices, and the piloting of the SCM-process at three sites in the company. Team 2 met regularly in 2–5-day co-located workshops at the different sites (Toronto, Canada; Stockholm, Sweden; Cleveland, UK and Oregon, US). Between the co-located workshops, the team made three releases of the SCM-process. Before the last two workshops, it conducted three pilots (in Bangkok, Halmstad and Halifax) of the SCM-process and assisted the local software development teams in implementing the SCM-process. Team 2 mostly used email and telephone to mediate their work, and never used the Lotus Notes database that was established for the project.

3.3 The shared meaning context of Team 1 and Team 2

In order to facilitate a comprehensive understand of the organizational context forming the foundation for building shared meaning in the two teams, we present a conceptual map in Figure 17.2. The company (labelled distributed organizational context in Figure 17.2) can be analytically delineated into lifeworld, organizational structures and work practices. The lifeworld consists of taken-for-granted background knowledge and assumptions related to the company's culture. Since the company is global, the lifeworld of the distributed organizational context is related to the 'local' lifeworlds comprising the basic assumptions constituted within the local geographical sites (local organizational contexts) such as the taken-for-granted knowledge about human interaction in Thailand or Canada. Similarities exist between the lifeworlds of the local organizational contexts. These similarities comprise the lifeworld of the distributed organizational context: the global company.

The organizational structures of the distributed organization comprise the explicit and articulated roles and norms formulated by the company (e.g. 'the vision

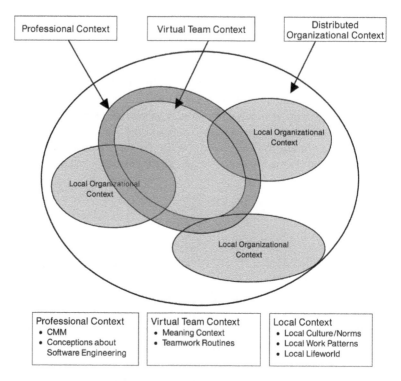

FIGURE 17.2 Shared meaning context of virtual teams is a conglomeration of pieces

of one global company using one set of common software processes') typically communicated by internal magazines, memos and newsletters. The organizational structures articulated by the global company influence those structures within local organizational contexts. However, the organizational structures from the global company are often translated to fit local organizational contexts, and additional structures particular to local organizations are often enacted with local stories and rituals supportive of the local organizational contexts.

Work practices as constituted by the profession-specific norms and language used by all employees also differ between the local organizational contexts. [...] The model in Figure 17.2 shows how the organizational context of a virtual team is a conglomeration of pieces related to lifeworlds, organizational structures and work practices that participants bring from their local organizational contexts. Developing shared meaning within virtual teams thus comprises negotiation processes, where the local organizational contexts serve as the foundation for building shared meaning.

In Team 1, the participants had to develop shared meaning across six local organizational contexts situated in Denmark, Germany, Finland, Thailand and two locations in Sweden. In Team 2, the participants had to develop shared meaning across four local organizational contexts situated in Canada, the UK, the US and

Sweden. In no team had the participants collaborated previously; however, they shared the professional context of software improvement processes.

[...]

4 Creating translucence in virtual teams

The development and maintenance of shared meaning requires translucence in communication structures at different levels: lifeworld, organizational structures and work practice. Without translucence, the risk of communication breakdowns increases. Our analysis suggests that breakdowns occur due to a lack of translucence on different levels, and that the recovery process requires critical reflection to create translucence. Sub-sections address each level of breakdown.

4.1 Translucence at lifeworld level

The lifeworld level comprises assumptions, knowledge, culture, beliefs and the taken-for-granted knowledge that organizational members use to act on and interpret the actions of others. All participants in a virtual team have their own lifeworld that is grounded on earlier experiences in the organization's life and is forming their expectation to collaborate. Experiencing communication breakdowns at the lifeworld level often makes taken-for-granted knowledge salient, such as cultural differences. Thus, creating translucence at the lifeworld level is an alignment process where participants negotiate the basic assumptions about working in the virtual team by, for example, negotiating the norms, values and beliefs.

4.1.1 Communication breakdowns at the lifeworld level

In our case, the differences in expectations and processes and the need for creating translucence emerged at the co-located workshops. Co-located workshops are known to be important to shaping virtual teamwork (Maznevski and Chudoba, 2000; Kirkman *et al.*, 2004). Living in different countries with different cultural norms and habits, Team 2 tried to establish the newly formed context by bringing gifts and greetings to the scene.

> This other interesting thing that this team has that I've never seen before is this international gift thing. When I pack, here's Louis's pile, here's Michael's pile and by the way Sven wants to see pictures of the new kid ... There's always stuff going or coming in. And Louis brings chocolate. Sven brings liquorice. Michael usually shows up with fudge. We take baby gifts for Michael's baby. And the latest thing as of the huggy-huggy, kissy-kissy thing – Michael has always done that. Not in Zurich, he kissed me in Toronto though. OK, from Michael you get one kiss, from Louis you get two. It's like this bee sting we had to go work it out, because how does this work? I'm from the States, we shake hands! (American member, Team 2)

The cultural exchange had a positive impact on the development of shared meaning in the virtual team. However, the collaboration within the co-located workshop was also associated with communication breakdowns experienced as a conflict on the work practice level, caused by the differences at the lifeworld level. The various working habits grounded in various lifeworlds crashed at the co-located workshops. Below, Team 2's project manager articulates how cultural working habits crashed at the co-located workshops.

> If you look at my team, there are things like, some members were working, and worked very hard, they worked weekends, they have families and they work 15–20-hour days. [Not a Dane or a British person] but to a lot of the Americans and the Canadians they will sacrifice weekends and leave their kids, and they will fly off to Australia and … So there is a very high expectation that the rest of the people in the team will do the same. […] [Working remotely] people can take work, they can have some work and then send it back. There is not deadline pressure. So, if the Canadians or the Americans wanna work weekends they can, and it doesn't affect me and you. But when you get to these meetings, where you show up, that's when you get the problems, because all of a sudden it's like, we are gonna start at 8 in the morning and work until 9 o'clock in the night, and we are gonna do that for five days. And if we don't finish, then maybe work Saturday, so the expectation is really very high … specifically within this five member group, you only get the real problems when we meet in one room, because then you have the clash of the cultures. (project manager of Team 2)

The participants' expectations and assumptions of how the work at the co-located workshop should be conducted were not aligned. There were different interpretations of what it meant to work hard, especially between the Swedes and the Briton on one side, and the Canadian and American on the other. The cultural gap had a bad influence on the co-located collaboration. At the first workshop in Toronto, all came and stayed through the entire process. In Stockholm everyone attended the first day that was used for organizing the workshop, but some left before the end. In Cleveland some came late, and in Oregon people came and went at different times so they did not have a full 5-day workshop. The participants tried to change these patterns by using an external consultant to moderate the workshop in Oregon, but did not succeed.

For Team 1 the main communication breakdown at the lifeworld level concerned the negotiation of the project objectives. This breakdown occurred the first day and was never resolved, and eventually led to the disbanding of the team after a year. Through our investigation, we find that this communication breakdown was located at the lifeworld level. The project manager of Team 1 prepared a program for the initial workshop so that the participants could develop relationships and trust (Jarvenpaa et al., 1998). Reflecting on the situation at the initial workshop, the project manager contemplated that the foundation for doing these kinds of activities was not present then and was still not present 8 months later.

> The idea was to drive, and the group was called process, methods and tools, and no one had a clue of what we should do. [...] Seeing this today, the difficulties were that most of them never worked in this environment, they have no experience using English as the business language. The first time as such, and they didn't, and even today many of them don't know, the details of what to do. We started this educational thing, but I think it's far away from being finished. [...] The next day we continued until 10 o'clock, and then we had this brainstorming session discussing many things. And it was a real brainstorming session; it was very, very difficult to get real benefit from it, because the people had to find in their own language what they were talking about. And if you don't have English as your mother language, then it's much more difficult than if you have. (project manager of Team 1)

It is assumed that international team members have access to a common language. In Team 1 some of the participants were not fluent in the business language of the company, which further complicated the development of a shared language making it impossible for the team to initially negotiate the general objective.

[...]

4.2 Translucence at organizational level

The toughest issues in information system design are those concerned with modelling cooperations across heterogeneous worlds, of modelling articulation work and multiplicity (Bowker and Star, 2002). Members of virtual teams are, like everyone else, participating in various local organizational contexts. However, the boundaries between the contexts become more challenging when geographical distance is the demarcation line. Virtual team members are participants in both the virtual team context and the local contexts in which they are physically located. The organizational level consists of the explicit and visible organizational structures forming the virtual team context; thus the physical location of management and the project manager is a part of the organizational level affecting the negotiated shared meaning.

4.2.1 Communication breakdowns at organizational level

In Team 2, top management and one team member were located in Toronto, Canada. The project manager was located in Cleveland, UK. When top management wanted information about the team, they usually went to the member in Toronto rather than the project manager in the UK because it was easier than calling Cleveland – that involved a 5-hour time difference.

> And they all sit in Toronto, and it's a hell of a lot more convenient to wander down the hall or to call [the team member], than it is to call [the project manager] with this 5-hour difference. (US team member in Team 2)

The various locations of the team members, top management and the project manager resulted in communication breakdowns. Communication between management and the team did not go through hierarchical structures mediated by the project manager. Instead, communication was often mediated by the Canadian team member and not the project manager in the UK. Hence, important decisions affecting the work were communicated through invisible structures. When people collaborate, they become involved with extra activities such as dividing, allocating, coordinating, scheduling and interrelated activities and tasks between participants. This extra work is referred to as articulation work (Schmidt and Bannon, 1992; Bowker and Star, 2002). Articulation work is seamlessly interrelated with tasks and actions. Invisible communication between top management and the team influenced by the geographical location of management caused team members (including the project manager) to feel left out of important decisions. Participants saw assignments, tasks and actions as appearing or disappearing behind the inaccessible negotiations between management and the Canadian team member.

> ... and it all kind of ended up in the project schedule all of a sudden. From one day to another. The original was that we were doing pilots in Bangkok and Halmstad. [...] And what I can remember all of a sudden, Halifax showed up in the monthly power point of some document somewhere. (Swedish team member from Team 2)

The number of pilot projects changed unbeknown to the team members. This gave an impression that the pilot project in Halifax suddenly appeared. Strategic discussions resulting in activities disappearing were also inaccessible to the team members.

> I don't know how this works exactly ... It just disappears. Or gets re-negotiated, gets shuffled or [project manager] and [team member in Toronto] had some discussion where to push it through another project. There is a strategy discussion going on there that the other three of us don't know about. We just see the action go away. (US Team member from Team 2)

The articulation work required for collaborative planning of actions was constrained by the invisible and opaque communication structures at the organizational level. The invisible structures prevented team members from knowing when work was transformed and re-negotiated. They felt they could not rely on former decisions since they could be changed without their involvement. They felt they were ignored and overruled by decisions made elsewhere. The communication breakdown experienced at the work practice level (e.g. tasks disappearing) stemmed from the conflict regarding organizational structures at the organizational level. In an organizational context, well-socialized actors have taken-for-granted knowledge and a set of pre-interpreted patterns of meaning about the organization which serves as a reference scheme and enables actors to act and interpret the actions of others (Ngwenyama and Lee, 1997). The interpretation of others' actions is complex in the virtual teams if participants do not develop a shared practice, thus, lacking a reference scheme enabling them to interpret each other's actions. Opaque communication structures at the organizational level constrain the building of shared meaning. Lack of a reference scheme increases complexity in interpretation of others' work and doing articulation work, aligning individual actions to the actions of others. The team members in the study experienced incongruence in frames of reference (Orlikowski and Gash, 1994), and articulation work became constrained. The team members functioned under this condition knowing that they could not influence important communication that was taking place. The actions of some team members were culturally influenced (i.e. based on work ethics and issues of convenience in this case) and were inaccessible and too complex for interpretation by global team members abroad.

The project manager of Team 1 tried to establish a shared meaning at the organizational level by, for example, providing the symbolic artefact of knights. This artefact had the purpose of representing the organizational structures of the team by being present all the time locally (at the computer screens), reminding the geographically distributed participants that they are a part of a virtual team context.

> [I wanted] to have some kind of symbol and to create some kind of community. So I had this idea of how the group was fighting for one set of common processes. And they get Playmobile, small figures you can sample together; it was a small knight, so that everyone can put them on their desk. You are isolated, so now you have something on your desk, which reminds you of where you belong to. (project manager of Team 1)

However, the unresolved breakdown at the lifeworld level meant that the team members lacked a common language in which to negotiate and construct meaning related to the symbolic artefact. Thus, the knights on the local computer monitors did not serve to make the participants feel less isolated.

[...]

4.3 Creating translucence at work process level

The work process level consists of profession-specific norms and work practices. All communication breakdowns manifest at the work practice level; however, not all breakdowns are grounded at this level, as we have illustrated above.

4.3.1 Communication breakdowns at work process level

Team 2 experienced communication breakdowns related to the work assignment: developing the SCM-process reflecting the software development practice of the 10 divisions around the globe. However, prior to the project, SCM-processes existed locally, thus, bringing the four highly skilled group members (excluding the project manager) together challenged the negotiation, since each member had its own locally preferred SCM-process causing a strategic discussion (Ngwenyama and Lyytinen, 1997). The strategic discussion entailed convincing the others of how to develop the SCM-process using existing local best practices. Participants focused on achieving an advantage over the others. Consider the quote below:

> [The department] in Toronto has a process description already. So does Oregon. They are all over the place. They are multiple. But the two best ones are in Oregon and Toronto. ... Locally these exist. Oregon already had one, Toronto already had one. We looked at all the divisions. Here is where the SCM-process already exists. Now we are gonna build one? Well why start from a blank sheet, if you have all these pieces already. The idea was: Take this survey – take the best from the process – and that became [the organization's] SCM. It makes sense based [on] inter-sustainable standards. Does ours look exactly the same – the one we build in Oregon? No, but the content are the same. OK. All right then you get down to the documents, the deliverable. The process description documents. If we use the table's content would I be OK? Sure. Do I have the same activities and deliverables? Sure. But do I fundamentally wanna start with Toronto's process description and turn it into the organization's process description? No. (US member in Team 2)

In Team 1, most of the participants continued to work on their former projects after the initial kick-off and only three people were fully released to participate in Team 1. These three people (one Dane and two Swedish employees) formed a sub-project aiming at developing a code standard. They, however, had many disagreements about how to achieve this outcome. Investigating the existing code standards within the company, they found that each site had its own local standard. The sub-group tried to locate a tool for validating code standard. However, having nine different code standards, they had to define a common standard before locating the validation tool. When they began by reviewing the code standard at the Swedish site, a communication breakdown related to the professional context emerged. The review was situated in a co-located setting in Sweden, where two of the sub-group members introduced the standard – created primarily by one of the Swedish members – to software engineers. The last member of the sub-group had called in sick that day. After observing and talking to the engineers, the two team members assessed the result.

We totally disagree about how the review went. [A Swedish member] thought that it went well and there only were small corrections to be made. I, on the other hand, was of the opinion that the programmers did not have a clue of the meaning behind the code standard. (Danish member in Team 1)

The Danish member perceived that introducing a code standard comprising approximately 200 rules to all software engineers in the company was unrealistic. Instead he suggested they implement an industrial code standard, since the chance of engineers already being familiar with an industrial standard was high and it would also be easier to locate a generic tool for validation. However, the Swedish member totally disagreed.

Bringing highly skilled and motivated people together to agree on a common task is a challenge that is well known from software development practice (Ngwenyama and Lyytinen, 1997). Specialists often follow different goals and find themselves in conflict during teamwork; however, they still collaborate to produce the expected product, as did the sub-group. The conflict did not have anything to do with antagonism, but it was embedded in the task. Since the participants of Team 1 and Team 2 had prior experiences working with SCM-processes or code standards, they had their own ideas, assumptions and expectations of how the work should be done.

[…]

References

Bell, B. and Kozlowski, S. (2002) A typology of virtual teams: implications for effective leadership. *Group and Organization Management*, 27, 14–49.

Bjørn, P. and Hertzum, M. (2006) Project-based collaborative learning: negotiating leadership and commitment in virtual teams. In: *5th Conference on Human Computer Interaction in Southern Africa (CHI-SA)*, Greunen D.V. (ed.), pp. 6–15. Association for Computing Machinery Special Interest Group on Computer–Human Interaction (ACM SIGCHI), Cape Town, South Africa.

Bowker, G.C. and Star, S.L. (2002) *Sorting Things Out: Classification and its Consequences*. The MIT Press, Cambridge, MA, USA.

Carstensen, P. and Schmidt, K. (1999) *Computer support cooperative work: new challenges to system design*. CTI Working Paper, vol. 43, February 1999.

Chudoba, K.M., Wynn, E., Lu, M. and Watson-Manheim, M.B. (2005) How virtual are we? Measuring virtuality and understanding its impact in a global organization. *Information Systems Journal*, 15, 279–306.

Clark, H. and Brennan, S. (1991) Grounding in communication. In *Perspectives on Social Shared Cognition*, Resnick, L., Levine, J. and Teasley, S. (eds), pp. 127–149. American Psychological Association, Washington, DC, USA.

Cramton, C.D. (2001) The mutual knowledge problem and its consequences for dispersed collaboration. *Organization Science*, 12, 346–371.

Daft, R.L. and Weick, K.E. (1984) Toward a model of organizations as interpretation systems. *Academy of Management Review*, 9, 284–295.

Ebling, M.R., John, B.E. and Satyanarayanan, M. (2002) The importance of translucence in mobile computing systems. *ACM Transactions on Computer – Human Interaction*, 9, 42–67.

Eisenhardt, K.M. (1989) Building theories from case study research. *The Academy of Management Review*, 14, 532–550.

Erickson, T. and Kellogg, W.A. (2000) Social translucence: an approach to the designing systems that support social processes. *ACM Transactions on Computer–Human Interaction*, 7, 59–83.

Fiol, C.M. and O'Connor, E.J. (2005) Identification in face-to-face, hybrid, and pure virtual teams: untangling the contradictions. *Organization Science*, 16, 19–32.

Gerson, E.M. and Star, S.L. (1986) Analyzing due process in the workplace. *ACM Transactions on Office Information Systems*, 4, 257–270.

Giddens, A. (1984) *The Constitution of Society*. Polity Press, Cambridge, UK.

Gioia, D.A. (1986) Symbols, scripts, and sensemaking: creating meaning in the organizational experience. In: *The Thinking Organization*, Sims, H.P. and Giola, D.A. (eds), pp. 49–74. Jossey-Bass, San Francisco, CA.

Glaser, B.G. and Strauss, A.L. (1967) *The Discovery of Grounded Theory: Strategies for Qualitative Research*. Aldine De Gruyter, New York, USA.

Griffith, T., Sawyer, J. and Neale, M. (2003) Virtualness and knowledge in teams: managing the love triangle of organizations, individuals, and information technology. *MIS Quarterly*, 27, 265–287.

Habermas, J. (1981) *Theorie des kommunikativen Handelns*, 2 Bände (*The Theory of Communicative Action*, 2 Vols.) McCarthy, T. (trans.). Suhrkamp, Frankfurt, Germany.

Heath, C., Svensson, M.S., Hindmarsh, J., Luff, P. and Lehn, D. (2002) *Configuring awareness. Computer Supported Cooperative Work (CSCW): An International Journal*, 11, 317–347.

Hertzum, M. (1999) Six roles of documents in professionals' work. In *Sixth European Conference on Computer Supported Cooperative Work*, Bødker, S., Kyng, M. and Schmidt, K. (eds), pp. 41–60. Kluwer Academic Publisher, Copenhagen, Denmark, 12–16 September.

Hinds, P. and Mortensen, M. (2005) Understanding conflict in geographically distributed teams: An empirical investigation. *Organization Science*, 16, 290–307.

Holmqvist, B. (1989) Work, language and perspective: An empirical investigation of the interpretation of a computer-based information system. *Scandinavian Journal of Information Systems* 1, 72–96.

Huysman, M., Steinfield, C., Jang, C.-Y., David, K., Veld, M.H.I.T., Poot, J. and Mulder, I. (2003) Virtual teams and appropriation of communication technology: exploring the concept of media stickiness. *Computer Supported Cooperative Work (CSCW): An International Journal*, 12, 411–436.

Jarvenpaa, S.L. and Leidner, D. E. (1999) Communication and trust in global virtual teams. *Organization Science*, 10, 791–815.

Jarvenpaa, S.L., Knoll, K. and Leidner, D.E. (1998) Is anybody out there? Antecedents of trust in global virtual teams. *Journal of Management Information Systems*, 14, 29–64.

Kirkman, B., Rosen, B., Tesluk, P. and Gibson, C. (2004) The impact of team empowerment on virtual team performance: the moderating role of face-to-face interaction. *Academy of Management Journal*, 47, 175–192.

Klein, H. and Truex, D. (1996) Discourse analysis: an approach to the investigation of organizational emergence. In *Signs of Work: Semiosis and Information Processing in Organisations*, Holmqvist, B., Andersen, P.B., Klein, H. and Posner, R. (eds), pp. 227–268. Walter de Gruyter, Berlin, Germany.

Klein, H.K. and Myers, M.D. (1999) A set of principles for conducting and evaluating interpretive field studies in information systems. *MIS Quarterly*, 23, 67–93.

Lipnack, J. and Stamps, J. (2000) *Virtual Teams: People Working Across Boundaries with Technology*. John Wiley & Sons, New York, USA.

Lundberg, C. (1989) An organizational learning: implications and opportunities for expanding organization development. In: *Research in Organizational Change and Development* (Vol. 3), Pasmore, W.A. and Woodman, R. (eds), pp. 61–82. JAI Press, Greenwich, CT.

Lyytinen, K.J. and Ngwenyama, O.K. (1992) What does computer support for cooperative work mean? A structurational analysis of computer supported cooperative work. *Accounting Management and Information Technology*, 2, 19–37.

Majchrzak, A., Rice, R.E., Malhotra, A., King, N. and Ba, S. (2000) Technology adaption: the case of a computer-supported inter-organizational virtual team. *MIS Quarterly*, 24, 569–600.

Malhotra, A. and Majchrzak, A. (2004) Enabling knowledge creation in far-flung teams: best practice for its support and knowledge sharing. *Journal of Knowledge Management*, 8, 75–88.

Mark, G. and Poltrock, S. (2003) Shaping technology across social worlds: groupware adoption in a distributed organization. In: *International ACM SIGGROUP Conference on Support Group Work: GROUP*, Schmidt, K., Pendergast, M., Tremaine, M. and Simone, C. (eds), pp. 284–293. Sanibel Island, FL.

Maznevski, M.L. and Chudoba, K.M. (2000) Bridging space over time: global virtual team dynamics and effectiveness. *Organization Science*, 11, 473–492.

Ngwenyama, O. and Klein, H. (1994) An exploration of the expertise of knowledge workers: towards a definition of the universe of discourse for knowledge acquisition. *Information Systems Journal*, 4, 129–140.

Ngwenyama, O. and Lyytinen, K. (1997) Groupware environments as action constitutive resources: a social action framework for analyzing groupware technologies. *Computer Supported Cooperative Work (CSCW): An International Journal*, 6, 71–93.

Ngwenyama, O.K. (1998) Groupware, social action and organizational emergence: on the process dynamics of computer mediated distributed work. *Accounting Management and Information Technology*, 8, 127–146.

Ngwenyama, O.K. and Lee, A.S. (1997) Communication richness in electronic mail: critical social theory and the contextuality of meaning. *MIS Quarterly*, 21, 145–167.

Olson, G.M. and Olson, J.S. (2000) Distance matters. *Human–Computer Interaction*, 15, 139–178.

Orlikowski, W. and Hofman, D. (1997) An improvisational model for change management: the case of groupware technologies. *Sloan Management Review*, 38, 11–21.

Orlikowski, W.J. and Gash, D.C. (1994) Technological frames: making sense of information technology in organizations. *ACM Transactions on Information Systems*, 12, 174–207.

Rennecker, J. and Godwin, L. (2005) Delays and interruptions: a self-perpetuating paradox of communication technology use. *Information and Organization*, 15, 247–266.

Robinson, M. (1991) Double-level language and co-operative working. *AI and Society*, 5, 34–60.

Schein, E.H. (1992) *Organizational Culture and Leadership*. Jossey-Bass, San Francisco, CA, USA.

Schmidt, K. and Bannon, L. (1992) Taking CSCW seriously: supporting articulation work. *Computer Supported Cooperative Work (CSCW): An International Journal*, 1, 7–40.

Schütz, A. (1982) *Lifeforms and Meaning Structures (Lebensformen und Sinnstruktur)*. Wagner, H.R. (trans.). Routledge and Kegan Paul, Abingdon, UK.

Strauss, A. (1988) The articulation of project work: an organizational process. *The Sociological Quarterly* 29, 163–178.

Suchman, L. (1987) *Plans and Situated Actions. The Problem of Human Machine Communication*. Cambridge University Press, Cambridge, UK.

Suchman, L. (1995) Making work visible. *Communications of the ACM*, 38, 56–64.

Townsend, A.M., DeMarie, S.M. and Henrickson, A.R. (1998) Virtual teams: technology and the workspace of the future. *Academy of Management Executive*, 12, 17–29.

Tyre, M. and Orlikowski, W. (1994) Windows of opportunities: temporal patterns of technological adaptation in organizations. *Organization Science*, 5, 98–118.

Walsham, G. (1995) Interpretive case studies in IS research: nature and method. *European Journal of Information Systems*, 4, 74–81.

Weick, K. (1969) *The Social Psychology of Organizing*. Addison-Wesley, Reading, MA, USA.

Weick, K. (1993) The collapse of sensemaking in organizations: the Mann Gulch disaster. *Administrative Science Quarterly*, 38, 628–652.

Weick, K., Sutcliffe, K. and Obstfeld, D. (2005) Organizing and the process of sensemaking. *Organizational Science*, 16, 409–421.

PART V

The darker side of collaborative arrangements

Introduction

Jill Mordaunt

In this section of the reader we explore why things go wrong in organisations and cross-boundary collaborations and examine the feasibility of proposals to prevent and resolve problems. Recognising problems in organisational relationships is not as straightforward as it might first appear. There is, as the saying goes, '20/20 vision with hindsight', but when problems are emerging recognition is often slow and diagnosis of the reasons for them can be the subject of much dispute. It does seem that the 'dark side' encompasses problems ranging from institutionalised acts and omissions that lead to failure to outright corruption. The readings selected for this section seek to illustrate the debates about how these processes operate and examine some of the solutions that are suggested for dealing with the (often spectacular) problems that can arise such as the collapse of the financial markets, failure of disaster response mechanisms and cover-ups over wrong-doing.

The first reading by Vaughan is an extract from the United States Senate Inquiry Report conducted after the *Columbia* disaster – when a space shuttle exploded on re-entry to the earth's atmosphere in 2003. This accident was caused by a foam debris strike damaging the heat resistant tiles on the wing of the shuttle. The National Aeronautics and Space Administration (NASA) knew about this problem but had discounted it as a threat to the shuttle, although there were concerns among the engineering staff about its implications. What is more perturbing about this accident is that it was almost a repetition of a similar accident that had befallen the *Challenger* shuttle, which had exploded on launch 17 years earlier in 1986. In that case the problem was the failure of an O-ring seal in the rocket booster. This was also a known problem and again engineers' concerns were over-ruled. Vaughan questions why it was that NASA seemed not to have learnt the lessons from this when something so similar seemed to have occurred with the *Columbia* shuttle. She concludes that the problems arose from issues of conflicting goals, the organisational culture of NASA, a structure and hierarchy that blocked communication channels, and that this was made worse by outsourcing which led to a 'silent safety system'. Her recommendations therefore focus on issues of leadership and organisational structure.

There are essentially two responses to dealing with organisational problems. The first is *post hoc* – dealing with problems that have arisen. The second is preventative – tackling problems before they arise. The second article by Jackall offers a critique of 'whistle-blowing' which is a way for those within organisations with problems to expose the wrong-doing they see occurring. Much has been made of whistle-blowing over the last 15 years or so as a way of dealing with organisational problems. In the UK the last Labour Government enacted the Public Interest Disclosure Act 1998 to provide some protection for those who 'blew the whistle'. There are similar provisions now across the globe. What has been interesting about whistle-blowing is how often those who expose the wrong-doing seem to suffer more in terms of their career prospects than the apparent 'wrong-doers'.

Jackall's short piece is a response to another in the same journal where a professor of legal ethics discusses his discomfort and that of his colleagues about whether to expose a colleague who has lied about a peer review he was supposed to have undertaken. Jackall's piece points out a number of issues and quandaries that face both those who blow the whistle and those who have to make a judgment of the 'truth' of their allegations. If we take the view that the causes of problems are 'socially constructed', then that implies that it is not generally so clear-cut about where these causes lie in the organisation. Jackall suggests that there are complex games played to create 'plausible deniability' particularly in large organisations where there are fragmented authority structures. Moreover, although organisations often have elaborate codes of ethics, the values in use emerge out of the organisation's culture, which is more pragmatic than the abstract values enshrined in these codes. Even where there are obvious breaches of standards, the exposure of these may not be in the individual's best interest nor in the organisation's, for example where people are urged not to 'rock the boat'. Then there is the problem of where the truth of the matter lies. Also, alliance with the media can leave the whistle-blower compromised in their own organisation when the media frenzy moves on.

The other response to dealing with these problems is preventative. Accountability is often seen as a way of ensuring that people working both within and across organisational boundaries may literally be held to account for their actions. The article by Mordaunt explores this issue particularly with reference to non-profit and public sector boards and managers. However, this issue has wider application. As Mordaunt reveals, this terminology masks a considerable amount of complexity and is, she argues, a 'slippery concept' that means very different things to different actors. Like the other authors in this section, she suggests that there are dilemmas and paradoxes inherent in dealing with problems and that accountability may be likened to a game. Moreover, the problems that accountability seeks to address are not amenable to easy solutions. Forcing people to comply may lead to what she calls 'formulaic compliance'.

Ultimately, dealing with the 'Dark Side' of organisation is fraught with difficulty. None of the material selected here suggests that problems should not be addressed, but they do suggest that problems are neither easy to diagnose nor easily amenable to resolution. Managers working in such settings would do well to recognise this complexity and to accept that some problems have sub-optimal solutions.

18

HISTORY AS CAUSE
Columbia and Challenger

Diane Vaughan

Source: Edited from Columbia Accident Investigation Board (CAIB) *CAIB Report Volume 1*, August 2003, Chapter 8, Columbia Accident Investigation Board.

This chapter is an extract from the Senate Inquiry Report conducted after the Columbia *Disaster.*

The investigation began with two central questions about NASA decisions. Why did NASA continue to fly with known foam debris problems in the years preceding the *Columbia* launch, and why did NASA managers conclude that the foam debris strike 81.9 seconds into *Columbia*'s flight was not a threat to the safety of the mission, despite the concerns of their engineers?

1 Echoes of *Challenger*

Ironically, the Rogers Commission investigation into *Challenger* started with two remarkably similar central questions: Why did NASA continue to fly with known O-ring erosion problems in the years before the *Challenger* launch, and why, on the eve of the *Challenger* launch, did NASA managers decide that launching the mission in such cold temperatures was an acceptable risk, despite the concerns of their engineers?

The echoes did not stop there. The foam debris hit was not the single cause of the *Columbia* accident, just as the failure of the joint seal that permitted O-ring erosion was not the single cause of *Challenger*. Both *Columbia* and *Challenger* were lost also because of the failure of NASA's organizational system. Previous political, budgetary, and policy decisions by leaders at the White House, Congress, and NASA impacted the Space Shuttle Program's structure, culture, and safety system and these in turn resulted in flawed decision-making for both accidents. The explanation is about system effects: how actions taken in one layer of NASA's organizational system impact other layers. History set the *Columbia* and *Challenger* accidents in motion. What happened in the political environment, the organization, and managers' and engineers' decision-making, the three worked together. Each is a critical link in the causal chain.

This chapter shows that both accidents were "failures of foresight" (Turner 1978, Turner and Pidgeon 1997). First, the history of engineering decisions on foam and O-ring incidents had identical trajectories that "normalized" these anomalies, so that flying with these flaws became routine and acceptable. Second, NASA history had an effect. In response to White House and Congressional mandates, NASA leaders took actions that created systemic organizational flaws at the time of *Challenger* that were also present for *Columbia*. The final section compares the two critical decision sequences immediately before the loss of both Orbiters – the pre-launch teleconference for *Challenger* and the post-launch foam strike discussions for *Columbia*. It shows how past definitions of risk combined with systemic problems in the NASA organization caused both accidents.

Connecting the parts of NASA's organizational system and drawing the parallels with *Challenger* demonstrate (that) despite all the post-*Challenger* changes at NASA and the agency's notable achievements since, the causes of the institutional failure responsible for *Challenger* have not been fixed. The recommendations for change are not only for fixing the Shuttle's technical system, but also for fixing each part of the organizational system that produced *Columbia*'s failure. Whilst individuals are responsible and accountable, NASA's problems cannot be solved simply by retirements, resignations, or transferring personnel.

The constraints under which the agency has operated throughout the Shuttle Program have contributed to both Shuttle accidents. Although NASA leaders have played an important role, these constraints were not entirely of NASA's own making. The White House and Congress must recognize the role of their decisions in this accident and take responsibility for safety in the future.

2 Failures of foresight: Two decision histories and the normalization of deviance

Foam loss may have occurred on all missions, and left bipod ramp foam loss occurred on 10 percent of the flights for which visible evidence exists. How, after the bitter lessons of *Challenger*, could NASA have failed to identify a similar trend? This section gives an insider perspective: how NASA defined risk and how those definitions changed over time for both foam debris hits and O-ring erosion. In both cases, engineers and managers conducting risk assessments continually normalized the technical deviations they found (Vaughan, 1996). In all official engineering analyses and launch recommendations prior to the accidents, evidence that the design was not performing as expected was reinterpreted as acceptable and non-deviant, which diminished perceptions of risk throughout the agency.

The initial Shuttle design predicted neither foam debris problems nor poor sealing action of the Solid Rocket Booster joints. To experience either on a mission was a violation of design specifications. The engineers decided to implement a temporary fix and/or accept the risk, and fly. For both O-rings and foam, that first decision was a turning point. It established a precedent for accepting, rather than eliminating, these technical deviations. Anomalies that did not lead to catastrophic failure were treated as a source of valid engineering data that justified further flights and was acceptable. Both O-ring erosion and foam debris events were repeatedly "addressed" in NASA's Flight Readiness Reviews but never fully resolved.

Before *Challenger*, the problematic Solid Rocket Booster joint had been elevated to a Criticality 1 item on NASA's Critical Items List. The joint was later demoted to a Criticality 1-R (redundant), and then in the month before *Challenger*'s launch was "closed out" of the problem-reporting system. Prior to both accidents, this demotion from high-risk item to low-risk item was very similar, but with some important differences. Damaging the Orbiter's Thermal Protection System, especially its fragile tiles, was normalized even before Shuttle launches began: it was expected due to forces at launch, orbit, and re-entry. (Roland, 1987) So ingrained was the agency's belief that foam debris was not a threat to flight safety that in press briefings after the *Columbia* accident, the Space Shuttle Program Manager still discounted the foam as a probable cause, saying that Shuttle managers were "comfortable" with their previous risk assessments.

From the beginning, NASA's belief about both these problems was affected by the fact that engineers were evaluating them in a work environment where technical problems were normal. Although management treated the Shuttle as operational, it was in reality an experimental vehicle. Many anomalies were expected on each mission. Another contributing factor was that both foam debris strikes and O-ring erosion events were examined separately, one at a time. What NASA engineers and managers saw were pieces of ill-structured problems (Turner op. cit) [...] NASA managers and engineers were receiving mixed signals. (Vaughan op. cit) Some signals defined as weak at the time were, in retrospect, warnings of danger. Finally, because foam debris strikes were occurring frequently, like O-ring erosion in the years before *Challenger*, foam anomalies became routine signals – a normal part of Shuttle operations, not signals of danger. Other anomalies gave signals that were strong, like wiring malfunctions, which had a clear relationship to a "loss of mission." On those occasions, NASA stood down from launch, sometimes for months, while the problems were corrected.

Each time an incident occurred, the Flight Readiness process declared it safe to continue flying. Taken one at a time, each decision seemed correct. The consequences of living with both of these anomalies were, in its view, minor. The dominant view at NASA – the managerial view – was, as one manager put it, "we were just eroding rubber O-rings," which was a low-cost problem (Vaughan op. cit.). The financial consequences of foam debris also were relatively low: replacing tiles extended the turnaround time between launches. In both cases, NASA was comfortable with its analyses. Prior to each accident, the agency saw no greater consequences on the horizon.

3 System effects: The impact of history and politics on risky work

NASA's own history encouraged this pattern of flying with known flaws. Seventeen years separated the two accidents. NASA Administrators, Congresses, and political administrations changed. However, NASA's political and budgetary situation remained the same in principle as it had been since the inception of the Shuttle Program. NASA remained a politicized and vulnerable agency, dependent on key political players who accepted NASA's ambitious proposals and then imposed strict budget limits. Post-*Challenger* policy decisions made by the White House, Congress, and NASA leadership resulted in the agency reproducing many of the failings identified by the Rogers Commission. Policy constraints affected the Shuttle Program's organization culture, its structure, and the structure of the safety system. The three combined to keep NASA on its slippery slope toward *Challenger* and *Columbia*. NASA culture allowed flying with flaws when problems were defined as normal and routine; the structure of NASA's Shuttle Program blocked the flow of critical information up the hierarchy, so definitions of risk continued unaltered. Finally, a perennially weakened safety system, unable to critically analyze and intervene, had no choice but to ratify the existing risk assessments on these two problems.

Prior to both accidents, NASA was scrambling to keep up. Not only were schedule pressures impacting the people who worked most closely with the technology – technicians, mission operators, flight crews, and vehicle processors – engineering decisions also were affected. For foam debris and O-ring erosion, the definition of risk established during the Flight Readiness process determined actions taken and not taken, but the schedule and shoestring budget were equally influential. NASA was cutting corners. Launches proceeded with incomplete engineering work on these flaws. [...] Available resources – including time out of the schedule for research and hardware modifications – went to the problems most likely to bring down a Shuttle. The NASA culture encouraged flying with flaws because the schedule could not be held up for routine problems that were not defined as a threat to mission safety.

Why, since the foam debris anomalies went on for so long, had no one recognized the trend and intervened? The O-ring history prior to *Challenger* had followed the same pattern. This question pointed ... toward the NASA organization structure and the structure of its safety system. Safety-oriented organizations often build in checks and balances to identify and monitor signals of potential danger. If these checks and balances were in place in the Shuttle Program, they weren't working.

Prior to *Challenger*, Shuttle Program structure had hindered information flows, leading to the conclusion that critical information about technical problems was not conveyed effectively through the hierarchy. The Space Shuttle Program had altered its structure by outsourcing to contractors, which added to communication problems. The Commission recommended many changes to

238 Organizational Collaboration

remedy these problems, and NASA made many of them. However, those post-*Challenger* changes were undone over time by management actions (McDonald, no date). NASA administrators, reacting to government pressures, transferred more functions and responsibilities to the private sector. The change was cost-efficient, but personnel cuts reduced oversight of contractors at the same time that the agency's dependence upon contractor engineering judgment increased. When high-risk technology is the product and lives are at stake, safety, oversight, and communication flows are critical. The Shuttle Program's normal chain of command and matrix system did not perform a check-and-balance function on either foam or O-rings.

The Flight Readiness process only affirmed the pre-*Challenger* engineering risk assessments. Equally troubling the Flight Readiness process, which is built on consensus verified by signatures of all responsible parties, in effect renders no one accountable. Managers at the top were dependent on engineers at the bottom for their engineering analysis and risk assessments. Information was lost as engineering risk analyses moved through the process. At succeeding stages, management awareness of anomalies, and therefore risks, was reduced either because of the need to be increasingly brief and concise as all the parts of the system came together, or because of the need to produce consensus decisions at each level. The Flight Readiness process was designed to assess hardware and take corrective actions that would transform known problems into acceptable flight risks, and that is precisely what it did. The 1986 House Committee on Science and Technology concluded during its investigation into *Challenger* that Flight Readiness Reviews had performed exactly as they were designed, but that they could not be expected to replace engineering analysis, and therefore they "cannot be expected to prevent a flight because of a design flaw that Project management had already determined an acceptable risk" (U. S. Congress, 1986). Those words, true for the history of O-ring erosion, also hold true for the history of foam debris.

The last line of defense against errors is usually a safety system. But the previous policy decisions by leaders also impacted the safety structure and contributed to both accidents. In neither problem did NASA's safety system attempt to reverse the course of events. In 1986, the Rogers Commission called it "The Silent Safety System." Pre-*Challenger* budget shortages resulted in safety personnel cutbacks. Without clout or independence, the safety personnel who remained were ineffective. In the case of *Columbia*, the Board found the same problems were reproduced and for an identical reason: when pressed for cost reduction, NASA attacked its own safety system. The faulty assumption was that a reduction in safety staff would not result in a reduction of safety, because contractors would assume greater safety responsibility. The effectiveness of those remaining staff safety engineers was blocked by their dependence on the very Program they were charged to supervise. Also, the Board found many safety units with unclear roles and responsibilities that left crucial gaps. Post-*Challenger* NASA still had no systematic procedure for identifying and monitoring trends. Problem reporting and tracking systems were still overloaded or underused, which undermined their very purpose. Multiple job titles disguised the true extent of safety personnel shortages. There were cases in which the same person was occupying more than one safety position – and in one instance at least three positions – which compromised any possibility of safety organization independence because the jobs were established with built-in conflicts of interest.

4 Organization, culture, and unintended consequences

At the same time that NASA leaders were emphasizing the importance of safety, their personnel cutbacks sent other signals. Streamlining and downsizing, which scarcely go unnoticed by employees, convey a message that efficiency is an important goal. The Shuttle/Space Station partnership affected both programs. Working evenings and weekends just to meet the International Space Station deadline sent a signal to employees that schedule is important. When paired with the "faster, better, cheaper" NASA motto of the 1990s and cuts that dramatically decreased safety personnel, efficiency becomes a strong signal and safety a weak one. This kind of doublespeak by top administrators affects people's decisions and actions without them even realizing it (Douglas, 1987, Burawoy, 1979).

Changes in Space Shuttle Program structure contributed to the accident in a second important way. Despite the constraints that the agency was under, prior to both accidents NASA appeared to be immersed in a culture of invincibility, in stark contradiction to post-accident reality. The Rogers Commission found a NASA blinded by its "Can-Do" attitude, a cultural artifact of the Apollo era that was inappropriate in a Space Shuttle Program so strapped by schedule pressures and shortages that spare parts had to be cannibalized from one vehicle to launch another. This can-do attitude bolstered administrators' belief in an achievable launch rate, the belief that they had an operational system, and an unwillingness to listen to outside experts. Even after the loss of *Challenger*, NASA was guilty of treating an experimental vehicle as if it were operational and of not listening to outside experts. Engineers and program planners were also affected by "Can-Do," which, when taken too far, can create a reluctance to say that something cannot be done.

How could the lessons of *Challenger* have been forgotten so quickly? First, if success is measured by launches and landings the machine appeared to be working successfully prior to both accidents. *Challenger* was the 25th launch. Seventeen years and 87 missions passed without major incident. Second, previous policy decisions again had an impact. NASA's Apollo-era research and development culture and its prized deference to the technical expertise of its working engineers was overridden in the Space Shuttle era by "bureaucratic accountability" – an allegiance to hierarchy, procedure, and following the chain of command (McCurdy, 1989). Prior to *Challenger*, the can-do culture was a result not just of years of apparently successful launches, but of the cultural belief that the Shuttle Program's many structures, rigorous procedures, and detailed system of rules were responsible for those successes (Vaughan, 1997).

5 History as cause: Two accidents

Risk, uncertainty, and history came together when unprecedented circumstances arose prior to both accidents. For *Challenger*, the weather prediction for launch time the next day was for cold temperatures that were out of the engineering experience base. For *Columbia*, a large foam hit – also outside the experience base – was discovered after launch. For the first case, all the discussion was pre-launch; for the second, it was post-launch. This initial difference determined the shape these two decision sequences took, the number of people who had information about the problem, and the locations of the involved parties.

For *Challenger*, engineers at Morton-Thiokol, the Solid Rocket Motor contractor in Utah, were concerned about the effect of the unprecedented cold temperatures on the rubber O-rings. Because launch was scheduled for the next morning, the new condition required a reassessment of the engineering analysis presented two weeks prior. A teleconference began at 8:45 p.m. Eastern Standard Time (EST) that included 34 people in three locations. Thiokol engineers were recommending a launch delay. A reconsideration of a Flight Readiness Review risk assessment the night before a launch was as unprecedented as the predicted cold temperatures. With no ground rules or procedures to guide their discussion, the participants automatically reverted to the centralized, hierarchical, tightly structured, and procedure-bound model used in Flight Readiness Reviews. The entire discussion and decision to launch began and ended with this group of 34 engineers. The phone conference linking them together concluded at 11:15 p.m. EST after a decision to accept the risk and fly.

For *Columbia*, information about the foam debris hit was widely distributed the day after launch. Rather than a tightly constructed exchange of information completed in a few hours, time allowed for the development of ideas and free-wheeling discussion among the engineering ranks. The early post-launch discussion among engineers and all later decision-making at management levels were decentralized, loosely organized, and with little form. The diffuse form and lack of structure in the rest of the proceedings would have several negative consequences.

In both situations, all new information was weighed and interpreted against past experience. Formal categories and cultural beliefs provide a consistent frame of reference in which people view and interpret information and experiences. Pre-existing definitions of risk shaped the actions taken and not taken. Worried engineers in 1986 and again in 2003 found it impossible to reverse the Flight Readiness Review risk assessments. These engineers could not prove that foam strikes and cold temperatures were unsafe, even though the previous analyses that declared them safe had been incomplete and were based on insufficient data and testing. The obstacles these engineers faced were political and organizational. They were rooted in NASA history and the decisions of leaders that had altered NASA culture, structure, and the structure of the safety system and affected the social context of decision-making for both accidents. In the following comparison of these critical decision scenarios for *Columbia* and *Challenger*, the systemic problems in the NASA organization are in italics, with the system effects on decision-making following.

NASA had conflicting goals of cost, schedule, and safety. Safety lost out as the mandates of an "operational system" increased the schedule pressure. Scarce resources went to problems that were defined as more serious, rather than to foam strikes or O-ring erosion.

In both situations, upper-level managers and engineering teams held opposing definitions of risk. [...] When confronted with the engineering risk assessments, top Shuttle Program managers held to the previous Flight Readiness Review assessments.

The effects of working as a manager in a culture with a cost/efficiency/safety conflict showed in managerial responses. In both cases, managers' techniques focused on the information that tended to support the expected or desired result at that time. In both cases, believing the safety of the mission was not at risk, managers drew conclusions that minimized the risk of delay.

[...]

NASA's culture of bureaucratic accountability emphasized chain of command, procedure, following the rules, and going by the book. While rules and procedures were essential for coordination, they had an unintended but negative effect. Allegiance to hierarchy and procedure had replaced deference to NASA engineers' technical expertise.

In both cases, engineers initially presented concerns as well as possible solutions – a request for images, a recommendation to place temperature constraints on launch. Management did not listen to what their engineers were telling them. Instead, rules and procedures took priority. For *Columbia*, program managers turned off the Kennedy engineers' initial request for Department of Defense imagery, with apologies to Defense Department representatives for not having followed "proper channels." Both *Challenger* and *Columbia* engineering teams were held to the usual quantitative standard of proof. But it was a reverse of the usual circumstance: instead of having to prove it was safe to fly, they were asked to prove that it was unsafe to fly.

Ignored by management was the qualitative data that the engineering teams did have: both instances were outside the experience base. In stark contrast to the requirement that engineers adhere to protocol and hierarchy was management's failure to apply this criterion to their own activities. The Mission Management Team did not meet on a regular schedule during the mission, proceeded in a loose format that allowed informal influence and status differences to shape their decisions, and allowed unchallenged opinions and assumptions to prevail. In highly uncertain circumstances, when lives were immediately at risk, management failed to defer to its engineers and failed to recognize that different data standards – qualitative, subjective, and intuitive – and different processes – democratic rather than protocol and chain of command – were more appropriate.

The organizational structure and hierarchy blocked effective communication of technical problems. Signals were overlooked, people were silenced, and useful information and dissenting views on technical issues did not surface at higher levels. What was communicated to parts of the organization was that O-ring erosion and foam debris were not problems.

Structure and hierarchy represent power and status. For both *Challenger* and *Columbia*, employees' positions in the organization determined the weight given to their information, by their own judgment and in the eyes of others. As a result, many signals of danger were missed.

Early in the *Challenger* teleconference, some engineers who had important information did not speak up. They did not define themselves as qualified because of their position: they were not in an appropriate specialization, had not recently worked the O-ring problem, or did not have access to the "good data" that they assumed others more involved in key discussions would have (Vaughan, 1997).

In the more decentralized decision process prior to *Columbia's* re-entry, structure and hierarchy again were responsible for an absence of signals. The initial request for imagery came from the "low status" Kennedy Space Center, bypassed the Mission Management Team, and went directly to the Department of Defense separate from the all-powerful Shuttle Program. Information was lost as it traveled up the hierarchy. A demoralized Debris Assessment Team did not include a slide about the need for better imagery in their presentation to the Mission Evaluation Room. The uncertainties and assumptions that signaled danger dropped out of the information chain when the Mission Evaluation Room manager condensed the Debris Assessment Team's formal presentation to an informal verbal brief at the Mission Management Team meeting.

Location in the structure empowered some to speak and silenced others. For example, a Thermal Protection System tile expert, who was a member of the Debris Assessment Team but had an office in the more prestigious Shuttle Program, used his personal network to shape the Mission Management Team view and snuff out dissent. The informal hierarchy among and within Centers was also influential. When asked why they didn't voice their concerns to Shuttle Program management, the Langley engineers said that people "need to stick to their expertise" (Wong 2003). Status mattered. For those with lesser standing, the requirement for data was stringent and inhibiting, which resulted in information that warned of danger not being passed up the chain. In perhaps the ultimate example of this, *Challenger* astronauts were told that the cold temperature was not a problem, and *Columbia* astronauts were told that the foam strike was not a problem.

NASA structure changed as roles and responsibilities were transferred to contractors, which increased the dependence on the private sector for safety functions and risk assessment while simultaneously reducing the in-house capability to spot safety issues.

A critical turning point in both decisions hung on the discussion of contractor risk assessments. Although both Thiokol and Boeing engineering assessments were replete with uncertainties, NASA ultimately accepted each. NASA was dependent on Thiokol for the risk assessment, but the decision process was affected by the contractor's dependence on NASA. Not willing to be responsible for a delay, the contractor did not act in the best interests of safety. Boeing's Crater analysis was performed in the context of the Debris Assessment Team, which was a collaborative effort that included Johnson, United Space Alliance, and Boeing. In this case, the decision process was also affected by NASA's dependence on the contractor. Unfamiliar with Crater, NASA engineers and managers had to rely on Boeing for interpretation and analysis, and did not have the training necessary to evaluate the results. They accepted Boeing engineers' use of Crater to model a debris impact 400 times outside validated limits.

NASA's safety system lacked the resources, independence, personnel, and authority to successfully apply alternate perspectives to developing problems. Overlapping roles and responsibilities across multiple safety offices also undermined the possibility of a reliable system of checks and balances.

NASA's "Silent Safety System" did nothing to alter the decision-making that immediately preceded both accidents. No safety representatives were present during the *Challenger* teleconference – no one even thought to call them. In the case of *Columbia*, safety representatives were present at all meetings. However, rather than critically question or actively participate in the analysis, the safety representatives simply listened and concurred.

6 Changing NASA's organizational system

The echoes of *Challenger* in *Columbia* have serious implications. These repeating patterns mean that flawed practices embedded in NASA's organizational system continued for 20 years and made substantial contributions to both accidents. An organization system failure calls for corrective measures that address all relevant levels of the organization, but NASA has shown very little understanding of the inner workings of its own organization.

NASA managers believed that the agency had a strong safety culture, but the agency had the same conflicting goals that it did before *Challenger*, when schedule concerns, production pressure, cost-cutting and a drive for ever-greater efficiency – all the signs of an "operational" enterprise – had eroded NASA's ability to assure mission safety. The belief in a safety culture has even less credibility in light of repeated cuts of safety personnel and budgets – also conditions that existed before *Challenger*. NASA managers stated confidently that everyone was encouraged to speak up about safety issues and that the agency was responsive to those concerns, but the Board found evidence to the contrary. NASA's bureaucratic structure kept important information from reaching engineers and managers alike. The same NASA whose engineers showed initiative and a solid working knowledge of how to get things done fast had a managerial culture with an allegiance to bureaucracy and cost-efficiency that squelched the engineers' efforts. When it came to managers' own actions, however, a different set of rules prevailed. Mission Management Team decision-making operated outside the rules even as it held its engineers to a stifling protocol. Management was not able to recognize that in unprecedented conditions, when lives are on the line, flexibility and democratic process should take priority over bureaucratic response (Weick, 1993).

During the *Columbia* investigation, the investigation consistently searched for causal principles that would explain both the technical and organizational system failures. These principles were needed to explain *Columbia* and its echoes of *Challenger*. They were also necessary to provide guidance for NASA. The analysis of organizational causes supports the following principles that should govern the changes in the agency's organizational system.

Leaders create culture. It is their responsibility to change it. Top administrators must take responsibility for risk, failure, and safety by remaining alert to the effects their decisions have on the system. Leaders are responsible for establishing the conditions that lead to their subordinates' successes or failures. The past decisions of national leaders set the *Columbia* accident in motion by creating resource and schedule strains that compromised the principles of a high-risk technology organization. The measure of NASA's success became how much costs were reduced and how efficiently the schedule was met. But we cannot explore space on a fixed-cost basis.

Changes in organizational structure should be made only with careful consideration of their effect on the system and their possible unintended consequences. Changes that make the organization more complex may create new ways that it can fail (Clarke, 1999). When changes are put in place, the risk of error initially increases, as old ways of doing things compete with new. Institutional memory is lost as personnel and records are moved and replaced. Changing the structure of organizations is complicated by external political and budgetary constraints, the inability of leaders to conceive of the full ramifications of their actions, the vested interests of insiders, and the failure to learn from the past.

The Shuttle Program's structure is a source of problems, not just because of the way it impedes the flow of information, but because it has had effects on the culture that contradict safety goals. NASA's blind spot is it believes it has a strong safety culture. Program history shows that the loss of a truly independent, robust capability to protect the system's fundamental requirements and specifications inevitably compromised those requirements, and therefore increased risk.

Strategies must increase the clarity, strength, and presence of signals that challenge assumptions about risk. Twice in NASA history, the agency embarked on a slippery slope that resulted in catastrophe. Each decision, taken by itself, seemed correct, routine, and indeed, insignificant and unremarkable. Yet in retrospect, the cumulative effect was stunning. NASA's challenge is to design systems that maximize the clarity of signals, amplify weak signals so they can be tracked, and account for missing signals. For both accidents there were moments when management definitions of risk might have been reversed were it not for the many missing signals – an absence of trend analysis, imagery data not obtained, concerns not voiced, information overlooked or dropped from briefings. A safety team must have equal and independent representation so that managers are not again lulled into complacency by shifting definitions of risk.

References

Burawoy, Michael, *Manufacturing Consent* (Chicago, IL: University of Chicago Press, 1979).

Clarke, Lee, *Mission Improbable: Using Fantasy Documents to Tame Disaster* (Chicago, IL: University of Chicago Press, 1999).

Douglas, Mary, *How Institutions Think* (London: Routledge and Kegan Paul, 1987).

McCurdy, Howard E. "The Decay of NASA's Technical Culture," *Space Policy* (November 1989), pp. 301–10.

McDonald, Harry (no date) Report of the Shuttle Independent Assessment Team.

Presidential Commission on the Space Shuttle *Challenger* Accident (Washington, DC: Government Printing Office, 1986).

Roland, Alex, "The Shuttle: Triumph or Turkey?" *Discover,* November 1985: pp. 29–49.

Turner, Barry, *Man-made Disasters* (London, Wykeham, 1978).

Turner, Barry and Pidgeon, Nick, *Man-made Disasters*, 2nd ed. (Oxford: Butterworth Heinneman, 1997).

Vaughan, Diane, *The Challenger Launch Decision: Risky Technology, Culture, and Deviance at NASA* (Chicago, IL: University of Chicago Press, 1996).

Vaughan, Diane, "The Trickle-Down Effect: Policy Decisions, Risky Work, and the Challenger Tragedy," *California Management Review*, 39, 2, Winter 1997.

Weick, Karl E., "The Collapse of Sensemaking in Organizations: The Mann Gulch Disaster." *Administrative Science Quarterly*, 38, 1993, pp. 628–652.

Wong, Edward, "E-Mail Writer Says He was Hypothesizing, Not Predicting Disaster," *New York Times*, 11 March 2003.

19

WHISTLEBLOWING AND ITS QUANDARIES

Robert Jackall

Source: *Georgetown Journal of Legal Ethics*, 2007, 20 (4), pp. 1133–6.

Whistleblowers are men and women who publicly call individuals in their own organizations to account for behavior that they, the whistleblowers, deem inappropriate by some standard. The metaphor that the word invokes – that of a referee in striped shirt who enforces agreed-upon rules in a football or basketball game – is misleading. Instead, whenever one calls attention to others' perceived "wrongdoing" in big organizations, one finds oneself in a tar pit of quandaries. This is an initial attempt to explore some of those perplexities.[1]

First, it's often difficult to ascertain responsibility for wrongdoing in large bureaucracies. The fantastically complicated division of authority that marks all large organizations separates most actors from the consequences of their actions. In particular, it insulates the highest authorities from accounting for any problems that their organizations create. Plausible deniability is part and parcel of these fragmented authority structures. If actors have networked well – a prerequisite for survival, let alone success, in the bureaucratic wilderness – they can count on loyal allies and subordinates to circle the wagons and protect them when arrows begin to fly. Moreover, if things go drastically wrong, a boss can always blame his underlings for poor judgment.

Second, such deniability is enhanced by the constant doublethink, doublespeak, backing and filling, and systematic obfuscation that characterize organizational actors' public speech to both internal and external audiences about their work,

---

[1] These remarks are based on thirteen case studies involving extensive interviews with eighteen self-described whistleblowers. I conducted these studies between 1981 and 1986. I describe a few cases of corporate whistleblowing in my book, *Moral Mazes: the world of corporate managers* (1988). Other cases from this set of materials – which range from case studies of whistleblowing in the National Aeronautics and Space Administration to the New York City Human Resources Administration – have not yet been published. In addition, in this Essay I draw on my extensive fieldwork with the New York Police Department and with prosecutors in the office of the District Attorney of New York.

their institutions, and especially any of their own decisions that might prove problematic. Virtually all bureaucracies in every institutional arena have elaborate written codes of ethics crafted by attorneys, compliance officers, moral philosophers, public relations and advertising practitioners, and other interpretive experts, all of whom are part of the ethics industry. Such written codes always stake out lofty moral ground and are seen as essential for gaining and maintaining public good will. In some bureaucratized professional worlds – law is the paradigmatic example – these codes are taken seriously and are enforced by professional associations. Violations still occur, of course, such as when lawyers deliberately misrepresent matters to courts. But if other lawyers catch them in such lies, and decide to act on this knowledge, the penalties can be heavy indeed.

In the corporate world, different standards are typically at work. There, up-and-coming young people must exhibit dexterity at invoking ethical codes and their accompanying rhetoric if they wish to triumph in the ongoing scramble for authority, power, and prestige. But few big corporations adhere to the high moral standards that their interpretive experts assert publicly as their lodestars. It's important to remember in this regard that Enron had an elaborate, formal code of ethics in place well before a young Williams College alumna asked embarrassing questions about the company's questionable accounting; these were in fact relatively simple inquiries that had never before been posed by a great many Wall Street financial analysts or Enron's corporate directors.[2] For the most part, formal guidelines have little to do with day-to-day behavior, and all corporate players know it. Instead, the moral rules-in-use that emerge directly out of a specific milieu's particular ethos – itself forged in addressing exigencies – shape day-to-day behavior. These rules-in-use regularly conflict with corporate actors' necessary public embrace of abstract virtues, designed for internal audiences who know better but have a stake in maintaining fictions, or for external audiences who know nothing about the specific worlds at issue. Thus, men and women in big corporations strive to do "what has to be done" while maintaining the public appearance of moral probity. The resultant ambiguity of meaning and intention makes accurate assessment and interpretation of others' actions precarious.

Third, even when there are relatively clear-cut instances of wrongdoing – defined here as actions that multiple insiders with different interests and perspectives deem moral leprosy – rules of etiquette and protocol restrict prerogatives to draw attention to them effectively in a way that is analogous to courts' limitation of standing to litigants with direct stakes in the outcome of cases. Denizens of the academy need look no further than to their own world for interesting examples of the invocation of jurisdictional rulings, even – and, perhaps especially – when crucial matters affecting the reputation and standards of a whole institution are at stake, such as the evaluation of faculty scholarship and teaching at promotion-

---

[2]For Enron's Code of Ethics from July 2000, see http://www.thesmokinggun.com/graphics/packageart/enron/enron.pdf.

decision time. Whatever their expertise, their long service to their institutions, and their *bona fides* in looking out for their institutions' best interests, faculty who are outside specific departmental and disciplinary loops and associated circles of affiliation where promotion decisions are made find even their most grounded observations about, say colleagues' misrepresentation of source materials, strident ideology passing as scholarship, indoctrination of students, or even plagiarism, quite unwelcome.

Fourth, all big organizations – however formal the delineation of their hierarchies – consist ultimately of dense social networks of men and women, each possessing elaborate cognitive maps of the organizational biographies of all players at their own level and above. When one chooses to point out the wrongdoing of colleagues, or especially that of superiors, one inevitably jars these intricate affiliations and the prevailing commonsensical moral rules-in-use. Such assertion of principles, even when moral leprosy is widely acknowledged, threatens established social order and makes everyone wonder whose actions will next come under unwanted scrutiny with unforeseeable results. Watchwords in big organizations, however banal, are telling in this regard: "Don't rock the boat."; "Go along to get along."; "Do what you're told to do, and keep your mouth shut." And most denizens of large organizations do keep their mouths shut, adopting the peculiarly modern stance of knowing and not knowing. In other words, even when men and women have direct knowledge of catastrophic mistakes, legal boundary crossing, sleight-of-hand accounting, the passing off of mediocre goods or people as first-rate, the manipulation of rules to achieve desired interpretations, outright deception, and, of course, the time-serving laziness endemic in all bureaucracies, most choose to turn a blind eye to such abuses in order to "live and let live." Of course, some organizational denizens decide to keep quiet about particular abuses that they've observed because they choose to store up knowledge of such depredations against the rainy day when their own survival or ascendancy might turn on their knowing where bodies are buried.

Fifth, the profound intellectual and moral confusion that permeates American society prevents many men and women from achieving the clear-mindedness necessary to see where bright lines are drawn, when and how others have crossed them, and what to do about it. The extreme form of epistemological relativism typical of the various postmodern approaches to the humanities, social sciences, and even the law, has migrated from the academy into the world of affairs. It has undercut the Aristotelian notion of truth – the conceit that human beings are capable of stating propositions that accurately describe events in the world outside of themselves – a minimalist idea of truth essential for any conception of responsibility that links actors to their own deeds. The Aristotelian framework has largely been replaced by a shadow-world of hermeneutics, language games, and fleeting images that place a premium on deciphering the nuances of meaning in a world where nothing is fixed, and nothing certain. In such a world, assertion of the wrongdoing of a colleague or superior is considered "judgmental," and is thought to be a character defect in the person *making the assertion*.

Moreover, strident moralism goes hand-in-hand with the rejection of the bedrock condition of rational argument. Those who eschew any reliable way of ascertaining even minimalist truth in the Aristotelian sense regularly assert their own morally-freighted views on particular situations. Would-be whistleblowers face not only the problem of how to convince others of the truth of what they've observed, but also how to counter the welter of moralistic obfuscations that permeate the public sphere of our society. The matter is still more complicated. There are situations in human affairs where the truth of things is simply inaccessible, where the differences between action with clear motive, or vague intent, or simple inattentiveness become extremely difficult to discern with any accuracy. How then do those who would call attention to others' wrongdoing proceed?

Some whistleblowers turn to the all-powerful media to expose wrongdoing in their organizations, always a dangerous tactic. At times, this is done through "leaks." Leaks regularly precipitate plumber expeditions to search for unwanted breaches of secrecy. When whistleblowers have followed organizational procedures, including secrecy protocols, but have nonetheless been thwarted – and perhaps sanctioned for their truth-telling – matters almost inevitably become public, often through discovery materials in lawsuits. Journalists become temporary allies of whistleblowers because their own vocation demands that they hunt constantly for man-bites-dog sensational stories, and there are none better than those that recount courageous employees exposing the sins of higher authorities. But actors in all the occupational and professional worlds that I've studied see journalists as snapshot-taking tourists, largely uninterested in the ambiguous nuances of the dilemmas that men and women of affairs face. Those who turn to journalists to right perceived organizational wrongs are not only thought to be party to washing dirty linen in public, but also to have turned their backs on colleagues facing troubling issues in favor of fleeting celebrity. And journalists inevitably move on to still other stories, leaving whistleblowers with compromised standing in their organizations, however they might be lionized in print or on the air. One can't underestimate the importance of the morally-freighted notion of betrayal. Even those who welcome the consequences of betrayal mistrust the betrayer.

In the end, blowing the whistle is a lonely business, even when one has definitive evidence against colleagues or superiors. Whistleblowing demands the stomach for controversy and the willingness to subject oneself to one's colleagues' enduring suspicions.

20

THE EMPEROR'S NEW CLOTHES
Why boards and managers find accountability relationships difficult
Jill Mordaunt

Source: Edited from *Public Policy and Administration*, 2006, 21 (3), Autumn, pp. 120–34.

Introduction

In their book on corporate governance, Lorsch and MacIver (1989) document that board members said they felt confident in their ability to question the CEO of their organisation about matters of concern. Yet in their observed performance, board members rarely did this. If board members raised problems, they did it covertly and outside the board. Similar accountability issues occur in non-profit organisations. Board performance rarely reflects the rhetoric implicit in regulatory and legislative requirements. There are competing and at times contradictory expectations and demands. How do boards and managers seek to balance these in ways that allow them to maintain their integrity and yet still satisfy the expectations of different stakeholders?

Accountability as paradox

This chapter aims to explore the paradoxes of accountability. If we are to understand organisations as experienced by practitioners then it is essential to understand the effects of tensions and inconsistencies without always looking for neat solutions. These paradoxes raise dilemmas for managers and boards as they seek to find ways of balancing the apparently inconsistent demands on, and expectations of, them. This chapter seeks to link up some existing management ideas in different ways to offer insight into how, what we might conceive of as an *accountability game*, is played.

Accountability requirements often have a negative impact on organisations and the people who work in them, for example, housing association staff operating the repair service became more concerned to comply with targets than actually getting the repairs done (Seddon, 2003). Public organisations are established for social purposes to deliver benefits to their end users, yet they often seem to be focusing their energies on meeting the demands of other external stakeholders. This raises issues such as 'In whose interests does (should) this organisation operate?'

The concept of accountability is riven with confusions and dilemmas that arise at different points. What are the sources of this complexity and are there ways in which some reconciliation between competing demands may be achieved? Broadly, the different accountability relationships may be typified as:

- *Market* accountability is about those who buy from, choose to use or fund the organisation. In this view the organisation's managers and trustees are accountable to the customer.
- *Managerial* accountability is concerned with rules and regulations that specify criteria against which the organisation's (and individuals within it) performance is measured.
- *Political* accountability is concerned with wider concepts of civic and democratic obligation and implies notions of reciprocity of rights and responsibilities.

As Newman (2001) observes these differing forms of accountability are not necessarily in conflict with each other, but under the last Labour government which was apparently obsessed with delivery and centralised control (Maddock, 2002), they made uneasy bedfellows as they each drew on differing value systems about what matters in organisational governance. Beside these tensions, the word 'accountability' is often used in a 'policy speak' way – at broad levels of generality without making explicit the meaning that is operating in particular contexts. This leads to communication difficulties because each party to the relationship assumes that the others are using the word with the same intended meaning whereas in reality the intentions may vary substantially without becoming explicit. Thus accountability is a 'slippery concept'.

As Figure 20.1 shows below, the many near and distant stakeholders in the non-profit organisational environment all have different concerns about organisational performance and therefore the issues they expect to be addressed can differ, at times very substantially.

However, these various stakeholders have differing abilities to hold the organisation to account. *Required* accountability flows from the organisational environment: the legal, political and economic context in which the organisation operates (Leat, 1988). Those who demand this kind of accountability generally have strong powers of redress for failure to comply with their demands. For example, the English Charity Commission has powers to disqualify people who fall below standards from acting as trustees (Charity Act, 1992).

By contrast, *proactive* or *voluntary* accountability flows from organisational values: the belief that the organisation should in its actions and working methods consciously seek to align itself with certain groups and interests. This is also called *offered* accountability. Here the organisation chooses to be accountable because it is

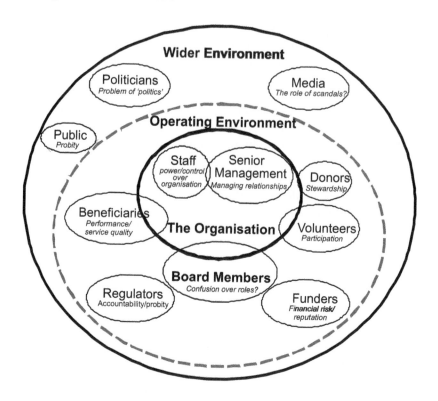

FIGURE 20.1 Stakeholder concerns in the Governance System
(Source: Cornforth and Mordaunt, 2004)

deemed appropriate. Such accountability is offered to beneficiaries and the wider public for example through meetings or via a website. These options combine with the *discretion* (in theory at any rate) to choose between different policies or courses of action and create dilemmas for boards and managers. In voluntary organisations, the cause of the end user is often the passion that drives the organisation. Yet, the differential powers of stakeholders to hold the organisation to account, means that some external stakeholders generally wield greater power than beneficiaries do. Figure 20.2 illustrates this.

The strength of external stakeholders is interesting. Regulators and funders have clear powers to demand accountability via legal sanctions or withholding funding. Although the media has no formal status vis-à-vis voluntary organisations – the potential power that bad publicity has to destroy public trust in an organisation disciplines many in the sector (Horton, 2006). There may be congruence of interest between internal and external stakeholders in ensuring organisational performance but faced with divergences of interest there is a tendency for the demands of those with the ability to apply strong sanctions to prevail. This differential power between stakeholders to demand accountability and to apply sanctions, poses serious dilemmas for non-profit managers. Too much attention

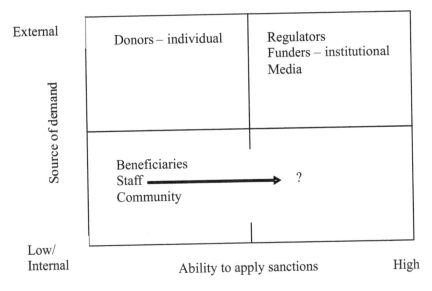

FIGURE 20.2 Differing demands for accountability

to the powerful stakeholders means that the interests of beneficiaries may be overlooked or ignored: the organisation's purposes may drift from serving beneficiaries to ensuring that external accountability demands are met. Equally insufficient attention to these stakeholders can lead to the organisation losing legitimacy and therefore losing resources.

These tensions and paradoxes in policy-making, leadership and management are now widely recognised (Lewis, 2000). These can be described in many different ways, but in the present context, dilemma theory (Hampden-Turner, 1990; Hampden-Turner and Trompenaars, 2000) is particularly appropriate. Dilemma theory arises out of social psychology and sees the ways of addressing the inevitable conflicts and tensions of managerial life as a dialectical process by which managers, as they seek to resolve these, reach higher synergies. This is personally risky for managers or board members as it means dealing with issues where the understandings and therefore the responses of others is uncertain and potentially negative. But Hampden-Turner (op. cit.) argues that 'we have no choice but to choose' and his work offers practical ways of charting dilemmas and finding ways of reconciling these.

As an illustration, the earlier discussion of competing accountabilities is represented in a dilemma diagram below. It shows how what is commonly seen as a zero-sum trade-off (tending to polarised viewpoints) can be reconstructed as a *shared* dilemma that needs to be navigated and negotiated. Both the external demands for accountability and the sense of obligation on the part of manager and trustees to offer account to members and service users are real. However, they often sit in tension with one another and external stakeholders increasingly want evidence of performance that may interfere with work with beneficiaries or may direct organisational energies elsewhere. The problem facing managers and boards is how to take the demands of external agencies and their beneficiaries seriously without being taken over by them. Depending on the orientation adopted, differing problems emerge. This may be posed as in Figure 20.3.

Because of the power to 'hold to account', there is a tendency for organisations to be driven by external requirements and to drift towards the lower right hand quadrant of this diagram. Fry (1995) contends that more and more formalised control procedures that focus on external control and sanctions to ensure compliance are counter-productive. If individuals are forced to be accountable, they comply, but then accountability is then frequently seen as an imposition. While this may achieve results in the short term, it does not necessarily secure commitment. Yet this has been a major focus of the political and funding environment that surrounds non-profit organisations in the UK and beyond for the last several years.

This concern with 'holding to account' has a detrimental effect on the capacity of organisations to become confident and act as external regulators and funders would wish. The focus on rational performance management of activities leads to a constant search for the 'right' way to manage to satisfy externally driven performance criteria and distracts organisations from living according to their values. As Meyer (1999) has argued, performance management by setting targets and accounting for these is like the search for the unobtainable. It never quite meets expectations, as the only way to do this effectively is to measure everything. As this is not possible, a selection is made focusing on particular aspects of

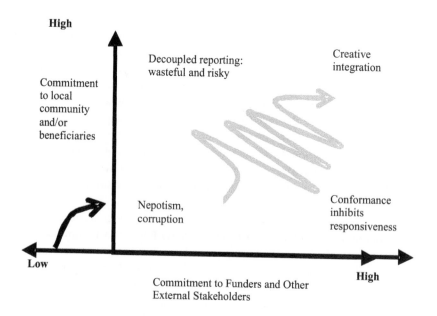

FIGURE 20.3 Dilemmas of accountability

performance that are deemed problematic. This has a distorting effect as Seddon's (2003) story of the housing association, referred to above, illustrates. Seeking to ensure accountability in this way often means that the target rather than the task to be completed takes precedence.

The accountability game

Although managers take accountability seriously in that they generally take great care to comply with the demands made of them, particularly by funders and regulators, paradoxically they generally do not appear to think very deeply about accountability. This frequently compounds the lack of conceptual clarity and the ambiguity and complexity that surrounds accountability. For example when conducting interviews with trustees about their uses of financial information, we asked to whom they thought they were accountable. The most frequent responses were either that they had not thought about it or they did not really know. The answers varied greatly and ranged from the service users to the Charity Commission (Cornforth and Edwards, 1998). Thus, it seems that mostly accountability is enacted by means of *'formulaic compliance'*. In some senses it seems that accountability is an *'hurrah'* word – obligatory to use, but with little concern for practical application.

However, it also seems that much *'offered'* accountability may be just as formulaic as *'required'* accountability. It is not unusual for voluntary sector Annual General Meetings to be short rituals, where little of significance occurs. There may be great defensiveness when questioned about the performance of the organisation. Evaluations can be designed to puff up achievements or user consultations used to legitimise the *status quo*. Meaningless statistics may be produced. This is not to say that all efforts to hold to account or to offer accountability are useless and futile, but that there may be something else happening as well. This leads to accountability appearing like a game played to appear compliant but, in Fry's terms (op. cit.), without commitment and it often appears that a ritual is taking place. As Paton (2003) has argued the fact that often accountability processes do not work as intended, does not mean they may not 'work' in other ways.

Some paradoxes therefore arise. Although supposedly accountability is a means of taking stock and learning from problems – quite the opposite may happen in reality. Kegan (1994) notes the case of the schoolteacher who sees the staff appraisal process turned into a compliance with state requirements rather than a learning process for teachers. Similarly, at a seminar of local authority officials, Chief Executives complained about the extent to which subordinates wanted to tell them what they thought they wanted to hear rather than what they needed to hear. Learning opportunities are missed and the goal of obtaining more effective and meaningful forms of accountability that are not just self-serving or formulaic seems elusive.

The game is reinforced by the formulaic and idiosyncratic way in which accountability regimes are implemented and exercised. It may be that those devising them had 'good intentions' but the actual operation of the system is often viewed as whimsical, dysfunctional and troubling. This response from a manager in an FE college on a university discussion area illustrates a practitioner view:

Q *What characterises non-profit management?*

> Answering to the requirements of people from outside bodies, in my case external moderators, inspectors, funding bodies. They don't seem to know what they really want and change their focus with the trends. I had to attend a meeting this term on 'The new inspection framework'. What was wrong with the old one? We only had it about 4 years ago.
>
> (Quoted with permission)

This sense of constant and apparently irrational churn that she depicts, probably stems from the paradoxes of accountability outlined above, but it appears to those on the receiving end that they are victims of individual game-playing.

Indeed, accountability regimes often appear not to be devised in a considered way. Instead 'mimetic isomorphism' (DiMaggio and Powell, 1983) occurs where regulators and organisations look at what others have done and seek formulae that may be implemented without deep thinking about what forms of accountability are required in specific contexts. For example, for many years housing associations in Scotland all used the same ill-thought-out business planning mechanism because the regulatory body imposed the formula used by the first association to provide a business plan on all other associations. The fact that some of the information this produced was completely meaningless seemed not to be an issue. No one in the housing associations raised that this was an issue – they simply produced the information they were required to and then the game had been played according to the rules.

Those who do try to make accountability meaningful to their organisation may bring in expert advice. The advice may be something that the organisation does not want to hear. Then the organisation may distance itself from the problem and fail to listen to the advice. But even when managers and board members do listen, the advice offered leaves unspecified the behaviours that are actually required to bring about change. For example, the Charity Commission expends much public money and considerable effort on offering advice to trustees about their roles and responsibilities (Charity Commission, 2005). Despite efforts to make this more user-friendly much of the advice is exhortative, abstract and disconnected from the realities that people face. There is little mention of the need for process skills in addressing what to do when the organisation is not legally compliant. As noted above this leads to 'formulaic compliance' rather than organisational learning and change. This is not really surprising when the language in which the accountability requirements is couched is examined. For example, when the Charity Commission introduced a new SORP reporting requirement on risk, the opening paragraph stated:

Risk is an inherent feature of all activity and may arise from inaction as well as new initiatives. Charities will have differing exposures to risk arising from their activities and will have different capacities to tolerate or absorb risk. A charity with sound reserves could perhaps embark on a new project with a higher risk profile than, say, a charity facing solvency difficulties. Risk tolerance may also be a factor of the activities undertaken to achieve objectives. Thus a relief charity operating in a war zone may, in order to achieve its objectives, need to tolerate a higher level of risk to staff than might be acceptable in its UK-based activities. A charity will also need to understand its overall risk profile, i.e. the balance taken between higher and lower risk activities.

(Charity Commission, 2004)

The language used is open to many interpretations and the criteria by which risk may be judged is not set out explicitly. For example, the document suggests that a risk might be that the trustee body lacks the necessary skills or commitment, without anywhere in the guidelines actually specifying what these skills and commitments might be. This language does not communicate with the audience who are often left bemused about what is expected of them.

All of these issues can make accountability seem like an empty ritual. However, there does seem to be some point to the game, for changing it is really difficult. There is often deep discomfort when things go wrong and paradoxically huge anger when people do expose shortcomings.

When accountability raises uncomfortable issues external stakeholders can seem to prefer to ignore the difficulties (Mordaunt and Cornforth, 2004) than deal with them. In an urban regeneration project where funds had been misspent, it appeared to our informant that council officers would rather pretend that this was not happening than tackle the chair, who was also prominent in the local political establishment. Experience suggests that this is not an isolated occurrence. When evaluating a community development project, serious problems emerged about the work of the local authority staff member involved. The responsible local authority official indicated that he did not want to hear this 'for then I would have to do something about it ...' Similar issues arise for trustees. One observed at a focus group meeting that he often did not ask questions that he knew he should 'because then I'd be responsible for the consequences of the answer' (Mordaunt and Cornforth, 2004).

In addition it appears that despite boards and managers advocating that people expose 'wrong-doing', in many cases, it is often the whistle-blower as much as the wrong-doer who is punished (Public Concern at Work, 2004).

Again, paradoxes emerge. Accountability appears formulaic and yet to be very important when wrongdoing is exposed. At the same time, it appears that there are moments, when both external and internal stakeholders seek to avoid engaging with problems. So to return to Paton's question in the preceding section – how do accountability regimes 'work'? Trust is an essential ingredient of this. It is beyond the scope of this chapter to engage with all the debates around the nature of trust but public trust and confidence are key to charity donations and funding. Where the organisation has a solid reputation and its legitimacy is high, it seems that the accountability reporting appears formulaic. In the absence of indications that anything is wrong, board members and external stakeholders may take it on trust that all is well and the reports made are not examined closely.

There do however appear to be some circumstances where the accountability game is played for high stakes. It may operate as an insurance policy to be called in when a serious concern arises. When the legitimacy of an organisation is questioned (appropriately or not), the full panoply of the accountability armoury is mustered. Then the audit or inspection regime is galvanised to look for any infringement of regulations or failing which will justify the withdrawal of funding or other penalties. However, audit failure may be more to do with being a *post hoc* justification for action than being the trigger for that action in the majority of cases. In other words, the judgment that the organisation is failing arises from other more qualitative concerns about its performance and the accountability reports then justify this. An example is the investigation of War on Want by the Charity Commission in the late 1980's after accusations in the press about their contentious General Secretary's behaviour (Wikipedia 2006).

Neither of these scenarios, however, explains why people work so hard to avoid owning problems that accountability regimes do expose.

The Emperor's new clothes

So why, when individual managers and board members are often so articulate and clear about the problems, do so many continue to play the *accountability game*? Why do people behave like the courtiers in the story of the Emperor's New Clothes? This issue is explored by both Argyris (1990) and by Kegan and Lahey (2000).

What is happening according to Argyris goes beyond cynical manipulation of accountability to suit particular purposes. He suggests that the problems arise because people want to avoid upsetting values deeply embedded in the organisation. In the context of the voluntary sector where many accountability demands are external to the organisation, these values are often shared across the domain and thus the game extends to a wider arena. Organisational defence regimes are developed to minimise the embarrassment or threat caused by negative reports. This stems from defences that manifest as what Argyris calls Mode 1 approaches to management and organisational learning. Although managers and board members' 'espoused theory' holds values of being in control, winning and not upsetting people – their actual behaviour sustains defences that act against these. Thus senior managers in non-profit organisations and funders often state that they value 'feedback', participation and involvement by those they fund or support. Although their 'espoused theory' emphasises partnership and participation, their 'theory in use' emphasises unilateral control, dependency, submissiveness and crucially not embarrassing others but allowing them to maintain 'face'.

These organisational defensive regimes are, Argyris suggests, anti-learning, overprotective and self-sealing. The effect is to produce a logic that:

- Crafts messages that contain inconsistencies
- Acts as if the messages are not inconsistent
- Makes the ambiguity and inconsistency in the message undiscussable
- Makes the undiscussability of the undiscussable also undiscussable.

(Argyris, op. cit., pp. 26–27)

When senior managers are challenged over their actions '(they)' used mixed messages to talk people out of their natural response to (their) actions – for example 'It's a very interesting idea ...', when as Argyris points out '*Interesting* is the word we most commonly use to express either our indifference or objection, while acting as if we want to be supportive'.

Because these defensive routines are not open to influence (because they are undiscussable), people feel a sense of helplessness in addressing them. There seems to be no way out of the impasse and the way in which organisational defence patterns are structured means that the problems get driven underground, for example, by blaming others or the organisation for problems or not confronting the ways in which individuals reinforce that which they complain about. These defence patterns are, of course, even more pernicious in an inter-organisational setting where the problems are compounded by lack of management authority to address them in any direct way unless powerful external stakeholders are willing to wield their, often rather heavy-handed, sanctions such as withdrawing funding.

Likewise, Kegan and Lahey (2000) suggest that cover-ups are created by the ways people talk about the organisation. On the surface, they espouse particular strong commitments. In the case of accountability, they will say they care deeply about being responsive to service users or about ensuring that they serve their local community. However, in fact they take no responsibility for ensuring that the espoused aim happens, because underlying these value commitments are competing commitments such as making sure that you do not upset people or avoiding conflict at any cost. These competing commitments are stronger than the stated commitment as they expose people's most deep-seated and greatest fears. For example, 'If I were really responsive and accountable to the community, I might lose control of the situation. Then I might be seen as a failure and I would lose my status in my profession.'

Once understanding dawns that deeply-held emotional commitments perhaps take precedence over the espoused values of, for example, serving the community, it readily becomes apparent that rather than being puzzling, the failure to deliver begins to make sense. Although leaders in public and non-profit organisations work hard to reform public and voluntary services and to make them accountable by creating widely shared viable missions, they fail to foster the ways of talking about these issues within their organisations to deal with the (often more personal and emotional) competing commitments. At an inter-organisational level, the silence on these issues is deafening. The Emperor may be naked but no one is willing to say so. The price of 'failure to hit the mark' if the message is not heard – is too high (Hampden-Turner, op. cit.).

Changing the game – is it possible?

On the one hand there appears a strong desire on the part of external stakeholders to ensure that those they fund and support act in appropriate ways that are fit for purpose and deliver the services that the end user needs and wants. On the other hand, the operation of the accountability game seems to work against this. For example, the international development field has become more and more constrained by external accountability demands and there is little sign of will on the part of the major players to deal with problems, despite the obvious impact on the likely success of their work (Wallace and Mordaunt, 2007). Striking the balance between the problems of 'decoupled reporting' or 'conformance' referred to earlier in Figure 20.3 appears elusive to many. So, can these dilemmas and paradoxes be addressed? To answer this question we need a better understanding of the ways in which some people manage these dilemmas more successfully than others.

All the approaches reviewed in this paper suggest that the answers lie in the realm of action: of personal development and management practices that are transformative of human behaviour. Argyris suggests that the solution lies in moving towards what he calls a Mode 2 approach to organisational problems. This holds the values of valid information, informed choice and responsibility to monitor the implementation of that choice. This leads to action strategies where problems or issues are proposed and inquiry into and confirmation of those strategies is sought and that face-saving is minimised. It implies new social virtues of help and support, respect for others, strength, honesty and integrity. This involves double-loop learning that besides focusing on the presenting problem also pays attention to the implications of the underlying values. The task is to change the mind-set of the actors in the organisation by people learning to be more reflective.

Similarly, Kegan and Lahey (2000) advocate an educative strategy to achieve organisational change. They advocate developing ways of talking that give organisational members better ways of discussing the competing commitments that prevent their espoused commitments becoming reality. This means moving from positions of negative critical thinking and taking responsibility for problems within the organisation rather than seeing the problems lying with others. It means creating agreements that allow all involved to point to shortcomings. Kegan and Lahey conclude that by developing these different ways of talking, leaders, managers and front-line staff will also be able to change the way in which they approach their work.

However, these concerns have permeated the management literature for many years. Yet there are real dilemmas here. How do you get sign-up throughout the organisation to its values and commitments? Fry (op. cit.) raised the question of how organisations and managers can move from holding to account and offering account to 'felt' accountability, where performance is delivered because the ethic has been internalised. His approach has some resonances of that of Kegan and Lahey (2000) in that he advocates 'conversations for accountability'. He argues that this has the effect of shifting the emphasis away from what was done wrong to what has been done well.

But is this enough? There is little research in this area and the issues that need investigation are many. All these solutions seem to involve transformative conversations and agreements about how to go forward. No one would dispute that, where in-depth work of the kind advocated occurs, that it has effects but it also has huge resource implications. How many organisations are prepared to take the amount of time needed to do this? What degree of unanimity does this demand within organisations? Additionally, strategies such as this raise further questions. How do you get individuals to address the difficulties and challenges of good performance by means of the developmental approaches advocated when there is a chance of personal pain and risk of failure? The reasons people adopt Argyris' Mode 1 strategies (outlined in the earlier section) when dealing with accountability is to avoid losing control and dealing with embarrassment.

However, these solutions also ignore the external pressures on organisations that maintain the *status quo*. How may such strategies be adopted in the interagency context that typifies voluntary sector accountability relationships? It is one thing to engage in such conversations within organisations, but it is much more challenging to do this across organisational boundaries especially when there is no sanction for not participating. In the inter-agency context the demands of external stakeholders and their perceived power is part of the problem. There are some glimmers of light, however, if there is will on the part of external stakeholders to address problems. The voluntary sector compacts that operate in the UK exemplify Kegan and Lahey's (op. cit.) approach. Although these do not resolve the problems of voluntary/state relationships, they provide a benchmark for expected standards of behaviour to which the aggrieved can point. However, achieving even this small measure of success in redressing the balance of power has taken years of negotiation. Time and commitment issues are to the fore.

This means that in this area of inter-agency accountability, we urgently need to conduct research that reveals the ways in which both managers and boards and all those engaged in the accountability game may address the dilemmas and paradoxes of accountability. If this can uncover the ways in which some managers have developed 'creative integration' (see Figure 20.3) and address the concerns of all stakeholders then we may find ways of making accountability more than an empty but resource-hungry and time-consuming shell.

References

Argyris, C. (1990), *Overcoming Organisational Defenses*, (Needham Heights, MA: Allyn & Bacon).

Charity Commission (2004), Charities and Risk Management – Appendices I, II and III, available at: http://www.charity-commission.gov.uk/investigations/charriskapp.asp#a3.

Charity Commission (2005), The Essential Trustee: What you need to know, available at http://www.charity-commission.gov.uk/publications/cc3.asp#b2.

Cornforth, C.J. and Edwards, C. (1998), *Developing Effective Board–Management Relations in Public and Voluntary Organizations*, (London: Chartered Institute of Management Accountants Research Foundation).

Cornforth, C.J. and Mordaunt, J. (2004), 'The governance of the voluntary and community sector – the starting point', *Developing an Integrated Governance Strategy for the Voluntary and Community Sector: volume of evidence*, (Newcastle upon Tyne: The Foundation for Good Governance), pp. 7–14.

DiMaggio, P. and Powell, W. (1983), 'The iron cage revisited: institutional isomorphism and collective rationality in organizational fields', *American Sociological Review*, Vol 48, pp. 147–160.

Fry, R. (1995), 'Accountability in organisational life: problem or opportunity for nonprofits?' *Nonprofit Management and Leadership*, Vol 6, No 2.

Hampden-Turner, C. (1990), *Charting the Corporate Mind: from dilemma to strategy*, (Oxford: Basil Blackwell).

Hampden-Turner, C. and Trompenaars, F. (2000), *Building Cross-cultural Competence: how to create wealth from conflicting values*, (Chichester: John Wiley & Sons).

Horton, J. (2006), 'Confidence in charities returning after scandals', *Edinburgh Evening News* 7th June 2006 http://news.scotsman.com/topics.cfm?tid=865&id=345292006.

Kegan, R. (1994), *In Over Our Heads: The Mental Demands of Modern Life*, (Cambridge, MA: Harvard University Press).

Kegan, R. and Lahey, L.L. (2000), *How the Way We Talk Can Change the Way We Work* (San Francisco, CA: Jossey-Bass).

Leat, D. (1988), *Voluntary organisations and accountability*, (London, NCVO).

Lewis, D. (2000), 'International Aid Agencies: policy conflict and convergence', in M. Harris and C. Rochester (eds), *Voluntary Agencies and Social Policy: Perspectives on Change and Choice*, (London: Macmillan).

Lorsch, J.W. and MacIver, E. (1989), *Pawns or Potentates: The Reality of America's Corporate Boards*, (Boston, MA: Harvard Business School Press).

Maddock, S. (2002), 'Making modernisation work', *International Journal of Public Sector Management*, Vol 15, pp. 13–43.

Meyer, M.W. (1999), 'Permanent failure and organizational performance', in H.K. Anheier (ed.), *When Things Go Wrong*, (Thousand Oaks, CA: Sage).

Mordaunt, J. and Cornforth, C.J. (2004), 'The role of boards in the failure and turnaround of non-profit organizations', *Public Money and Management*, Vol. 24, No 4, pp. 227–234.

Newman, J. (2001) *Modernising Governance*. London: Sage.

Paton, R. (2003), *Managing and measuring social enterprises*, (London: Sage).

Public Concern at Work (2004) 'Case studies', available at: http://www.pcaw.co.uk/help%5Findivid/cases.html.

Seddon, J. (2003), *Freedom from Command and Control*, (Buckingham: Vanguard Education Ltd.).

Wallace, T. and Mordaunt, J. (2007) 'When is the price too high? Gaining funding from institutional sources', in J. Mordaunt and R.C. Paton (eds), *Thoughtful Fundraising*, (Routledge: Abingdon).

Wikipedia (2006), 'War on Want' http://en.wikipedia.org/wiki/War_on_Want.

INDEX